JOHN BURNSIDE

A Lie About My Father

VINTAGE BOOKS
London

Published by Vintage 2007

2 4 6 8 10 9 7 5 3

Copyright © John Burnside 2006

John Burnside has asserted his right under the Copyright,
Designs and Patents Act, 1988 to be identified as the author
of this work

First published in Great Britain in 2006 by
Jonathan Cape

Vintage
Random House, 20 Vauxhall Bridge Road,
London SW1V 2SA

www.vintage-books.co.uk

Addresses for companies within The Random House Group Limited
can be found at: www.randomhouse.co.uk/offices.htm

The Random House Group Limited Reg. No. 954009

A CIP catalogue record for this book
is available from the British Library

ISBN 9780099479536

The Random House Group Limited supports The Forest Stewardship
Council (FSC), the leading international forest certification organisation.
All our titles that are printed on Greenpeace approved FSC certified paper
carry the FSC logo. Our paper procurement policy can be found at:
www.rbooks.co.uk/environment

Printed and bound in Great Britain by
CPI Antony Rowe, Chippenham, Wiltshire

This book is best treated as a work of fiction. If he were here to discuss it, my father would agree, I'm sure, that it's as true to say that I never had a father as it is to say that he never had a son.

We stand upon the brink of a precipice. We peer into the abyss – we grow sick and dizzy. Our first impulse is to shrink from the danger. Unaccountably we remain. By slow degrees our sickness and dizziness and horror become merged in a cloud of unnameable feeling. By gradations, still more imperceptible, this cloud assumes shape, as did the vapor from the bottle out of which arose the genius in the Arabian Nights. But out of this *our* cloud upon the precipice's edge, there grows into palpability, a shape, far more terrible than any genius or any demon of a tale, and yet it is but a thought, although a fearful one, and one which chills the very marrow of our bones with the fierceness of the delight of its horror. It is merely the idea of what would be our sensations during the sweeping precipitancy of a fall from such a height. And this fall – this rushing annihilation – for the very reason that it involves one of the most ghastly and loathsome images of death and suffering which have ever presented themselves to our imagination – for this very cause do we now the most vividly desire it. And because our reason violently deters us from the brink, therefore do we most impetuously approach it. There is no passion in nature so demoniacally impatient, as that of him who, shuddering upon the edge of a precipice, thus meditates a plunge. To indulge, for a moment, in any attempt at *thought*, is to be inevitably lost; for reflection but urges us to forbear, and *therefore* it is, I say, that we *cannot*. If there be no friendly arm to check us, or if we fail in a sudden effort to prostrate ourselves backward from the abyss, we plunge, and are destroyed.

Examine these and similar actions as we will, we shall find them resulting solely from the spirit of the *Perverse*. We perpetrate them merely because we feel that we should *not*. Beyond or behind this there is no intelligible principle; and we might, indeed, deem this perverseness a direct instigation of the arch-fiend, were it not occasionally known to operate in the furtherance of good.

Edgar Allan Poe, 'The Imp of the Perverse'

Where, during all these years, was my free will? From what deep and hidden place was it called forth in a moment so that I might bend my neck under thy yoke, which is easy, and take up thy burden, which is light?

St Augustine, *Confessions*

BIRDLAND

. . . fell on his knees and looked up and cried out,
'No, daddy, don't leave me here alone,
Take me up, daddy, to the belly of your ship,
Let the ship slide open and I'll go inside of it
Where you are not human . . .'

Patti Smith

Every year, it comes as a surprise. The leaves flare, for a time, to crimson and butter yellow, the air shifts, in the early morning, from the damp greens of late summer to soft graphites and an occasional, miraculous quail grey. Everything brightens before it burns away, the way a dying man is suddenly filled with new hope, hours before they are laying him out to be washed and dressed for the last time in a cool side room. I was brought up, not necessarily to believe, but to allow for the possibility that the dead come back at Halloween; or rather, not the dead, but their souls: whether as individual wisps of fading consciousness or some single, aggregated mass, it didn't matter. All I knew was that *soul* was there, in one of its many guises: ghost, or revenant, breath of wind, figment of light or fire, or just some inexplicable memory, some snapshot filed away at the back of my mind, a picture I didn't even know I possessed until that moment.

So it is that, with the usual show of scepticism and something close to total conviction, I have celebrated Halloween all my life. Most years, if I can, I stay at home. I make an occasion of the day, a private, local festival of penance and celebration in more or less equal measure. I think of my own dead, out there among the millions of returning souls

3

permitted, for this one night, to visit the places they once knew, the houses they inhabited, the streets they crossed on their way to work, or to secret assignations, and I remember why, in my part of the world, the living spend this day building fires, so they can light them all at once, all over the darkening land, as night approaches. It's not, as mere superstition says, that they are trying to frighten off evil spirits. No: the purpose of these fires is to light the way, and to offer a little warmth to ghosts who are so like ourselves that we are all interchangeable: living and dead; guest and host; householder and spectre; my father, myself. One day we may all be ghosts, and the ghosts we entertain will live and breathe again. Perhaps, in the past, each of us knew what it was to wander home and find it strange, the garden altered, the kitchen full of strangers.

To make it work, Halloween has to be a collaboration. The dead have their part to play, but so have the living. The reason I stay close to home on Halloween – whatever *home* happens to be – isn't just because I am conscious of, even dutiful about, my part in the ritual, but also because I know how vulnerable I am at such times. Halloween is an occasion, not just for visitations, but also for subtle, yet significant shifts and slips in the psyche, near-imperceptible transformations that, by the time they become visible, have altered the path of a life for ever. At Halloween, when the ghosts are about, I feel more open; more open, and more alert, but also more threatened. It's best, at such times, to sit at home until the first light breaks, and send my personal spirits away satisfied.

There have been times, however, when I had to be away: out on the road, somewhere in transit, alone, exposed, capable of forgetting what I think I am. Ten years ago, for instance, I was driving in the Finger Lakes region of upper New York

4

State, alone in a rented car, as the day of the dead approached. I had arrived in Rochester, NY, towards the end of October, and now I was searching for the little town where a friend lived, not far from Lake Keuka. I get lost easily – willingly, perhaps – and it was an easy place to get lost in, all the little roads leading off to places that were more beautiful and silent than any I had seen till then. So I was thoroughly lost that morning, when I stopped to pick up the clown. I didn't know he was a clown when I picked him up, but I could have guessed as much from his looks, and from the way he stood by the side of the road, utterly indifferent to the absence of traffic, or to the question of whether I would give him a lift. Even though he didn't appear to be a local, he looked like someone who knew the way.

It was the mid-nineties and I had been having a difficult year. I was stressed, tired, grateful to be alone and out on the road. I was tired of my work; tired of my history; tired, more than anything, of being *a person* (when St Paul tells us that God is no respecter of persons, he is saying more than we usually understand). I was tired of acting, tired of being visible. Driving around in that quiet corner of the world, passing through little townships where the children had set great grinning or mock-scary jack-o'-lanterns on the porches, I might as well have been invisible, a man from nowhere, as anyone is when he is passing through. I had been on the road for a while, and I was content just to drive around, stopping from time to time for a coffee and moving on, like a faint gust of wind that the local people, with their own dramas and hurts to enact, barely noticed, if they noticed it at all.

So I was happy being alone, enjoying the quiet of who I am when I am not with others, and I had no wish to change my situation till I stopped in a small town for lunch. I don't remember where it was, or why it 'appealed to me particularly, all I recall is the narrow, sparsely furnished diner, and the fact that it was empty. Empty, that is, but for the woman who brought me the menu, a painter working as a waitress (I have never met a waitress working as a painter, or an actor playing Hamlet till the next busboy position frees up, but I believed her, that day, and I still do today). She was a very beautiful woman, which struck me as odd at the time, because I hadn't thought of American women as beautiful till I met her. Pretty, yes; attractive, very often; but not beautiful. To me, they usually looked too new, as if they had just come off an assembly line. But then, I was more accustomed to California, where *everything* looks too new.

As is the way of quiet days, I spent a little time talking to this beautiful woman – I'll call her Frances – then I paid my bill and left. It had been one of those brief encounters that happen in transit, of no significance to either party beyond the level of pleasant, courteous exchange. She hadn't seen me as anything other than a friendly face – an outsider, someone she could relax and chat with, on a far from busy day – and I hadn't planned for anything other than a light but leisurely meal, to break the tedium of driving; after a few miles, however, I realised that Frances had shocked me out of my solitary mood and I found myself thinking about her, wondering, speculating, as it is possible to do when there is nothing but road ahead, no home, no obligations, no basic facts of existence. I was annoyed, I was charmed, I felt silly, and I was a little touched by my own silliness. I imagine the mood would have passed after an hour or so, with some country music on the radio and the not at all pressing, even faintly amusing problem of finding the way to my friend's house, but I had been feeling more than geographically lost for a while when I came upon a hitch-hiker and stopped to pick him up.

I'm going to call him Mike. He had come up from the city, he said, on his way to visit his father. We got talking about New York, about the Lakes and, eventually, about his father who, according to Mike's account, was a rare, living example of those men who had come to seem, for me at least, a matter of myth: competent, quiet, broad-minded, solitary, he had run a building supplies store in a nearby town, but was now retired and, ever since his second wife died, living alone in a simple house out in the woods, among the red and golden trees, not far from his nearest neighbour, for all practical purposes, but far enough to afford him real privacy.

At the time, I had no idea why it mattered to me, but I immediately decided that Mike's father – whose name, in this story, is Martin – was one of those people who liked to wake alone in the early morning and stand on his porch looking out at the woods, or at the little dirt road that ran to his door, to see what he could see. A man – I can imagine him so easily in the telling – for whom every sighting of the local deer, or the woodland birds, was a significant event, no matter how common those sightings might be. A significant event for him because, every time a human being encounters an animal, or a bird, he learns something new, or remembers something old that he had forgotten. This is one of the four or five things Martin has learned in life, and he is one of those men who understands that knowing four or five things is more than enough. I could imagine him allowing himself a good half-hour or so to stand outside with a warm coffee cradled in his hands, watching the day begin, before he went indoors and made breakfast. The rest of his day would be spent in patient work: the good work of daily maintenance, the odd task that

7

had been waiting for the right moment or season to be carried out, the sudden emergency repair.

I don't mean to say that Mike told me all – or any – of this about his father, but I knew, from what he did say, that Martin was just such a man. I could see him married, then widowed: self-sufficient all along, and no less so when he was bound to his wife and children – and it wasn't even a matter of time before this man, this father, merged with the ideal I had grown up expecting to find, a man like Walter Pidgeon, say, in his best movies: a creature mostly removed from the world inhabited by others, sitting alone with his paper, or musing over his pipe. My childhood dream of a father had been just that conservative-seeming type: a man who willingly accepted his imposed silence, his easy invisibility, and lived inside himself, in a self-validating world that had gradually become richer and quieter, like a pond in the woods that goes undisturbed for years, filling with leaves and spores, becoming a dark continuum of frog life and the slow chemistry of generation and decay. By the end, I could imagine, everything would have been internalised. Others would think him reserved, even withdrawn; they wouldn't see the faint smile that played about his face or, if they did, they would think of it as self-effacing or conciliatory, or even slightly embarrassed, the smile of a man who had nothing to say for himself. Nothing to say, nothing to show, nothing to prove. But it might as easily be the smile of someone who has seen through all the usual aspirations: the wry, mocking expression of someone who had learned, early on, that being a successful man, in worldly terms, is the ultimate in pyrrhic victories.

Mike was a different kettle of fish. He was tall, perhaps too tall, a rather gangly boy-man who looked ten years older than I guessed he was. He had sandy, already receding hair and oddly dark eyes, as if he had dyed or tinted them in some way. He told me he had gone off to the city at nineteen, to study acting, but what he really wanted to do was become a clown. Now he was in clown school – I had no idea, till then, that people actually studied such things – and even though his father had been a practical man all his life, he had been supportive, if not always clear about what it was Mike wanted to achieve. 'My dad never disrespected me for doing what I wanted to do,' Mike said. 'He was always there for me.' He spoke in that way, like a character on television, but I recognised the shorthand he was using. 'I got to hand it to him.' He shook his head in appreciation. I imagined he might be a good clown: everything he did was exaggerated, every phrase he uttered was picked out of the great treasure trove of received ideas. 'I can do other stuff,' he added. 'I made sure of that, for his sake.' He looked out at the trees. 'I'm a pretty fair carpenter,' he said, with a hint of pride.

I nodded. I wondered, if these lines had come up in a script he was learning, whether he would recognise himself in them. Not that I mean this as a criticism. I liked Mike. As he talked, I drove along, trying to find a suitable place in his story to interrupt him, and find out where we were going. Before I could, however, he gave me the kind of *interested* look that is so arresting in Americans. 'So. John. Tell me about your dad,' he said.

'He's dead,' I replied.

This seemed to surprise him, though he was probably just taken aback by my un-American directness. 'I'm sorry to hear that,' he said, after a moment. 'How long has it been? If you don't mind me asking.'

It was my turn to take a moment. 'Ten years now,' I said. 'Ten years – more or less.' I had to think, but I didn't mind sounding vague, hoping that would prompt him to change the subject.

'And your mother?'

'She died a long time ago,' I said. 'When she was forty-seven.'

'That's young,' he remarked. I realised that this subject wasn't going to go away and I was beginning to feel that Mike was too interested in family history. Or maybe I was beginning to suspect that I wasn't interested enough. There was silence for a minute, then Mike put the question I'd known was coming. 'So – what was he like, your dad?'

Now it was my turn for a long pause. Looking back on the moment, after I had dropped Mike off and driven away, it occurred to me that there was so much I could have said. I could have said that I'd come to believe that, when a man becomes a father, he is – or he ought to be – transformed into something other than the man he had been until that moment. Every life is a more or less secret narrative, but when a man becomes a father, the story is lived, not for, but in the constant awareness of another, or others. However hard you try to avoid it, fatherhood is a narrative, something that is not only told to, but also told by those others. At certain points in my adult life, I have found myself talking, over dinner, about fathers and sons: the hour late, the coffee drunk, the candles burning to smoke, and men around the table reminiscing about the fathers they have lost, one way or another. The ones who died, and the ones who went astray; the weak and the false; the well-meaning and the malicious, and the ones who were never there in the first place, or not in any recognisable form. Regarding my own father, I could have told Mike the truth. I could have talked about the violence, the drinking, the shameful, maudlin theatre of his penitences.

I could have told him about the gambling, and the fits of manic destruction. I could have spoken for hours about his cruelty, his pettiness, the way he picked obsessively at everything I did when I was too small and fearful to defend myself. I could have told him that I had buried my father with gratitude and a sense of what he might well have called *closure* a long time ago: buried him, not only in the cold, wet clay of the defunct steel town where he died, but also in the icy subsoil of my own forgetting. Ten years before, I had returned him to the earth and walked away, ashes to ashes, dust to dust, abandoning his memory to the blear-eyed strangers who hadn't had time to move on or die before he had his last heart attack, between the bar and the cigarette machine in the Silver Band Club. I could have said that I had buried my father long ago and walked back to the funeral car in the first smirr of afternoon rain, thinking it was all over, that I was moving on. I could have added that, before my father died, I hadn't seen him in years, but I hadn't been able to relax, quite, as long as he was still alive. I had always known he was there, decaying in the old house, enduring a half-life tinged with whisky and heart pills, a dull gleam of anger and regret fading into the remaining sticks of battered and burn-scabbed furniture, into the glow from the absurdly large rented television in the corner, into cupboards emptied of everything except leftover dog food from his brief experiment in keeping a Dobermann and tattered packs of duty-free cigarettes his mates brought back from holidays in Torremolinos and Calais. I could have explained that I hadn't seen him for years because I had walked out on him, in nothing but my shirtsleeves, with no money and nowhere to go, two days after my mother's funeral. I could have said that, since that day in 1977, I hadn't sat down with him, other than on the odd family occasion, but

11

I had carried him with me everywhere, an ember of self-loathing in the quick of my mind, caustic and unquenchable. I could have said that, partly because of my father, I had always been – and still was – one of those binge drinkers you meet from time to time, out on a mission to do as much clandestine damage as possible. I could have explained that I carried myself fairly well, that I was responsible, hard-working, possessed of an almost excessive and clumsy affection for my own, 90 per cent of the time; that, in the normal course of affairs, I could take just about any insult or injury. I could have said that, like most men, I tried hard to maintain the front needed for ordinary social existence, all the time longing for one spontaneous, honest expression of vitality, but that I never saw it coming when, after weeks or months or even years of pained and shamefaced pretence, my control would snap – a far-off but resonant crack at the back of my mind – and I would find myself in the midst of a binge that might last for days, only to end miserably in some anonymous room, leaving me drained and ashamed. I could have told him that I on no account wanted to suggest that I'd had an abnormally difficult upbringing and that, even if I had, I had no intention of using it as explanation or excuse for anything. I just wanted to put all that behind me, to take responsibility upon myself alone for how I met present demands.

I could have said that I knew it was too simple to say that my father injured me, and that I had taken years to recover from that hurt. I knew, *of course I knew*, that life is always more complicated than our narratives. I could even have said – had I known – that I appreciated the fact that my father himself had been hurt in ways that I cannot begin to imagine, when he was abandoned, one May morning, on a stranger's doorstep, that he had no doubt spent his whole life looking back, wishing all the time to absolve or accept or expunge that original pain, if not for his own, then at least for his family's sake. It never occurred to him, I think, to look away, to forget himself: there was always that gap he had to fill, there was always a flaw in a self he could never really trust. I could have said all these things, and then I could have told Mike – a stranger on the road, whom I would never meet again – that, in my own way, I had forgiven my father for what he had done, but that I would never forget it. I thought about it, and I think I was tempted, not to spite this well-meaning, well-raised son, but for my own sake, to put into words something that had been buried for too long, something that needed to be worked out in the saying. Finally, however, and with some misgivings, I abandoned that idea and, as Mike wanted me to do, not just because his head was full of beautiful, simple scripts, but also because he was a certain kind of son, and because Martin was a certain kind of man, I told him a lie about my father.

FOUNDLINGS

We are what we imagine.

N. Scott Momoday

CHAPTER 1

My father told lies all his life and, because I knew no better, I repeated them. Lies about everything, great and small, were the very fabric of my world. The web of his invention was so intricate, so full of dead ends and false trails that, a few months before that encounter with Mike, I had only just uncovered the last of his falsehoods, the lie that had probably shamed him most, though it was an invention that, under the circumstances, he could hardly have avoided. It was an invention, an act of the imagination, when he managed to convince others, and so convince himself that, as a child, he had been wanted, if not by his real parents, then by someone. It's easy to understand why he didn't want to be a nobody; he didn't want to be *illegitimate* – but it was probably just as important to him to feel that he came from somewhere. It mattered, once upon a time, where a person came from, and my father didn't feel he had the luxury of saying, as I can, that it doesn't matter where a man was born, or who his ancestors were. Nobility, honesty, guile, imagination, integrity, the ability to appreciate, ease of self-expression – in his time, most people believed that these were handed down by blood. The notion amazes me, now; but I think my father believed, till the day he died, that he was inferior, not only because he was illegitimate (*that*, he could have lived with), but because he was a nobody from nowhere, a lost child that no one had ever wanted.

And no one ever did find out where my father came from. He really was a nobody: a foundling, a throwaway. The lies he told were intended to conceal this fact, and they were so successful that I didn't know, until after he died, that he'd been left on a doorstep in West Fife in the late spring of 1926, by person or persons unknown. He had gone to considerable lengths to keep this secret; in the end, I only discovered the truth by accident, when I was visiting my Aunt Margaret, seven years after we had buried him. To me it was shocking news that, as soon as I heard it, made perfect sense. For a while, I even managed to convince myself that it explained everything.

It was the first time I'd visited any of my relatives since I returned to live in Scotland in the mid-nineties. Margaret was my favourite aunt, mostly because she was so close in age and temperament to my mother. I had gone round to her house, more or less unannounced, and she had welcomed me in, a little surprised to see me, but just as hospitable as I remembered her. An hour later, I was asking if she knew anything about my dad's adopted family, who had supposedly come from High Valleyfield, not far from where she lived. According to my father's stories, he had been adopted by his biological uncle, a miner and lay preacher, after his real father, a small-time entrepreneur and something of a rogue, had abandoned a girl – a sometime employee in one of his shady business ventures – he had made pregnant. A slight variant was that he was the son of a moderately wealthy industrialist who had paid one of his factory girls to move away when she turned out to be in the family way. Or he was the son of a lay preacher who had strayed. Or he was the son . . .

It went on, depending on his mood and how much he'd had to drink. All that mattered was that he was *somebody's* son. He'd had a father and a mother. For practical, or social reasons, they had given him over to the care of others, but they had at least existed. I had heard all manner of variation on these basic stories over the years, some of them patent contradictions, some elaborately styled; the only consistent details were that his foster-family, usually the Dicks, though sometimes the McGhees, had lived in High Valleyfield, that my father had had a half-sister, much older than himself, possibly by the name of Anne, and that his foster-father was a quiet, upright man, well respected in the pits, and an occasional preacher.

Aunt Margaret was confused. 'I'm not sure I understand you, son,' she said, looking faintly worried, when I enquired about these imaginary half-relatives.

'Well,' I said. 'I know my dad was adopted.' I went on to explain what I knew about his history, including the lay-preacher detail, which made her smile grimly.

'Oh, your father,' she said. 'He had some stories in him, right enough.'

'How do you mean?'

I watched as she considered her words carefully. My aunt is a good woman, and she has always been kind to me; she is also a person of particular tact. Like my mother, she moved to Cowdenbeath when she married, and the two sisters had stayed close, supporting one another through the various trials of life until my father moved us all, suddenly, to an East Midlands steel town, in the mid-sixties. During that time, she must have seen – and guessed – much more about what went on in our house than she had ever acknowledged. Now she was an old woman, still bright of eye, still capable of lighting up with a smile whose warmth had always cheered me; but I imagine she was also tired, and perhaps a little fed up with the very mention of her brother-in-law Tommy Dick, or George McGhee, or whatever his name was. He had brought too much pain to her favourite sister, he had embarrassed too many people she cared about, and I think she had heard a little too much nonsense over the years to let this particular deception pass. 'Your dad wasn't adopted,' she said. 'Or, not in the way you mean.'

'No?'

'He was a foundling child,' she said. 'The people who found him did take him in, but only for a little while. I don't think they were from High Valleyfield, though.' She fell silent, thinking back to a time just before she was born. 'Those were hard times,' she said. 'It was around the time of the great strike, and people didn't have much. From what I heard, he was passed about quite a bit. Of course, there weren't the social services they have now.' She studied my face, looking for a reaction, before she went on. 'So, I wouldn't say he was adopted. When you adopt someone, you make a choice. But nobody chose your father. He wasn't chosen so much as – passed on.'

A foundling child. I don't think I had ever heard that phrase before, outside the world of fairy tales. It becomes confused with changeling, with the bewitched child left for innocents to take in, a cuckoo soul with a nature he cannot change, or even understand, marooned in the human world. I try from time to time to imagine the morning when he was found, wrapped in nothing but a blanket according to the story Aunt Margaret had heard, a thin, squalling child of the General Strike, wrapped in a blanket and left on a doorstep in a West Fife mining town. Nobody I have ever known was there to

20

witness his abandonment, so I can imagine it as I like: as a scene from a fairy tale, perhaps, the unknown baby left at the door of some unsuspecting innocents, who take him in and try, as well as they are able, to bring him up alongside their own children, only to tire of him after a while and pass him on, first to relatives and then, as seems to have been the way of such things, to near strangers. I could imagine it wet and windy, the blanket sodden, the child crying plaintively, weak with hunger and terrified. My father wouldn't have liked that image, which is why he put so much work into imagining alternatives, some fairly close to the truth, though never as desolate or as cruel as this abandonment must have seemed.

I could stick to that kind of grainy, wet Thursday morning realism, and I would probably be fairly close to the truth; but what I choose to imagine is a summer's morning. It would have been sometime in late May or early June, so there is a slim chance that it was one of those days when the sun comes up warm and, in a matter of minutes, burns off the dew on the privet hedges and the little drying greens between the houses. At that hour, it would have been quiet in the coal town: the men on early shifts already gone to work; the children drowsing in their beds; women in their kitchens, boiling great bundles of linen in huge cauldrons, or kneeling at the door to polish the front step and the little bit of linoleum at the threshold. Though early June offers no guarantee of warmth in West Fife, I try to imagine a pleasant day because, in this story, the baby on the doorstep of one of those coal-town houses is my father. He is about to be discovered by one of the many foster-families he will know during his childhood, people with whom he will dwell for a few years before being passed along, in the years when the General Strike was turning into the Great Depression. He will learn the names and faces of each family in turn, and he will try to feel that he belongs to them as much as any child belongs to its given parents; then they will explain, awkwardly and with as much kindness as the occasion allows, that he is going to stay with an aunt, or a cousin, or a neighbour, someone more able to feed him, someone with fewer children of their own. He will move several times between this June morning and the day he signs up for the air force and leaves the coalfields for what he always thought of as the best years of his life, yet the houses he knows, the people, the towns, the self he feels himself to be, will not differ much from one temporary home to the next. The houses are tenements, mostly; the families working-class miners. The General Strike hit them hard, perhaps the hardest of all, and nobody had much to spare. It is possible that my father had been abandoned for some reason connected with the strike, or with the conditions that had preceded it; either way, people had other things to worry about that year. Once they had passed him on, they would soon have forgotten the sad waif in his pitiful blanket. After a while, he would be a boy: big, hungry, awkward, always underfoot. Someone they would rather keep a week as a fortnight.

Until he joined the air force, my father lived in Cowdenbeath and its environs. I don't know what the town was like during the thirties and forties, when he was a boy, growing into a young man, but I cannot imagine it was very different from the Cowdenbeath I knew in the fifties and early sixties. The town had been known for its poverty and overcrowded housing conditions early in the century; when I lived there, things had improved, but the overall impression was of an ordinary pit town, with its slag heaps and grey streets. Opposite St Bride's, the school I attended for six years, the pithead still stood, its wheels turning; even if, by then, the onshore mines were starting to run down. In my father's day, everything would have been going full tilt, though the miners wouldn't have seen much of the fruit of their labours. So I'm guessing that my father's Cowdenbeath was nearly identical to the town where I grew up, only a little darker, a little more crowded, a little smokier. The houses he passed through, as he moved from family to family, would have been dimly lit and almost bare, but there would have been gardens and allotments where people grew essential vegetables to supplement their meagre incomes, or wartime rations. Later, no matter where he lived, my father tended a garden of sorts, but he never grew flowers. I used to think it was a masculine thing, that he thought flowers were sissy; but he probably just remembered those allotments of the Depression, the taste of fresh leeks or new potatoes dug from your own patch of ground. The most obvious sign of his collapse, later in life, was the fact that the last garden he had was overrun with weeds and volunteer bedding plants, and not a potato or a cabbage plant in sight.

It's odd, imagining my father as a baby, or a growing boy. The first image I have of him is a wedding photograph: in it he is gawky, but proud of his air force uniform. His prominent teeth suggest that a smile was a calculation for him, a calculation he has failed to get quite right as he looks straight at the camera and gives it all he has. My mother is more natural-looking: pretty, already a little roundish, she is obviously happy. They were married on another June day, twenty-six years after my father had been abandoned and, again, it is easy to imagine a warm summer's morning, the lilac in bloom in her father's garden and sparrows brawling in the hedges around St Kenneth's Church. I try to imagine bells, but all I hear is the crank of the pithead wheel across the street and someone unloading crates of soft drinks in the yard of the nearby pub. Yet here they stand, arm in arm: her waxy-looking bouquet curdling in her hands, while he adopts that smile I never saw in thirty years, boyish and awkward and marred by his buck teeth, yes, but at the same time *almost* confident, and only a hint in his eyes of what he knew was fear, before he learned to call it love. I have always been puzzled by this picture. Were these my parents? Why did they never look like this, all the time I was growing up? Most of all, did they really have not the least inkling of what was to come? On their wedding day, did they really know nothing at all about one another?

I've seen other weddings. Strangers in California, friends in Croydon or Devon; Mexican weddings, Russian weddings, Finnish weddings. In one of the most beautiful ceremonies I have ever seen, I've watched processions of couples coming from the *casa de matrimonios* in a mid-Transylvanian town, the dark-eyed Romanian girls smiling, the men solemn, as they stand for photographs in the gusts of charcoal smoke and the burnt-sugar scent from the braziers along the river bank, where local women cook little sweets called *floricele* especially for the newlyweds and their guests. Every time I see a wedding, I wonder what the bride and groom expect from it all, and why none of the others there, the old ones, the long-married, do not step up and warn them about the enterprise. I think this, because I watched my parents torture themselves and one another for twenty-odd years, before my mother finally gave up and died, from disappointment more than anything, leaving my father to sit alone in the house, rehearsing what, for him, approximated grief. At my own wedding, I remember the fear I had of making a false promise, but also the sudden

24

realisation that this was exactly what mattered: that we were here to take exactly that risk, to make promises we could only hope to keep, in sickness and in health, madness and sanity, joy and fear, all of them inexplicable, even inexpressible, so that, as often as not, one is mistaken for another.

I imagine that, for the first time perhaps, my father felt wanted that day in a way he had never felt wanted before. It's in my mother's face, that small, but perfect victory a woman of her nature feels when she chooses to love a man who is loved for the first time. I have no idea what goes on in the human heart, but I do know, if I know anything, that men and women love for different reasons. I imagine most men love what pleases them, and think no more of it − but for women, love is an imaginative act, a choice, an invention, even. Maybe it has to be. I don't doubt that there were people who wondered aloud what she saw in him. He was a nobody from nowhere, an illegitimate child, and a non-Catholic into the bargain. Not a great catch, even in his uniform. If they'd known the man she'd supposedly jilted when my father came along, their thoughts that day might well have been with him.

There is something sad about wedding photographs seen long after the event. The picture I have of my mother and father shows hopeful, brave, smiling people that I never knew: all I saw were the disappointments and the lies that, for them, were still to come, still unimagined. Yet now, looking at him in his RAF uniform, with his white bride by his side, I can feel a little better about my father than I did when he was alive. He lied all the time, even when there was no need to lie, but I don't think he ever thought he was being dishonest. I think he had a sense of himself as someone who had as much right to a history as anybody else, but when he asked his 'relatives' to tell him about himself, he must have been

25

received in embarrassed silence, or with kind inventions, part-truths that had served, for strangers and others, in the absence of anything else. That wouldn't have been enough for him, though. He needed a *history*, he needed the sense of a self. By a process that demanded some wit – perhaps a little more than he possessed – and only very casual deception, he invented that self. It took more than a little doing, and who can blame him if he wasn't altogether successful or wholly consistent. If the world says you are nobody from nowhere, then you can choose not to argue, or you can invent yourself as someone other than you first seemed. Nobody wants to be a foundling child, and being something has to be better than being nothing.

CHAPTER 2

It's unsettling, when a child realises for the first time that his parents existed before he was born – and from that moment on, it gets ever more complicated and worrying: not only did they have a *life* before they became his parents, but there was also a time before they were married, a time before they had even met, when they were other people, with their own ideas, their own hopes, their own fleeting moments of hapless understanding. Perhaps they were in love with other people, or they swore they would never get married, never have kids. Tracing the line back to its origin, there was a time before all that, when they were children, and even a time before that, when they didn't exist. As a child, I came to this idea with a horrified fascination. Once upon a time, I wasn't here. Before that, my parents weren't here. And before that . . . What kind of world was it, when nobody I knew existed? What did people do? How could anything have been there at all, if I wasn't there to see it?

As far as my father is concerned, I know absolutely nothing about who he was, or what he did, before he was my father. I was shown photographs of my mother when she was a young woman: dark-haired, pale, her lipstick too freely applied, she is standing on a beach, or posing with friends in a garden or park, surprisingly slim in her striped jersey and black slacks.

To me, this *girl* was an impossibility. She was nothing like my mother: carefree, even a little wild-looking, she bore no resemblance to the preoccupied woman who kept trying to make something of our condemned home, trailing offcuts and sale items back from the shops, knitting and sewing all the time so we would have decent clothes, scavenging old magazines and notebooks from anywhere she could find them so she could teach me to read and write before I got to school.

My mother was a maze of contradictions. A dutiful, if not devout Catholic of the simple faith variety so beloved of the clerical trade, she hated Communism which, to her, was politics of any variety. Yet, perhaps because my father wasn't, and every other male member of her family either was, or had been, associated with the pits, she revered the miners, and she could tell us all about the hardships they had endured, about what they had done in the war, about how the pit bosses had brought in people from all over Scotland to break their will during the General Strike, and how they had stood fast when everyone else had crumbled and given in. She could also tell you how, according to family lore, her father, a devout Catholic, had been picked up by the police, supposedly for drunkenness, and taken to the cells. This was part and parcel of the routine harassment of Catholic men, or 'the Irish' as the Protestants called them – and the police in those days were all Protestants in that corner of Scotland. A known Catholic emerged from the pub, none the worse for wear, and was pulled in, to pass the night in a damp cell, his pockets emptied, his belt and shoes removed, all the routine humiliations. My grandfather had endured all this in the steady, stoic manner bred of daily necessity, but when he came to be discharged, the rosary beads he always carried were missing. My mother's voice brimmed with pride when she told how he finally left the police station that morning, after being threatened with a charge, but kept coming back, day after day, asking for his rosary beads till, one evening, the desk sergeant finally relented.

'They arrested him for being drunk,' she would say. 'Your grandfather has never been drunk in his life.'

This was true. My grandfather could put away as much whisky as anyone, but he would never have been seen out on the street with a drink on him. He always dressed well to go out, in a worn, but clean black suit, a flat cap or bunnet, very polished shoes. He kept a picture of the Virgin Mary in his breast pocket, and his rosary beads in his jacket. He took me aside at a family occasion once – one of the many weddings a man with twelve children was obliged to attend – and offered me a small card, like those collectors' cards you used to get with cigarettes, or tea. It was a picture of the Virgin.

'Every man should carry a picture of the Blessed Virgin Mary with him at all times,' he told me.

I stared at the card and nodded.

'Take it,' he said. 'It's for you.'

I took it.

'Look after her,' he continued, as I put the card in my blazer pocket. 'And she will look after you.'

It was from her parents that my mother's values came. Like her father, she disliked people who loved money, yet what she wanted, more than anything, was the most routine form of chintzy respectability. Like her mother, she loved flowers and gardening. She had a reverence for learning that sat heavy on my childhood: every spare moment, I was set to work, studying, reading, writing – yet she herself never once read what she thought of as a 'real book' in all the years I knew her. She was quiet and secretive, and she had the air about her, even when I was very young, of a woman whose loves and friendships were all in the past, or at a distance. She was fierce about family, even when family let her down. Perhaps most of all when they let her down.

My mother's pictures – photographs of her family, of her friends, of herself on days out with fellow workers from the Co-op, all the scraps and images she treasured – were kept in a large, shabby handbag that my father had brought her from Egypt, when he was stationed out there, but there were no photographs of my father before his air force days, when he is always the one at the back of the group, usually with a glass lifted to his mouth and obscuring his face, a man making it all too clear that he wasn't interested in posing for snapshots. But then, photographs can be misleading. What we remember, when we truly remember, rather than when we recall the memories that are planted in our minds by others, is the only testament that can be trusted; not because it is precise, but because it is our own. A photograph, a family story, the re-collections of some old-timer at a wedding or a funeral, recol-lections of a time when nobody else in the room was even born, are works of art, not facts. I knew, at a fairly young age, that anything my father told me about himself, anything he told me about *anything*, was to be treated with suspicion. But why was he the exception? Why should anything I was told be treated as definitely true or absolutely false? When they told stories, when they showed pictures, when they reminisced together with a room full of family, all people communicated was their intentions. Whatever was true, was secret.

My father had no history that he could talk about with others. Nobody reminisced with him about the old days, nobody brought snapshots out of an old box and handed them around so the assembled company could see what he was like as a boy. All he had were his own, unverified stories. His own apocrypha. By the time he was my father, he wasn't so much a man as a force of nature, something that came out of nowhere, an unpredictable, wild, occasionally absurd creature who could be all smiles and charm one moment, and utterly venomous the next. He was a square-built man of around five eleven, strong, physically ruthless, very quick. *Quick with his hands*, was the phrase people used when they wanted a euphemism for domestic violence, but my father was almost never actually violent. At some instinctual level he understood that a threat is much more potent than an actual blow: after the first few times, a blow can lose its power, because – as he himself liked to say – people can get used to almost anything. He'd got used to working in a rubber-products factory, standing all day in the heat and stench, at the age of fifteen, and he'd got used to the smell of burning flesh when he worked on the disposal squads during the foot-and-mouth epidemic of the early sixties. He'd got used to a few blows himself, no doubt, over the years, and he could take as good as he gave. He'd come home a few times, when I was a child, with blood on his face and shirt, cuts on his arms, bruises on his knuckles. Yet his injuries never troubled him. 'It's a scratch,' he would say, when my mother tried to get him to go to the hospital; then he'd wash the blood away with warm water and throw his shirt in the dustbin.

So he rarely hit out. He knew the threat of violence is always stronger than violence itself. It works much the same way horror movies work: if you see the big rubber shark, or the killer from beyond the grave in his ghostly make-up, you're more inclined to laugh than scream. My father was one of those men who sit in a room, and you can feel it: the simmer, the sense of some unpredictable force that might, at any moment, break loose and do something terrible. Now and again, he would break something: carefully, deliberately, letting us see how much he enjoyed it, letting us register how easy it was. The worst thing that could happen was when he fell into one of his dark silences and sat brooding all day, waiting for the small provocation that would set things going. I don't think he could control it, once it began, any more than he could stop drinking, or gambling until all the money in his pockets was gone. Yet he hardly ever hit anybody inside the house. Not in those early days, at least. Maybe I was just sheltered from the worst when I was still so young. Later, he seemed a changed man, a kind of monster; but he might have been that same monster all along, transmuted, by my child's need, into something like a father, if not a protector. As I grew up, I wondered what was happening to him. I wondered why he was changing. But he didn't change: he just became real. For years, I would have sworn that I remembered better days, but when I stop to look back, I remember nothing about him, other than what I was told. I do not see him. I barely even see myself.

For me, memory begins in King Street, in the condemned house where my parents lived after they were first married. I was told so much about the time before I was born that I can imagine I was actually present at the death of my mother's first child – a girl she called Elizabeth, after her own mother – or if not present *at* the death, then certainly *for* it. I seem to know this girl, first as a baby, then as a toddler, a girl who was just over a year ahead of me all the way through childhood. Pretty, fair-haired, but with my mother's dark, almost motionless eyes, she comes and goes through the home movie of King Street that runs inside my head, a child in a white hand-me-down dress standing beside me in the garden, squinting into the sun; a girl who set off for school one day and came home different, with ink stains on her hands and the smell of dried paint in her hair. I remember this girl because my father talked about her when he was upset, or when he came home drunk and sat in the kitchen muttering to himself. It was characteristic of how they were, I see now, that my mother never once mentioned Elizabeth's name, while my father talked about her all the time. Even in grief, they were separated.

I seem to know my ghost sister, but the truth is that she died before I was born. I could never find out how long she was in this world; some stories suggest she died in hospital after a few hours, or a few days; others that she lived for some time before succumbing to whatever it was that ailed her. I always felt kin to her, though, even when my father took me aside, one drunken Saturday afternoon – the first time, this may have happened when we still lived in King Street, but it happened more often than I can recall, and it went on for years – and told me that he and my mother had had another child before me, that her name was Elizabeth, that she had died and that he wished she had lived, and I had died instead. He always told me this as if it would come as a surprise, a piece of unexpected news about his, or my history, and he always went through the steps in the same order, with due solemnity, building up to those final, brutal words, which he uttered without the least hint of brutality, without anything that might, on the surface, be taken for malice. I think he thought, as he confided in my three-, or five-, or eight-year-old self, that I was supposed to feel sorry for him, that I was supposed to express my regret, not only for his loss, but for my own inability to reverse the twist of fate that had left him in such an unfortunate position.

After a while, I would see it coming. He would wait till my mother was out of the room, then he would tell me, very quietly, his voice just barely slurring, 'You know something?'

I would shake my head.

'You know, you had a sister once.'

I would wait. There was no point in saying anything. The first thing I learned was that there were times when you didn't say anything, even if you were called upon to talk.

'Her name was Elizabeth.'

I nodded dutifully. I knew all this. I knew what was coming. I just didn't understand why.

'And she died.'

Once upon a time, there was a little Indian boy who lived by himself in a cave in the mountains. He was all alone in the world, except for his friend, the timber wolf –

'But you know what?'

This boy had no parents, only the wolf, whose name was –

'It could have been you that died.'

Mungo. Chano. White Fang. I would try names out in my head, but I could never find one I liked.

'It could have been the other way around. You could have died, and she could have lived.'

Lobo. Tonto. Silverado. I have no idea where these names originated. Maybe radio.

'I wish – '

It was easy to block it out, after a while. I don't think I really hated him – not then. I suppose his telling of the story, and my defences against it, became more elaborate as the years passed, and we got to know one another better. I was always taking his measure, figuring out what I needed to do in order to get past him. The best I could come up with was to tell my own stories, stories that countered his half-truths with the pure actuality of fiction. It was self-defence, nothing more; but what better defence than a story, set somewhere in the far north, about a boy and a dog and the secrets they keep, in a country of perpetual snow?

I asked my mother about it. I must have felt guilty about being so damned healthy.

'Oh,' she said, 'you were a blue baby. We didn't know how things would turn out.' She gave me an inquisitive look. 'What has your father been saying?'

'Nothing,' I said. 'He was just telling me about Elizabeth—'

'Well, you know about that,' she said. 'She was our first baby, and she died. So we had you instead.' Even when I was very young, I knew she meant this well, but her words did nothing to make up for what my father had told me. It still sounded like I was second-best.

'What's a blue baby?'

'It's when — I don't know. You had to be looked after by a specialist.' She pronounced this word with all the reverence people of her class reserved for medical professionals. 'You had to be put in an oxygen tent, when you were first born.'

I tried to picture an oxygen tent. I knew oxygen was part of the air. When I was older, I decided I had been strangely privileged by this oxygen-rich birth, as if I had come into the world with sky in my lungs.

'Anyway,' she would always conclude, 'don't listen to your father. He doesn't know what he's talking about, half the time.'

I nodded. I knew she was right, but I wasn't sure which half of the time I should ignore. If it had been all the time,

I think I would have managed better. But things were never that straightforward. All his best lies were half-truths – I suppose the grain of truth in each of his stories helped him to remember, if not the lesser details, then at least the general arc of the plot – which meant there was something there to be sifted out, something that might have revealed him to me. I suppose, at the time, I wasn't quite ready to give up on that possibility – as my mother so obviously had.

I still don't really know what a blue baby is. At the time, I thought it meant that, when I was born, I almost died. This, oddly enough, was something of a comfort to me: it was something I had in common with my ghost sister, something special. It was as if a part of the soul I'd had at birth had been traded off for my earthly survival, as if part of me had gone into the beyond with Elizabeth. I'm told blue baby syndrome is fairly uncommon nowadays, that a blue baby is a child born with a congenital heart defect that causes a bluish coloration of the skin. Sometimes it happens that red blood cells in the infant's blood are destroyed by the mother's antibodies, and this can also cause cyanosis. Whatever the cause, my problems could not have been serious, because I was soon at home and, according to family lore, my father was dandling me on his knee, singing me old songs, delighted with his new son.

I hear these memories, like stories being told in my head, but I never see them. Growing up, I was always anxious about memory, at some undercurrent level: it wasn't, for me, a philosophical question, when I asked myself what a memory was, and why my own memories were usually so vague. When somebody said to me that they could see some incident happening in their mind's eye, I had no idea what they meant. Was it like a film, running on some screen behind the eyes? Was it only a figure of speech? Why did one thing – a smell, a taste – suggest something else – a moment, a girl's face – when there was no obvious connection between the two? Was I defective in some way? I remembered – I still remember – so little. I have a very weak notion of time. An hour can pass without my noticing. A day can pass. Or a single minute can seem to go on for ever. This was true then, and it was more exquisite because, as a child, I was never sure I would emerge from a moment's foundering, just I was never sure where the time had gone, when an hour, or a day, skipped by.

I do know, however, that my first real visual memory is of Smokey the Cat. The dilapidated houses on King Street were pretty thoroughly infested with rats and house mice. I'm told that this never bothered me, that my mother found me in the garden one afternoon, when I was three years old, watching a rat foraging around the coal bunker, and she noticed that I wasn't afraid, just fascinated. I have no recollection of this, naturally. What I do remember is that my mother had a horror of all animals: rats, mice, cats, dogs, horses, cattle. She was also worried about the risk of disease the rats posed – with one dead child, a blue baby and, in the year or so before we left King Street, a new baby girl to look after – she wanted to be rid of them. The irony was that, according to the accepted wisdom, the only reliable method of eliminating rats in such conditions was to go out and get a terrier, or a cat.

Which is where Smokey came in. My mother agreed to having him out of necessity, but she didn't like the idea. Naturally, Smokey sensed this immediately and decided he wanted to be my mother's special friend: no matter what she did, he would follow her around, or jump suddenly into her lap when she sat knitting. Worst of all, he would bring her little gifts: half-dead mice; songbirds; even, on one occasion, a large, rather lean rat that lay twitching on the floor till she gave Smokey permission to finish it off. I think she did her best to appear gracious, but the outcome was preordained from the first: disgusted woman, disappointed cat. My mother never did understand the concept of pets. She found it deeply unsettling that a cat could mistake her, at some basic level, for its own kin. At the same time, she couldn't help feeling sorry for the rats and, no matter how hard she tried to disguise this sympathy, the cat usually got the sense that all was not well, and so felt – who knows what a cat feels? Betrayed, was how it looked. Still, it never gave up. For as long as we lived on King Street, that animal followed my mother around with its tender, half-killed gifts. When we finally moved, Smokey did not come with us. I think he suspected it was some kind of trick to finally rid him of his hunting instinct. Or maybe he guessed that, where we were going, we had no use for him, and he didn't want us to forget him by degrees till, like most cats, he finally became invisible. After we moved, after we had settled, we noticed that he was gone, but nobody missed him.

Nobody, that is, except my father. He went out from time to time to try and find out where the cat had gone. King Street wasn't far away, and he would begin his search at our old house, checking the gardens round about, then tracing a path past the shops and on to the farm road, then up through the beech woods, past Kirk's chicken farm on the left and the dense woods on the right. He did that for quite a while, but he never found Smokey. I remember finding it a little strange: for as long as Smokey had been there, taken for granted, my father had paid him only the most passing attention, but now that the animal was lost, he couldn't quite put him out of his mind.

CHAPTER 3

Our new house was on Blackburn Drive, a sprawl of wartime prefabs close to the edge of Cowdenbeath and separated somewhat from the rest of the town by the Beath woods. At that time, the woods were a narrow strip of mixed trees, mostly beech, and the kind of undergrowth associated with that fairly dark woodland, invaded here and there, where trees had been cleared, by great swathes of rosebay willowherb and even, where it was moist, by Himalayan balsam. A damp, stony track that everybody called the farm road cut through the woods, running all the way from the Co-op and the little corner shop where my father bought his cigarettes, past the old abattoir, skirting Kirk's poultry farm on the way, and finally emerging, beyond the prefabs, to meet the Old Perth Road. Beyond that, there was nothing but open fields, and the odd derelict farm building, till you got to the place we kids called the Water Houses, a dark, mysterious set of sheds and storehouses that, to my mind, was both deeply sinister and infinitely exciting. I spent a good deal of time at the Water Houses, mostly because I had been forbidden ever to go near them. I spent as much time out in the woods and wetlands beyond, searching for moorhens' nests, or gathering blueberries. It's all gone now, of course: the woods, the prefabs, the chicken farm, the old slaughterhouse. The fields have been turned over to a light industrial estate; the Water Houses have collapsed. As a child, I thought Beath woods were magical: so close to home, yet so dark and damp, they were haunted by tawny owls and foxes; haunted, too, by strange noises and movements in the dark that nobody could explain. When I was around seven, I took to getting up on summer nights, after my parents had gone to bed, and sitting out on the window sill, listening to the owls, spooked by their weird cries, even more spooked by the fact that, no matter how close they sounded, I never saw them.

The woods further out were a different story. People went to those woods for all sorts of reasons: in the daytime, illicit couples stole up through the fields and into the undergrowth to lie, half naked and silent, coupling like joyous animals; after school, or on the weekends, gangs of older boys would hold secret drinking sessions, or they would haul a sack of trapped cats into the darker corners for arcane torture ceremonies. (I was present at some of these, by accident, before I was really old enough to be admitted, and I saw what was done. It was surprisingly casual, and surprisingly cruel. Those ceremonies involved rope, fire, fish-hooks, penknives and various brands of household cleaning products.) To go there alone, in the middle of the day, was to enter a dangerous realm of spent bonfires and burned fur, the half-decomposed bodies of unclaimed dogs, farmers with shotguns, stark displays of rats and crows, carefully suspended in the branches of elder or thorn bushes from pieces of muddy baling twine, like somebody's bizarre idea of avant-garde sculpture. I went there as often as I could. This was the place where I learned the deep pleasure of being alone, of being out in the open with an angel-haunted sky over my head, and the damp earth, packed tight with tubers and seeds and the bodies of the dead, under my feet. All that time, I was engaged in that search a child-hood sometimes becomes, a search for the perfect instrument, for some compass point, some line of cold steel, some buried filament of copper and smoked glass. I didn't know what it did; maybe it guided the trains through town, west to the rain, or north, into deeper snows. Once found, it might turn boys into something more interesting and much stranger than the handful of men I knew; perhaps it simply existed, part of the beautiful machinery of the world, calibrated, steady, hidden, uniting the human realm with all that lay beyond. It was imaginary – but it was more real than the business of school and home and minding my father; it was also very specific to me, something I alone could imagine, something I alone could find. I was a pit-town child, escaping into the woods or the wet meadows for the afternoon, entering a world that I knew must belong to somebody else and, at the same time, quite sure that those others had no right to it. I made it up in words I took from books: windflower, sorrel, pipit, old man's beard; I didn't really know anything, but I wanted to. All the time, I knew something else was there, waiting to arrive and touch me. When all the names I knew from memory and textbooks, all the world I thought to see had been assigned, another life began, crossing a field, fording a burn, stepping out on to the further bank and coming to light, but not quite taking shape: a running fox, a wind-gust in the grass, the dense, communal silence of beasts. Rabbit and weasel, wed to their mortal dance; the farmer's cat, out stalking in the weeds; his ewes and cattle turning from a dream of salt and hay to where the earth began. It was darker and more dangerous than that, but you wouldn't see it at first; then, when the perfect moment came, it would take hold of your spirit, and you would never be the same again.

In those days, being a child was all about navigation. At eight years of age, my entire body was a map, a nerve chart of dogs and fruit trees, and the places where bottles might be found, to be rinsed out later and redeemed at Brewster's for a penny or two. My homeward routes were records of the movements of bullies, of teachers and priests, of beautiful strangers. At the same time, it was always a dress rehearsal for something else, something beyond my knowledge. When I was nine I ran away for the first time, and lasted the best part of a night in the woods, with a blanket from the press, a couple of potatoes I planned to bake in a fire, and a tin of beans that I couldn't eat, having forgotten to bring a can-opener. Later, after we had moved to Corby, I got as far as Edinburgh, or London, or – on one bizarre occasion – Market Deeping, but it was the same map I was following, the same limbo world of orange street lamps and owl-haunted woods. If there is an afterlife, for me it will be limbo, the one truly great Catholic invention: a no man's land of mystery and haunting music, with nobody good or holy around to be compared to – *they* will all be in heaven – just the inter-esting outsiders, the unbaptised and the pagan, and the faultless sceptics God cannot quite find it in Himself to send to hell.

When I look back at my time in the prefabs, I am touched by the life I led. My sister and I were haunted: Margaret, eighteen months younger than me, had ghostly visions of men in long white robes standing over her in the dark, or she would be on her way home from Brownies, and she would suddenly realise she was being followed by some spirit, some not-human presence. I would spend hours in the woods, or out by the Water Houses, looking for angels. I had seen an angel once, standing in a tree, staring down at me, and I'd been dizzy and confused for a long time afterwards, touched by something unbearable, yet also by a kind of magic. Even at home, I was never safe from such visions. There were times when I was sitting up at night (though, once or twice it happened in the clear afternoon), when the door of the press would open slowly and something appeared: not spirit, not flesh, but something between the two, like the faded stain of blood and salt on the sleeve of a fishmonger's coat, a creature that seemed less other than it ought to have done, a presence that I could barely distinguish from myself. I knew this was something I had to conceal from my parents, though I had no idea what it was: perhaps a fetch that possessed me, like the malevolent beings in old folk tales; perhaps nothing more than a memory and a competence beyond what I was deemed to possess by those around me, something angelic that had chosen a shape I couldn't quite believe in, coming out of a wall or a door and filling my room with brightness and a delicious fear. Delicious because it was fanciful, something I knew I was making up, or at least collaborating with – unlike the fear my father inspired, a real terror over which I had no control. It's hard to say what was most frightening: his body, which seemed so powerful and, at times, so dangerous; his moods, which see-sawed back and forth, jokey one minute, black and frightening the next; his voice. He had an amazing voice: most of the time he was silent, or soft-spoken, as if he was thinking about something else while he talked; then, out of the blue, it would harden and go dark, not necessarily a shout, but always a threat, always the harbinger of damage and terror. But the worst aspect of his voice was when he nagged at me, quietly and persistently eating away at my confidence, questioning my right even to occupy space in his world.

'Stand up straight. Look at you. What is it? What's wrong with you? Are you a hunchback or something? Come on. Stand up. Straighten your shoulders. Straighten your back. Look at yourself.'

On and on. I would be walking along the street and he would be there, behind me, picking away. 'You walk like a girl. Look at you. Why can't you stand up straight?' He would ignore the people going by, focused entirely on me, watching my every move, ready to pounce. When I started to read, he would criticise the books I was reading. When I brought home a report card, he would take it silently, cast his eye over it then pick out the lowest grade.

'What happened here?' he would say pointing at the offending B. 'Geography. What's wrong, you can't remember the capital of Bolivia?'

The next time I brought home a report card, I had an A in Geography. He studied the grades, took in the comments, sat quiet for a moment, considering before he spoke. 'I see you're falling behind in science,' he said pointing to the A–. 'What's the minus for?' He looked at me, knowing I wouldn't dare to answer back. 'It's no good getting it right once, you know. You have to keep it up. Just because you did all right last time, it doesn't mean you can just sit back and take it for granted. You have to keep at it.' He set the card aside. 'I didn't get all the opportunities you're getting,' he said. 'I'm working hard to give you a chance to do something with yourself. But it's up to you. I can't do it for you. All right?' I nodded. He nodded in turn. 'All right, then,' he said, then went back to his paper.

At one level, I knew this was all happening for a reason – in his mind, at least. For my father, and for whole generations of working-class men, cruelty was an ideology. It was important, for the boy's sake, to bring a son up tough: men had to be hard to get through life, there was no room for weakness or sentiment. It wasn't what he would have chosen, but he didn't want me to get hurt by looking for something I couldn't have. What he wanted was to warn me against hope, against any expectation of someone from my background being treated as a human being in the big hard world. He wanted to kill off my finer – and so, weaker – self. Art. Music. Books. Imagination. Signs of weakness, all. A man was defined, in my father's circles, by what he could bear, the pain he could shrug off, the warmth or comfort he could deny himself. That my father was also a heavy drinker wasn't a contradiction in this ideology: he drank hard, not for pleasure; he could hold his drink; alcohol, in its own way, was a drug of ascesis, as well as release. The hangovers were pure murder, but he still got up and went to work. He'd never missed a day's work in his life through drink, he would say, and he never would. He didn't seem to notice that, as soon as he was out of the company of his cronies from the Woodside or, later, the Hazel Tree, all that self-control withered away, and he became a monster – like the night he came home late from the Woodside and, while I lay sleeping in the next room, burned my favourite toy, a teddy bear called Sooty. It seems he'd come in and found it, *strewn across the floor*, as he put it, and he'd tossed it into the fire to teach me a lesson. If I couldn't keep my things tidy, then I had to be prepared to lose them. The next morning, when I got up and went through to the living room, Sooty was gone. When I asked my mother if she'd seen him, she looked guilty, then she told me she hadn't. I should go and look, he would turn up, I needed to take better care of my things. She never mentioned that she'd found what remained of Sooty smouldering away in the grate at five o'clock that

45

morning. It was my father who told me what he'd done. 'I put Sooty on the fire,' he said. 'You're too big for a teddy now, anyway.' I was six.

'You did not,' my mother protested. 'Don't say things like that,' she said, 'even as a joke.' As soon as she spoke, I knew that she was covering up. I couldn't believe it. *Sooty*. I'd had that bear for as long as I'd existed.

'I burned him,' my father insisted. 'If you can promise to keep your things tidy, you can have something else,' he said.

'I don't want something else,' I said. 'I want Sooty.'

My mother looked a little desperate. 'You must have lost him,' she said. 'He'll turn up.' She shot my father a scary, warning look. 'If he doesn't, we'll get you another teddy just like him.'

I didn't say anything – but I swore I wouldn't have another bear. I never did. A few weeks later, my father brought a rocket set home for me, one of the items he occasionally got from 'a friend'. He brought it home in a plain cardboard box and opened it up, so I could see what it was. I didn't refuse the gift; I didn't reject him. I took the rocket set, but I didn't play with it that night and, the next day, I gave it away to a boy called Alan Smith, who was playing outside Stewart Banks' house.

Every winter my mother would knit me a new balaclava. This was what she did to keep me safe: the wool was the same colour every time – dark blue, though she never called it that, she always had a new name for it, Navy, or Midnight, or something. The new balaclava would appear at around the same time every year, a few days into November, when the first frosts came. The only thing she ever changed was the pattern: sometimes it looked rounded, like Norman armour, a helmet of woollen chain mail to cover the skull in a tight, meshed fit; sometimes it was almost square on top, with a thick seam that made the corners into pointed, lynx-like ears, but no matter what shape it was, it concealed a little more of my face each year, as if she were trying to cover me so well that I would become invisible. Maybe she thought that, this way, whatever terrible fall I had coming would let me pass unnoticed.

Meanwhile, I had started attending a primary school for the children of the poor, one of those institutions where to turn up at all and stay awake till the end of the day was an achievement. In that community, Catholics had to be very careful: their children should not stray, their schoolteachers should be seen to be diligent and strong on discipline. To encourage near-perfect attendance, the work was carefully designed so that it was not too difficult, while being mildly rewarding. At least, that was how it seemed to me. I was bored in school, most of the time; the only exception was in Scripture class, when we studied the life of Jesus and looked at beautiful, ancient-looking maps of Palestine and Judaea. I liked the teachers well enough. They lent me books and gave me special problems to solve.

At five, however, I didn't much like the children. I imagine this is something many children discover, on their first day of school, but there is so much pressure to socialise, at school and beyond, that they learn to adapt. I didn't have that pressure, however: my mother's efforts to improve me at home meant that I was – and stayed – at least a year ahead of my classmates. This meant I received special treatment, sitting off by myself with a book of my own, or more advanced sums to work out, while the others practised their pencraft, or plasticine-doggy-making. At the time, this was considered an

47

enlightened view, though there was no mistaking the look in the eyes of my teachers, a look that suggested they thought of me as a freak, not of nature, so much as of abnormal nurture. Looking back, I realise that the smartest of my primary schoolteachers, Miss Conway, recognised in me a boy made clever, but not particularly intelligent, by an ambitious, or rather, desperate, mother. It would take me another ten years to stop admiring that cleverness. Nevertheless, I was an anomaly in that little coal-town classroom: hypersensitive, overly polite, occasionally cruel, I thought other boys were the strangest little animals and avoided them as much as I could. Unlike the stereotypical 'sensitive' child, however, the one who likes books and nice pictures, I was big and ready to defend myself if the need arose. I also had the distinct advantage of being related to the hardest, leanest, most uncom-promising older boy in town, my bright, funny and utterly merciless cousin, Kenneth. Kenneth was a boy's boy, an outdoors type who knew every bird in the woods and every fish in the loch. I admired him from afar; but then, he seemed like an adult to me, the way he knew everything you couldn't learn from a book. Even then, I saw that there was more to life than my mother had taught me: all I had was words and diagrams, Kenneth had life itself. To me, he was more grown up than most grown-ups, and more alive than anybody I had ever met.

He was the exception, however. The other children at school, especially the boys, bored and annoyed me and, by the time I was eight, I liked them even less than I had at five. Truth to tell, though I didn't realise it at the time, they reminded me of my father. They lived in the same world of minor grudges and willed confusion, and I felt fortunate to inhabit my own little universe of books for older children and logic problems, the scriptures and Church Latin. At the time, all Catholic children were supposed to acquire a smattering of medieval Latin, so they could follow the Mass, and I loved it. The words were so beautiful: strange in the mouth, tasting of unleavened bread and church incense, they carried an incontrovertible authority, the authority, not only of the divine, but also – as I had just begun to realise from my extracurricular studies in zoology – of the scientific. I had no words to articulate the feeling but, for me, the fact that Latin was the language of both priests and biologists was a source of excitement, even inspiration, and I was sure there was some great secret out there, waiting to be discovered, a private, arcane knowledge that only the privileged were allowed to share.

Looking back, I see that I disliked the Catholic children more than the Protestants I knew. This made for difficulties, because Catholics and Protestants, in our little Scottish town, were supposed to be enemies, either politely skirting one another, as adults, or waiting outside the rival school, as children, to administer a mild beating. The local Protestant school – the state school – came out five minutes before St Bride's, time enough for a gaggle of the bigger, and obviously stupider, Prod boys to gather around the school gates, leering and dangerous, ready to catch any stragglers who happened their way. They never caught me. I was the fastest runner in my class, and I would rather have died than be humiliated by a gang of my obvious inferiors. Yet even then, in the midst of this community of visible, though fairly vague, discrimination, I knew there were Protestant kids on the other side who felt exactly as I did. One of these was Stewart Banks, who was nowhere near as good as me at book learning but, like my cousin Kenneth, knew a thing or two about the wider world.

Stewart was a neighbour. All our neighbours, on Blackburn Drive and the streets around, were Protestants, whether by accident or some unlikely demographic, I do not know. Stewart's parents were, by far, the most easygoing, tolerant and disorganised people I had ever encountered. They were the very opposite of my mother, with her obsessive neatness, and her almost desperate desire to get out of the prefabs and live a better life, but they got on with her very well – and they were the only neighbours who did not make it obvious, one way or another, that they disapproved of my father's goings-on. At the time, even though I had just begun to disapprove of him myself, that mattered a great deal to me. Like most children, I wanted my home life to be just like everybody else's: in spite of the fact that I *knew* I was not like other people in that little town, I wanted to appear normal.

Normal was a big word, back then. If anybody did anything even remotely interesting, they were considered abnormal. Abnormal children were taken off to special places, never to be heard of again. Abnormal men posed a terrifying, though undefined, danger to children. The most abnormal people I knew were the Mormon family who lived a few streets away from us. It was said that Mormon men had several wives, and that Mormon boys could make babies with their sisters. Though I had no clear idea how babies were made – Elizabeth Banks told me, once, that men and women did it by sticking their bottoms together and taking deep breaths – I was certain that brothers and sisters couldn't do it. It had to be a man and a woman who were married to each other. That much I knew from Scripture class.

Stewart was normal; I was not. Stewart had a normal family: his father went to work in the morning and came home at the end of the day, even on the weekends. His job had something to do with the distribution of D.C. Thomson products, which meant that he was allowed to bring home as many magazines and comics as he liked. My mother would not allow me to have comics, partly because of money, but mostly because she didn't approve of them. Now and again, I got a copy of *Look and Learn*, which she considered mind-improving, but to have seen me reading the *Beano* would have broken her heart.

In Stewart's house, on the other hand, every available surface was piled high with comics, newspapers, magazines. His mother read all the women's magazines, *The People's Friend*, anything to do with knitting and jam recipes, anything with those 'Stranger Than Fiction', true-life stories that were all the rage. Stewart liked strip cartoons of the *Eagle*, *Roy of the Rovers*, *Boy's Own* variety. I liked the funny stuff. Every Saturday, I rose early and hopped over the fence to the Banks'. Stewart and his family would stay in bed till late – ten thirty, eleven, even, which I assumed was one of the bad habits of Protestants – but the back door was never locked, and I was welcome to come in any time, Mrs Banks said, even if nobody was about. This meant that I usually had an hour or two to study the *Dandy* and the *Beano*, or whatever else Mr Banks had brought home that week. It was the first of many forbidden pleasures.

Stewart was my only friend. In the summer, we went bird-nesting together, or we filched pieces of linoleum and tobogganed down the slag heaps that surrounded the town, tumbling off when we reached the bottom and making delicious red scrapes on our hands and knees, those red scrapes with hard little pieces of coal and slag buried just under the skin. In winter, if it snowed, we climbed trees in the woods – it was more fun to climb trees in the winter, when the leaves had fallen; we could see so much further, out and away from the town, to the fields and the graveyard beyond – or we made our own sleds from oddments of timber and careered down the little hill opposite Stewart's house. Together, we were the best bottle collectors in town, traipsing along the rims of ditches and foraging in the mouse-scented undergrowth for anything we could take to the shops and redeem. Most weeks, we made enough money that way to get us into the matinée at the Picture House.

Stewart was almost obsessively interested in all things Catholic: what our God was like, whether we believed in the Devil, what the saints did, whether the host really turned to flesh when the priest placed it on your tongue and you walked back up the aisle, trying to stay serious, with all eyes on you as the wafer melted in your mouth. He was amazed when I told him what I had learned in confirmation classes: that it was a sin for a Catholic to marry a Protestant, that if we did, husband and wife and all their children would go to hell. (I worried about this sometimes, as my father was a non-Catholic, but my mother seemed to think we weren't going to hell because, even if my father rarely attended Mass, he had converted to Catholicism before they actually married. I also worried about the distinction between non-Catholic and Protestant, which seemed to exist, though it was never defined. In the end, I decided the way to look at it was that Protestants were actively not-Catholic, whereas non-Catholics didn't much care, one way or another.) Stewart wondered if I thought he was going to hell and I had to tell him that it was unavoidable, unless he became a Catholic. He thought about this for a while, then he laughed.

'So you'll be going to heaven,' he said. 'Guaranteed.'

'Not necessarily,' I said. 'You can't go to heaven if you die with a mortal sin on your soul.' I then proceeded to explain what a mortal sin was.

'So,' Stewart said, 'if you get run over by a bus on your way to confession, with the mortal sin still on your soul, you go to hell, but if you get run over by the next bus, on your way home from confession, you go to heaven.'

'I suppose so,' I said, though even I could see the absurdity of the notion.

I think, however, that Stewart was more in awe of *The Catholics*, the more he learned about the strangeness of our beliefs. I think he admired us for entertaining such preposterous convictions. Certainly, he never mocked my religion; he only seemed bemused, and strangely taken in, by it. For a while, I even wondered if he was going to ask me to lead him to the priests' house, where he would repent his evil ways and join the one holy, Catholic and apostolic Church. But he never did. He came to Mass with me once, and I skipped Mass the following week, to go with him to kirk. I think he liked the statues and the flowers; he couldn't take his eyes off the foot of the Virgin, crushing the head of the serpent in a damp, incense-flavoured alcove just inside the door. I liked the emptiness of the kirk: the white walls, the clear windows, the fact that you could miss it once in a while. I didn't go there again, though. When it was discovered, by the Catholic powers that be, not only that I had missed Mass, but that I had taken the opportunity to support the other team, all hell broke loose. My mother was summoned to the school; the priest came to our house and sat gazing at me mournfully, his mouth full of home-made Dundee cake. Eventually, he told me he was surprised by what I had done, as he'd come to think that I might – *Deo volente* – be a boy who had a vocation. For a while, Stewart and I saw a little less of one another, as the

53

danger to my mortal soul, and my possible vocation, was assessed. In the end, though – a full confession having been made – I was allowed to go on seeing the Protestant boy (or maybe he was just a non-Catholic), as long as I promised never to go to his 'chapel' again.

If Stewart was my first and, for a long time, my only friend, then the girl from the prefab next door – I'll call her Sandra Fulton – was my first and, for a very long time, my only love. She was a year and a half older than me, but we were friends nevertheless. What we had in common, to begin with, was a desire to be left alone, a native mistrust of other children; what we came to share, though I didn't understand it at the time, would stay with me for years to come. We were conspirators, collaborators in the creation of a world that included nobody but ourselves; some days, Margaret tagged along, and was even allowed to participate in the first stages of our little games, but she never became a full member of the club, and even she didn't know what happened when Sandra and I were alone.

At the time, we didn't really know what we were doing either. Gradually, by degrees, we concocted an exquisite game, but it was a mystery to us that it should be so very pleasurable. We knew enough to know that it wasn't the usual game played by boys and girls: it wasn't doctors and nurses, it wasn't 'I'll show you mine if you show me yours'. In fact, there was no obvious sex in the game at all. I'd played those ordinary games – to this day, I remember how odd Annie Simpson's naked, unfinished-looking little pubis looked, when she slipped off her knickers and showed me what she had in the woods by the chicken farm – and I knew what they were about. I had kissed a girl in school; I had carefully nurtured a crush on my favourite teacher; for a time, I had allowed myself to become infatuated with the classroom vamp. I can still see Geraldine MacInnes, the most beautiful girl in Cowdenbeath, standing on the touchline in the one football game where I gave my all, scoring three goals and bewildering everyone with my sudden enthusiasm. She didn't notice me at all, though, and I lost all interest in football after that. My father still took me to Cowdenbeath games, when they were at home, and we would stand on the cold terraces, eating hot pies and shouting at the referee, but my heart wasn't really in it. With Sandra, it wasn't some childish romance, or curiosity about the body's machinery that drew us together. It was the fact that we had discovered something together and, even if we had no idea what it was, we knew it had to be kept secret.

Sandra's mother was an intense, very private Englishwoman, who made friends with considerable difficulty. She was shy, unhappy, and had a tendency to withdraw into herself suddenly and for no obvious reason, like a hedgehog curling up into a prickly, featureless ball. The only person she liked – the one person she talked to, the only person for whom I ever saw her smile – was my mother. The two women seemed to be united by some common, unspoken grief that, by the time the Fulton story was fully played out, had deepened and spread, like a black stain on both their lives. I think what my mother saw, in Mary Fulton, was a woman so much like herself – in her hopes, and in her disappointments – that when the tragedy of Arthur's crime destroyed, first his family, then Mary Fulton herself, my mother could hardly bear it.

Arthur Fulton was the kind of man everybody refers to as a 'gentle giant'. He was basketball-player tall, but with a light heavyweight's build; when he walked into a room, everything stopped for a moment to adjust to his presence. The furniture dwindled, the atmosphere darkened. What made matters worse was that Arthur, a shy, painfully inarticulate man, had a horror of being the object of attention, and would gladly have crept through life unnoticed. It was written in his face, not just embarrassment, but a terror of all things social. My father was fairly asocial too – most of the men in our wider circle were unhappy at public gatherings, or with any form of polite intercourse – but Arthur's problem was pathological. The only people he ever seemed comfortable around were children. He adored Sandra. He had decided, early on, that she was his princess, his one and only. Nobody ever doted on a child so blatantly – partly, no doubt, because he loved her, but also, I am sure, because she gave him a focus, a reason for not giving up on affection altogether. He was unhappy in his marriage; that was obvious. His wife treated him like a child and, in return, he chose the company of children over adults whenever he could.

I sometimes wonder what Arthur Fulton would have done if he had ever caught Sandra and me playing our little game. Oddly enough, even though it gave us so much pleasure, even though we knew it had to be kept secret at all costs, we never thought of it as wrong, or even as anything other than an innocent and private matter. The game was simple: we began by acting out a scenario where I was a burglar breaking into the house and stealing something while her back was turned. Then, when I had made my escape, she had to guess what it was I had taken. This progressed to my 'breaking in' when she was there. I would do my best to sneak in and take something without her seeing, but at some point she spotted me, and I had to escape, either by hopping back out of the window, or by overpowering her and tying her up. Which is where it all got interesting. I knew nothing about sex, much less about bondage, but to my eight-year-old self, tying Sandra Fulton up with soft woollen scarves and the belt from her school Burberry was painfully erotic, causing in my pre-adolescent nervous system something close to overload. I have no idea how Sandra felt while all this was going on, though I do recall that she was the one, at every stage of our little game, who took the lead. For a grown-up, nowadays, this might immediately set alarm bells ringing, especially when you consider what her father is supposed to have done to his girlfriend later, but I don't think she had been schooled in any of this. She was just a year older and a whole lot more imaginative than I was. Where she is now, I have no idea, but I wonder, sometimes, if that game of ours left an enduring impression on her heart – as it did on mine. I hope so. I like to think that, somewhere, a bored housewife, or some tired professional, pauses a moment and remembers those games at the prefabs, when she was tied up with assorted oddments from her school clothes, and lay waiting (in vain, alas) to discover what might happen next, while I stood over her in my makeshift burglar's mask, flushed with excitement. Nothing ever did happen, of course; though, looking back, and considering the world we inhabited, we'd done pretty well to get that far. It was just bad luck that any further experiments we might have conducted were cut short by a terrible crime, and by my father's perennial dissatisfaction with his lot.

CHAPTER 4

My father disliked his new house. Looking back, I can see that the move was another defeat for him: the prefabs had been intended as temporary accommodation during the post-war period of austerity, but they had lingered on, cheap housing for poor people, an improvement, at least, on the ratty tenements on King Street and elsewhere. Every year, there was talk of demolition, but the fact was that most people who lived in the prefabs were happy with what they had, and nobody on the council was stupid enough to move us back into the overcrowded, noisy, unsanitary ruins from which we had just escaped. To my mother, and many like her, the prefabs were a godsend: detached houses, in effect, with their own gardens, in loose clusters at the greener end of the town, with neighbours just close enough to call on for help in emergencies or for a spot of tea and gossip, but not so close that they got to know all your business. That would have been import-ant to her, for during the seven years we lived in the prefabs, my father became more and more of an unknown quantity. For weeks on end, he would come home from work on a Friday night, or on a Saturday afternoon if there was over-time, and he would be tired to the bone, silent and dulled and uneasy, but he would hand over his wages, and there would be enough for the coming week, for cereals and sausages and cheap cuts of meat. Then, without warning, he would disappear, taking his wage packet with him, turning up drunk with 'friends' in the small hours of Sunday morning, loud and jovial and edgy, prepared to be loved, and ready to do damage if love was withheld. Or he would slip in quietly while we were playing in the garden, and sit weeping at the kitchen table, drunk and contrite, promising that this was the last, that, from now on, he would be fine. On those days, we would know, when we came indoors, that for a week or more every meal would be split-pea or lentil soup from the supply of dried foods my mother hoarded in the top cupboard for just such a rainy day, and the milk bottles would disappear from the doorstep for a while, replaced by a printed note, in her neat, slightly cramped hand, that said: *No milk today, thank you.*

I look back now and see that the move to the prefabs sealed my father's sense of himself as a failure. For as long as we had been at King Street, on the waiting list, there was a chance of going up in the world, but the simple fact was that, as a casual worker, doing mostly seasonal work, first at the docks, then in the building trade, he would always occupy the bottom of the social pile, just one rung above the unemployed and the unemployable. He was also a drinker, and everybody knew that. People know they cannot depend on a drunk. He could be hired, of course, but he would always be brought in on a seasonal or casual basis, so there were no obligations if anything went wrong. Things usually went wrong, sooner or later. It surprises me, looking back, that my father ever thought his problem with alcohol was a secret. Everybody knew. The child I was could tell, walking along the high street in Cowdenbeath, by the way people behaved towards my mother, combining respect and pity in more or less equal measure, admiring her for the tenacity with which she held her family together, but also pitying, and perhaps even despising a little, this woman whose lack of judgement had not only led her into the mess she was in, but kept her there, hoodwinked, self-deceiving, vainly hoping for something to change.

My father did not blame himself for his failure, of course. When he had been in the air force, he had been happy; he was always saying he should never have left the RAF, that he'd only come out because of my mother, who didn't like the idea of having to go and live wherever the MOD might send him, far from her family, maybe in some foreign country – Germany, or Cyprus, say – countries that sounded exciting and exotic to us, but to her would have been a living hell, so far from her own folk, in a place where she would never be able to speak the language. After my father left the RAF, he'd got work at the docks, and there had been some kind of scam going on there, where my father – a seasoned gambler, who could do pretty complex arithmetic in his head – had run a book, before betting shops were made legal. I don't know the whole story: he and my mother were just married, living in the King Street rat warren, and he was working at the docks, when this opportunity came up. I imagine it was fairly nickel-and-dime stuff but, according to my father, there were days when he came home and dropped a pile of cash on the kitchen table, on top of his wages for the week. In my mother's version, this did happen once or twice; mostly, however, he'd come home broke, having gambled away the extra – and, as she was always quick to point out, *illegal* – money he'd been paid. It was a frequent bone of contention and, later, when I was seven or eight, I would hear them arguing about it, my father playing the part of criminal entrepreneur headed for bigger things when my mother's nervousness had forced him to turn his back on a way of life that would have made us all rich. He would say nobody ever got rich working for somebody else; my mother would reply that she didn't want to be rich, she just wanted enough to get on with her life, no trouble, no fuss. It was like listening to a bad soap opera, and I couldn't take much of it. After a while, I'd be up and out of the window, or sitting in the press in the corner of the bedroom, curled up with my toys, blocking them out of my mind.

So time passed. I was happy enough, at times, playing in the woods, making dens, finding birds' nests in the scrap piles behind the old abattoirs. Sometimes, I would get to visit Uncle John and Aunt Margaret: Big John would take me out fishing in the loch with his younger sons, Kenneth and Anthony, even though I was too young to fish; sometimes I was allowed to stay over, and the oldest of my cousins, Wee John, who was a prize-winning chemistry student, would tell me about magnetism, or space. I remember he showed me odd experiments with water glass and metal salts, say, and I would wonder how he knew such things, when he was just like his brothers, just like me. When I grew up, I thought, I would know things like that: the periodic table, which cousin John had on a chart on his bedroom wall; the migrations of birds; the distances between stars. All that knowledge felt like something substantial to hold on to, against the vagaries of everyday life.

After a while, my mother was pregnant again. My parents were excited; even my father brightened up as they planned for a new baby and, for a while, he settled down and dug in. He got a steadier job at Grangemouth, doing something that kept him out from early morning till late at night, which meant we never saw him. I wasn't unhappy about that. They worked hard at this new beginning, and my mother tried to stay healthy, but things went badly in the latter months and, finally, when she came to deliver, the baby died. It was a baby boy; he would have been called Andrew. When my mother came home from the hospital she looked pale as death; she went to bed in the room at the back of the house and didn't speak to anyone for days. My father kept going to work, as if nothing had happened, but I knew he was unhappy, and the nights were quiet, very still, disturbed only by the calls of the tawny owls in Kirk's woods. I would lie awake, then, listening to the night and thinking about my brother. He was gone before he had even existed, and I'd never even got to see him, but I had a new ghost to entertain.

I knew this loss would have consequences – and, gradually, things got worse. My father was bitter about losing the baby, and this led to more frequent binges, but it was still a while before the late-night parties with the friends he'd picked up on his procession through Cowdenbeath's worst pubs became a regular thing. I remember the men who came as exact clones of my father – big, drunk, edgy, just this side of dangerous – and it seemed to me that they were always different, new names, new faces, new unknown quantities to appease and please and outmanoeuvre. I would be in bed when they arrived, though usually not asleep. By that time I was old enough to worry when he wasn't home, old enough to feel the tension when Margaret and I were put to bed – I have no explanation for this, but my mother always knew when he was about to go *off the rails*, as she put it – old enough to wonder whether we would all get safely through the night. I would be in bed, pretending to be asleep, not daring to slip out in case my father came home and found my bed empty when, as was more and more the case, he wanted me up and about, serving drinks, emptying ashtrays, mopping up spillages and the occasional pool of vomit or piss. All evening, I would lie awake, listening to my mother as she went about the house, hiding ornaments, tidying up, doing her best to make the place look good and, at the same time, concealing anything she thought my father and his friends might damage or abuse. Then she would go to bed and close her bedroom door. She would pretend to be asleep too – and when my father eventually got back, he would leave her to it. He didn't want her about at such times, watching him, making the odd innocent-sounding but wholly calculated remark, asking his friends about their own homes, their own families, trying to shame them into decency.

With me, though, it was different. My father took real pleasure in rousing me from my bed and having me come through, in my pyjamas, to do those little jobs he felt I could manage, all the time listening to what the men were saying, taking note, ready to speak when spoken to. He would have me perform tricks: feats of mental arithmetic or memory, or he would tell them to ask me questions. The capital of Bolivia came up a good deal, as did the spelling of Mississippi and the attribution of various, usually misquoted, lines from Burns. It was a difficult balancing act, showing off just enough so he would be proud (the father of a smart son, naturally, because he was so smart himself), but not so much that he would be embarrassed, or shown up (maybe the boy's too smart, a bit of a show-off, when all's said and done). I quickly learned which questions to answer confidently, which should be hesitated over and which should be left unanswered. A bright boy, bright as a button, and good-natured with it. Not too proud to fetch a rag from the scullery and help out when there was a wee accident, or pop out to the coal bunker for more coal on a chilly night. Bright, yes, but always willing.

'Hey, son. Pour us all another rum, will you?'

'Hey, son. Get us a towel here.'

'Where's the toilet, wee man?'

I would pour the rum, or the whisky, or the beer, and I would know I was pouring away our food for the week, the insurance money, probably the rent. I also knew never to let this show. On party nights, we were the richest people in the world. Our hospitality knew no limits. And we regretted nothing.

Sometimes my father came home earlier in the evening. This meant he was running out of money, and somebody had offered to chip in on a carry-out. When that happened, his usual partner-in-crime was Paddy, a friend of his from the Woodside, his favourite drinking hole. My mother had once made the mistake of saying that Paddy was a gentleman, which allowed my father to pretend, on these early returns from the pub, that he had brought Paddy home to say hello. On the nights when Paddy came back, my father would make sure they brought something for my mother to drink, a Babycham, say. My mother didn't like alcohol, but she would drink a Babycham now and then to be sociable. My father also knew that she wouldn't make a scene in front of Paddy, that she would sit nicely for a while, then excuse herself and go off to bed. Maybe she would venture a parting shot along the lines of 'Don't sit up too late, now', or 'Remember, they're asleep'. I would hear this as she stood in the hallway, on her way to bed, and I knew what would happen next.

One night my father came home about nine thirty and discovered that my mother had already turned in. All her life, she suffered from anaemia; she would get headaches and mysterious dizzy spells; if she sat down for any length of time, just knitting, or listening to the wireless, she would suddenly fall asleep and sit, head slumped forward on to her chest, lost

64

to us. Sometimes, when my father was out, she would send us to bed at the usual time, then she would go through to the living room, turn the lights off, stoke up the fire, and go to bed, presumably because she thought my father would be out for hours, and she could get some proper rest. I think that was when she was most content, alone in bed, drifting away, letting her worries slide. That night, she'd had a headache, though, and she looked pale and thin-mouthed, with dark blue circles around the eyes. When my father got in, I was pretty sure she was asleep, but I knew he wouldn't disturb her anyway.

Half an hour passed, before he slipped into my room. 'Hey, son,' he said, peering down at me. 'You're no asleep already, are you?' He could see I wasn't. 'Come on, put your jumper and your trousers on. There's somebody here to see you.'

I got up and slipped my clothes on over my pyjamas. I didn't really want to see Paddy – oddly enough, I felt more uncomfortable with him than with my father's other, less gentlemanly friends. With them, it was just a matter of doing what needed to be done, but Paddy embarrassed me. I think he embarrassed himself, when he'd had too much to drink. He at least knew he could do better.

Paddy was sitting in the living room, by the fire. There was always a fire in the grate, except in high summer: the prefabs had no other heating, and where we were, by the woods, it was damp. Damp was much worse than cold, everybody said so. You could walk miles in a freezing gale, as long as you stayed dry, but everybody knew stories about the wifie who'd just washed her hair, then popped out for some coal and died two days later, in a high fever. So the fire was there to keep out the damp, and it was a godsend to Paddy, who always looked a little damp himself, a man in a worn suit that looked like it had just come off a rail in a second-hand shop, and still needed a bit of an iron.

'You no sleeping yet, son?' was his greeting. As always, he looked embarrassed.

I shook my head.

'Paddy's not had his tea,' my father said. 'I bet you'd like some chips. Would you like some chips?' I didn't know who he was talking to, me or Paddy. He took a banknote from his pocket and held it out to me. 'Run down to the shop and get us a couple of fish suppers,' he said. 'And some chips for yourself.'

'Aw, come on, Tommy,' Paddy protested. He looked more embarrassed than ever. 'You're not sending him out like that, are ye?'

My father kept his eyes on me. 'He's all right,' he said. 'Aren't you, son?'

I nodded.

'Well, he'll need a coat on,' Paddy said.

My father gave a snort. 'He'll not need a coat,' he said. 'Will you?'

I shook my head. I didn't really have a coat. 'I'm fine,' I said.

My father nodded his approval. 'He never feels the cold,' he said. 'Do you, son? Takes after his Dad.' He looked at my feet. 'You better put your shoes on, though,' he said. 'We don't want your feet getting cold.' He turned away, heading off towards the kitchen.

Paddy sat staring at me dolefully. 'Aye,' he said. 'You have to keep your feet warm.' he said. He looked wretched and it suddenly occurred to me that he was going to die, not some day, but soon. He looked like he knew it, too. I couldn't help but feel sorry for him.

*

66

For the week or so after one of these parties, we ate soup and scraps. My mother would go traipsing around the high street, come Monday morning, asking the butcher for offcuts as a treat for our imaginary dog, bits of bone with a little meat on, or bacon rashers, to give the soup a little body. We had free milk in school, but we either didn't qualify, or were too proud to take, free dinners. Sometimes, Mr Kirk from the poultry farm would give us a few eggs, after I'd supposedly helped him out with his birds, and there was always plenty of flour in the house, for real emergencies. One autumn afternoon, when school was out and we were hungry, Margaret came home with a couple of turnips that she had found on the road. My mother was suspicious, but she started preparing vegetable soup, with barley and a few scraps of fat, right away. It was always a pleasure, watching the prefab windows steam up while my mother cooked us soup, and we were all gathered round, my sister and I sitting at the kitchen table, my mother standing at the cooker, when the farmer arrived. He explained that he'd seen a girl pulling turnips from his field, and that he'd followed her along the Old Perth Road. He wasn't annoyed with her, he said, he just wanted to say that, if she wanted a neep for Halloween, she should just come and ask, and he'd be happy to let her have one.

My mother didn't know what to say, other than to apologise. She was standing at the door, in her apron, the smell of boiled turnips filling the room.

'I hope she doesn't plan to eat thae neeps,' the farmer said. 'They're meant for fodder.' He looked past my mother to where we were sitting at the table. Margaret shrank into her seat. 'For the beasts,' he continued, being helpful.

'Oh, no,' my mother said. 'It's – something for school. An experiment. I'm sure she didn't know – '

'I don't mind,' the farmer put in quickly, sensing, now, what he had stumbled into. Maybe he knew all along, and had come to see if he could help. 'Just – well, if she comes and asks me, next time.'

My mother promised she would, and the man went away. I thought she would be angry and send Margaret to the bedroom for what she had done, but she wasn't angry, and she didn't say anything. She just walked back to the cooker and turned down the gas. Then she stood, stirring the soup, gazing out of the window. She was doing her best to seem calm, but I could tell she was crying.

Secretly, my father still had more than the odd flutter on the horses. I think my first real prefabs era memory is of running lines for him: think, rather than know, because there are other, earlier scenes in my head, incidents on a beach, or on our Sunday walks in the local cemetery, that have been described often enough, during family conversations, in the endless whiling away of time, to be imprinted in my mind, almost real, almost mine. Yet, in spite of that, if I were asked for a first memory, it would be of learning a series of words and numbers, taking possession of a fistful of banknotes, and running a mile or so to a shop on the edge of the next town, where a man who seemed to me extraordinarily old would take the money, listen to what I had to say, and send me away with a bag of sherbet lemons or a bottle of Cherryade. I'm not sure when all this happened: I was five, maybe six, and one day, when my father let me choose a horse from the list in the paper, I took Nicholas Silver, a big, strong grey who won the Grand National in 1960, at fifty to one. I got to bet a shilling – though at the time I would rather have had the money, or the sweets it would buy – and I liked it when I was presented with my winnings, an impossible sum that seems to grow magically out of mere guesswork.

How a grown-up comes to forget the terrors of childhood is a mystery to me, but he does. No one who remembered what it was like to thread his way through the backstreets haunted by the strange and violent dogs of my childhood would ever keep a Rottweiler or a bull terrier. But then, dogs were part of the pathology of all the places where I grew up. Big dogs, in particular. It's mostly about power, I suppose: a big dog makes a small man bigger; imagine what it does for a frightened child. At first I wanted a black Labrador, then I longed for a husky; then I didn't want a dog at all. I'd met a stray one day, when I was around seven, and it had followed me home, a black-and-white mongrel with a curious, intelligent face that no boy could resist. When I asked if I could keep it, my mother assumed that soft, quiet tone she reserved for non-negotiable situations. 'You're not having a dog,' she said. 'And that's that.'

'It doesn't belong to anybody,' I said. 'It's a stray.'

'I don't care what it is. You're not bringing a dog into this house.'

We'd had this discussion before and I knew it was no use, so I decided to wait and see what my father said, when he got home from work. My father liked dogs; he was always talking about the Alsatian he'd supposedly worked with in Germany, a big, brutally intelligent beast called Prince. I didn't believe him, even then: I'd seen police-dog handlers at Gala Days, and I knew it took a specialist to manage a dog like that. My father had been a flight sergeant. He wasn't a dog specialist. He did like dogs, though, and I had hopes he might talk my mother round. I had no idea, of course, what I was

69

letting us all in for. That night, with my stray friend gone, I asked him if I could get a dog.

'Ask your mum,' he said.

'I asked her. She said to ask you.'

He looked at me from behind a paper he'd brought home from Grangemouth. 'No she didn't,' he said.

I thought it best not to pursue this line. 'But can I?' I said. 'I'll look after it.'

My mother appeared at the kitchen door. 'You're not having a dog,' she said, 'and that's final.' I'd thought she was out of earshot.

My father didn't say anything. His paper went up, while he waited for his dinner to be on the table. He probably hadn't even heard what I'd said. *Ask your mother* was his standard reply when he didn't want to be bothered with me. I'd timed things wrong, I realised. He'd just come in from work, he was tired and, worse, he was sober. I'd made a mistake: there would be no dog.

But I was wrong. Or almost wrong. The following Saturday, my father appeared in the middle of the afternoon with the saddest excuse for a canine I had ever seen. It was the kind of dog that gets called Patch in movies and cartoons, a cross-bred, cross-eyed, unlovable runt of a thing that someone had given him at the Woodside, probably for the price of a pint. By the time he got it back to the house, it was missing something, or someone, whining miserably and pulling at the end of its ragged string leash, dirty, wild-eyed and as horribly unhappy with its new surroundings as my mother was with it.

'What have you done?' was all she could say, when she finally spoke.

'It's a wee dog,' my father replied. 'For the boy. He's always talking about getting a dog.'

70

I felt sick. This dog was so unappealing, even I didn't want it. I wanted the stray I had made friends with, and given a secret name. I would sooner have kept a cobra than this desperate thing, but I couldn't say so. My father would have been too upset. Now, he turned to me. 'Here,' he said, waving at the worried animal that was now abjectly plastered to the floor by the stove, aware of nothing but my mother's terrible gaze. 'I got you a dog. What do you want to call him?'

I didn't know what to say. All of a sudden, I knew I would never want a dog again for as long as I lived, that I had probably never really wanted one in the first place. I stared at the wretched beast, and I did feel sorry for it, but I felt sorrier for myself, and even sorrier still for my parents – at that moment, both my parents – so helplessly locked into the misery of wedlock. All I could do was stall. 'Where did he come from?' I asked.

'It's a good wee puppy,' my father said. He obviously didn't want to say anything more about provenance in front of my mother. 'All it needs is a good home – '

'It's not staying,' my mother said. 'For one thing, we can't afford – ' My father stiffened. If there was one thing he didn't want to hear, ever, it was the details of what he couldn't afford. Realising her mistake, my mother turned back to me. 'I'm sorry,' she said. 'You can have something else. But not a dog.'

I nodded. I wanted to be invisible. I looked at my father and saw the misery in his eyes. He'd been defeated again, this time by his own son. As tears came to my eyes, I turned quickly and ran from the room.

I never quite understood the balance of power in my parents' house. Usually, my father did what he liked and damn the consequences. Right after a binge, he would be remorseful, especially if he, or one of his cronies, had done any damage, and the month or so following one of my mother's occasional mysterious illnesses would always be a softly-softly period, but, mostly, he did what he wanted. Looking back now, I can see the underlying blackmailer's logic in this scene: my father does what he thinks, or can pretend to think, is a good deed, knowing all the time that his seeming kindness will be refused. My mother will feel guilty about the apparent rejection, even while she sees through it all, and also feels thoroughly manipulated. It's one of the facts of marriage: you don't get credit points for anything you can't explain in simple, everyday terms. My mother knew, at some level, what was going on, but she had no way of putting it into words; or if she did, my father would pretend he didn't understand. The moment would pass, but there would be a marker set against it, and later, when the opportunity arose, it would be used as an excuse to do something quite unconnected with that particular event, or it would be cast up to the other party in an argument, and the game would be complete. Sure enough, the following Friday, my father didn't turn up until close to midnight. He came straight into my room and woke me. 'Come into the kitchen,' he said. 'Alec's brought you a present.'

I knew who Alec was. He was the crony my mother most disliked, a sly, smiling man with very round eyes in a flat, pale face. He worked on the building with my father; he was also involved in other activities, though I didn't know what they were. All I knew was that my mother disapproved. Once, she used the word *criminal*, which was a big word in her vocabulary, but I never found out what she meant by it.

Alec was sober. He was standing in the kitchen, holding a big hessian sack of the kind people used for grain or animal feed. I'd seen them being delivered to the farms round about, and I loved how rounded they looked, the grain slipping around inside as the men unloaded them from the great lorries, the fat sides daubed with numbers and place names. This sack, though, was long and limp, hanging from Alec's hand, where the top was all rucked and bunched up in his fist, and it was empty, except for something at the very bottom, some live thing that was moving around restlessly, not so much afraid as curious, wanting to get out, but not necessarily to run away. Alec grinned. 'Come and see,' he said to me, jiggling the sack. 'What do you think this is?' He was trying too hard, as always. I'd noticed that before. He could be nice as you like, he could turn it on like a tap, but he always wanted to get something for himself out of any encounter. There were times when I felt sorry for him a little, thinking that even a boy my age could see right through him. Maybe he wasn't so bad after all. Maybe he was lonely.

I knew it was an animal. Obviously. After the argument about the dog, I also knew it had to be a pet of some kind – but it seemed too small in its hessian sack to be a dog. Maybe a kitten. I supposed it could be a small puppy, but I didn't think my father would do that again. He rarely made the same mistake twice; not when there were so many others to make. Probably it was a kitten. 'I don't know,' I said. My father was standing beside me, watching. He wasn't altogether drunk, but he was on the way. I felt a sudden exquisite shudder of dread. Something was about to go wrong.

Alec unclenched his fist and let the sack drop to the floor. For a moment, nothing happened. Then, slowly, their tiny black noses emerging first, two hedgehogs appeared: baby hedgehogs, I thought, tiny, far thinner and quicker than I would have imagined. I don't know what Alec and my father thought they would do, maybe curl up into a ball, or wait to be offered a saucerful of milk, but the hedgehogs had no time for that. As soon as they hit the linoleum, they took off: in spite of the light, and the huge presence standing over them, they scampered away, heading for the living-room door, and pattering on, into the hallway, into my parents' bedroom. Usually, when my father was out late, my mother would close the door, so she wouldn't be disturbed by his friends' antics; this time, perhaps because she had gone to bed early, and she wanted to listen out in case Margaret or I needed her, the door was wide open. In ran the hedgehogs, and in we all ran, chasing them: me, my father, even Alec, excited by the sound of those tiny claws on the floor, or by the speed, or perhaps by the apparent single-mindedness of the two hedgehogs, who had, without a moment's hesitation, made off at full tilt towards the bedroom. It was an eerie sound, that clatter of little nails on the floor.

I think my mother had been half asleep, but by the time we got to the bedroom, she was wide awake. She had been lying, not in, but on the bed, in her nightdress and house-coat, which was the moment's only saving feature. Still, nobody had ever seen her like that, much less one of my father's cronies. 'What in God's name is going on?' she cried, as we all tumbled into the little bedroom. She was staring at us, and I suddenly felt betrayed, implicated in a crime that wasn't my fault, a crime that had been perpetrated against me as much as anyone.

'Sorry, missus,' Alec said, not smiling for once, as he with-drew.

My mother barely noticed him. She was staring at my father. 'Well?'

He didn't answer. Something was under the bed; there was the sound of a scuffle, then both hedgehogs darted out and away, back towards the door. My mother watched them go.

'It's all right,' I said, wanting to keep the peace. 'It's just hedgehogs. They're not – '

'*Hedgehogs!*' My mother was on the verge of panic. She almost jumped off the bed; then she remembered her bare feet.

'Never mind,' my father said. 'It was a bad idea.' He sounded aggrieved, as if he'd done something, not only utterly blameless, but entirely logical, entirely benevolent, and was being unfairly punished for it. 'As usual,' he added, and I knew from the tone of his voice that we'd all pay for this night's business, one way or another. He looked at me, as if he expected some kind of useful intervention, then he shook his head sadly and retreated. After a moment I could hear him talking to Alec in the kitchen; then the back door banged shut and they were gone.

My mother looked at me. 'Go to bed,' she said.

I never did understand how it worked, that balance of power. There were times when my mother was completely in charge, the one sensible grown-up in a house full of children. Then, all of a sudden, for no obvious reason, things switched around. My mother was like a frightened child, trying to cope with a man who was, or could at any moment be, out of control. I didn't understand it, but I knew it well enough. So it was no surprise, a few nights later, when she came into my room and woke me. 'Get dressed,' she said. 'Quick.'

I got out of bed and picked up my clothes. I could hear voices – men talking, not shouting, but talking loudly, excited, just starting to slip out of control – and I knew someone was there, but *that* was nothing new. What was new was the expression on my mother's face: a look of deep apprehension, it seemed at first, and then, as she stood watching me, waiting

75

at the door while I pulled on my raggedy sweater and jeans, a look of fear.

'Quick,' she said again. I glanced over at the other bed, where my sister was sleeping. 'Never mind Margaret. He'll not bother her.'

I wasn't sure what this meant, but now I was afraid. Afraid for myself, and afraid for my mother. Afraid of what might happen. I slipped my plimsolls on over my bare feet and laced them up.

'Just go outside for a bit,' my mother said. 'Till things settle down.'

I started towards the door, where she was still standing, as if ready to bar it. She made me think of Catherine Douglas, who tried to save James I from his assassins by barring the door with her thin, bare arm. We'd had that story in school and I hadn't been able to put out of my mind the thought of that delicate, white arm cracking as the door was forced in.

My mother shook her head. 'Go out the window,' she said. 'You've done it often enough.' I was surprised: I didn't think she knew about my night sorties; then I realised that she was trying to make a little joke out of it all, as if what was happening was just some kind of game. 'Quick now,' she said. 'Just go out and round the back – ' She broke off to listen. Someone was coming, it seemed. I hopped up on to my bed and opened the window. The cool night air gusted in as the window swung open. I had been out at night often enough; it didn't frighten me in the least. Not the dark, not the woods. There was more to be afraid of indoors. I had learned a fondness for the cool darkness, the calls of the tawny owls in Mr Kirk's strip of woods, the sky full of stars that, when I was older, I would be able to name. I climbed up on to the window sill, then I turned back to her. I wanted to say something, to

76

make some arrangement about what I would do and when I should come back, but I didn't know what to say. 'Don't worry,' she said. 'And don't go far. Stay near the house. All right?'

I nodded.

'You'll be all right,' she said, more for her own sake than mine.

I nodded again, then I dropped down into the cool darkness. It was quiet outside, and I was stunned, for a moment, by how still it was, how nearly silent. Then an owl called, and I scampered away from the window. I felt like an animal, like one of the wolverines I had read about in *Look and Learn*, or in one of the Jack London novels Miss Conway had lent me. A wolverine, a coyote, a quick, lithe thing, slipping away in the night. I passed through the narrow gap in our front hedge, and I could smell the cold, the green of it, that privet and dust smell of a coal town in summer. Back in the house, I heard my father shouting, then more voices, arguing about something, coming to some agreement, and settling down, only to flare up again as the front door tilted open and my father stood there, in a shirt that, for that one moment, seemed impossibly, cinematically white. He looked out into the darkness a moment and I think he was on the point of coming out, then he turned aside and slammed the door shut. I waited, watched. I was still worried, though not for myself. Then, all of a sudden, as a wave of cold and utter detachment came over me, I realised that nothing more would happen – not that night, and not the next day. My father and his friends would sit drinking till the drink was gone, then the other men would leave, and my father would go to bed. The one thing he prided himself on was that he never hit my mother – and at that moment, I not only believed that this was true, but that he never would hit her. He had no need. That night, for the first time, I saw that. She was terrified of him, but she had given up being frightened for herself. Now it was her children she had to protect. It still hadn't registered that I was out there because, for the first time, she thought I was in physical danger. I thought she just didn't want me to see something that would shame me, or her, or my father. Tomorrow, I thought, things would go back to normal. It would be quite a time before I saw that, no matter what my mother or any of us did, there had never been a *normal* to go back to.

CHAPTER 5

As my father drifted through his thirties, he became more and more restless. In Cowdenbeath, he was unhappy to be so close to in-laws who thought so little of him, but he was also in the place where he had lived all his life, a place where he could not help but be seen for what he was. I understand, now, why he would have found that restrictive: he needed to lie, in order to *be*, or, at least, in order not to be the failure he would soon become, in his own eyes, as well as in the eyes of others, if he didn't get away. For the next several years, we would be flitting, if not in reality, then in our minds: my father talked about moving all the time, first to one place, then another. It was always the most seductive story he could offer us: a story about making a new start, about finding a better life. Margaret and I were all for that; we thought he would be happier somewhere else, and if he was happier, we would be happier too. As we understood it, all we had to do was move and we would have sunshine, bikes, rooms of our own.

While all these vague plans were being hatched, my mother sat tight, not arguing, just resisting with all she had. Silence. Patience. The momentum of daily routine. Even as a child, I knew she didn't want to go anywhere: in Cowdenbeath, she had family, friends, support. She had well-tried ways of getting through the bad times. There were places, there, where she could hide, and not seem to be hiding; an agreed etiquette that allowed her to beg and not seem to be begging. I knew the words for this, even when I didn't fully understand the system: coal towns were close-knit communities; everybody pulled together. The same machinery that allowed my father to get away with what he did also kept his family going, through fat and lean – though it was mostly lean, and that was also common knowledge. Meanwhile, I hopped out of the bedroom window a little more often. I even got to know, without telling, when it was time for me to go. My father never remembered, in the morning, that I'd been absent from my bed when he came looking for me to run errands, or entertain his friends, or whatever it was he wanted me to do. For him, mornings after were reserved for remorse and sweet tea, just as they were all over Scotland.

Our first move was to Birmingham. I was six. I had been to Edinburgh, so I knew what a city was like, but I had only ever seen the clean heartland of the capital: Princes Street, the Bridges, the Scott Memorial, James Thin's Bookshop. Edinburgh, for me, was crossing the Forth Rail Bridge on a special day's outing, when times were as good as they got. My mother would wear make-up, lipstick, her good coat, and she would give us a halfpenny each to throw out of the carriage window as the train crossed the firth. This was a tradition: a child tossed a coin out of the window and made a wish, right at the centre of the bridge; if you did it right, the wish would come true, no matter what you wished for. Naturally, I wished for extravagant, wild things: a big house at the edge of town, near Central Park; a car, like the one my uncle John had; happy parents. I didn't expect to get any of it, though – not because I didn't think it was possible, but because I knew I wasn't doing the thing right: a halfpenny wasn't enough, I wasn't throwing it out at exactly the midpoint, it wasn't hitting the water right.

Edinburgh was best clothes and afternoon tea with scones in the British Home Stores café. Birmingham was something else. To my six-year-old self, it was huge, dark and rainy, crowded with people who were unlike us in every way. I couldn't understand what they were saying; I couldn't figure out how the traffic worked; there were cars and buses everywhere. The house where we lodged was owned by a tall, striking Irishwoman called Maureen, who smoked all the time and watched over her tenants like a strict but benevolent head-mistress, a woman who would rather have died than be seen without her make-up and lipstick, routinely obsessed with her personal appearance, but prepared to live in a house that was, quite literally, a midden. 'I hope you like cats,' she said, as she showed us to the single room we would occupy at the top of the house. 'There's not usually this many. Both my girls just had kittens.'

I watched my mother suppress her disgust. The stairway was oddly golden, bathed in a cool, syrupy light; it also smelled terrible, a mixture of smoke, cat shit and boiled vegetables. The understanding was that Maureen's house was a cheap and decidedly temporary billet. On her side, Maureen seemed to think we were on the run from somewhere. She was careful not to ask questions, or act too curious, which only made my mother more awkward, as it began to register, over the first few days, that my father had spun our landlady a whole web of bizarre and unnecessary lies. The room was long and narrow, and contained two beds, an old wardrobe and a deal table. A mirror was screwed to the wall by the door, there was a battered bedside unit between the double bed where my parents slept and the narrower, not quite single bed Margaret and I had to share. The only light was a bulb overhead, almost obscured by a thick, crimson, velvety-looking lampshade with long, dusty tassels. Worst of all, it was unbearably noisy. As my mother said to Aunt Margaret, when we got back safely to Cowdenbeath, the walls were so thin, you could hear what the people next door were thinking before they said it.

We stayed in Birmingham for several weeks. In all that time, I never saw the centre, never went to any gardens or famous monuments, never had tea and scones. We were out in some anonymous, run-down district with all the other transient people who'd come looking for a fresh start – Irish and West Indians, mostly. I was fascinated by the Jamaican men, in their dowdy overcoats and trilby-style hats, like the detectives in old films, only black, with beautiful, soft voices that worked magic around them as they walked along, a magic I could hear but didn't understand. Most of the time, though, I was scared. One rainy afternoon, I was hit by a car, just lightly, enough to knock me down, but nothing was broken and the driver was very good about it, calming my mother down, asking if she needed anything. It had been my fault: I'd stepped out into the road without looking, something I'd never done at home, but nobody was angry and, afterwards, my mother bought me a book. I remember it still: *The Pomegranate Seeds and Other Stories*, a piece of ephemera that was only a step away from being a comic, but had a proper story as well as pictures. It was stories from Greek mythology, so I imagine my mother thought it educational. I kept that book intact and spotless for years.

A week after the car incident, I came down with chicken-pox. I had it first, then Margaret caught it. We didn't mind having to stay indoors – my strongest memory of Birmingham, other than raw, itchy spots and traffic, was of rainy days and nowhere to go – but it was hard for my mother, with my father out labouring all day, and Maureen trying to help, coming into the room without knocking, bringing Kaolin and Morphine for the invalids and cups of hot, steaming tea for my mother, who could hardly refuse all this well-meaning assistance. I believe she did like Maureen, in spite of everything, but she would have preferred to deal with things herself, not among strangers.

My father loved Birmingham. Perhaps, for a drunk, cities really are better: in a small town, a man runs out of goodwill pretty quickly, and people soon know where they stand with him. In a city, he can go from pub to pub, hotel bar to hotel bar and, if he makes a mistake in one, there's always another. Meanwhile, he can be anybody he chooses to be. He can walk into a strange place, strike up a conversation, gradually let slip the clues and revealing details of a life he has never known. A life he might have had, if things had been different. He can even believe, as he slips into the familiar-seeming role, that he came so close to making that life happen, his story might as well be the truth. If he hadn't married that particular woman. If he'd never had kids. If he'd stayed in the air force, he'd be just a few years from a pension by now.

He must have known that it couldn't last. He'd led my mother to believe that flitting to Birmingham was the beginning of new life, but he was just doing the same casual work on the building that he'd been doing at home. At least in Cowdenbeath, we'd had the prefab to ourselves; now, in Maureen's house, we were living with strangers, some of whom were fixtures, like the furniture and the smell in the hallways, while others came and went, men from Cork or Somerset who stayed a week or so, then disappeared, women who were almost indistinguishable from Maureen, some a little younger and fresher-looking, some older, caked in dark, wet-looking make-up. The men were mysterious and sullen, which made my mother think they were criminals; the women popped in for a cup of tea one afternoon, stayed for a few days, then wandered off somewhere, never to be seen again. They were so like Maureen, I thought they must be her sisters, or cousins; they dressed in similar clothes, smoked the same cigarettes, talked the same talk. They might as well have been the same woman, variant incarnations of the coarse, good-humoured, hard-headed landlady who beguiled and frightened me.

My mother waited for a few weeks, as I remember, before she went to work on talking us home. To begin with, she was careful: it wouldn't do to suggest that my father had been wrong, or that he was stuck in the dead-end work he'd been getting so far. It wouldn't do for him to feel that he'd failed. He would have to be talked around slowly, with great care, like a sulky child. Towards the end, though, when it became obvious that he had no intention of leaving, she never stopped talking about going back, and my father got more and more angry, more and more desperate to get out into the world and show people what he was capable of. I think he really believed he could change his life, given half a chance; but the truth was, he wasn't the type to charm success from the banal apparatus of the daily grind. As soon as he got ahead, he was in the pub, buying drinks for everybody; or he would spend the morning with the racing papers, studying the form, then he'd put everything he had on the one horse, to win. Soon, he was staying out late, or not coming back to the digs at all. One night, Maureen locked the door when she saw him coming back along the street, his face bloody, his clothes torn. It wasn't that she didn't like him, but she was afraid for him, and she had come to the point of believing that what he needed was a firm hand. She was afraid for my mother, too, and for the children of this unlucky pair, sick and thin, in cheap clothes, desperately homesick and frightened by what was happening to their father. She had said it before: one day, that man will say the wrong thing to the wrong people, and he won't come home at all.

My mother assumed it was the West Indians Maureen feared. She came from West Fife, where black people were unknown, and she'd heard all the usual stories that went the rounds. I'd been embarrassed more than once by the exaggerated care she took when she was in a crowded place, among 'the golliwogs', as she called them. It was a small, dark shock to me, that she was prejudiced.

'No, Tess,' Maureen said. 'They're all right. Some people don't like them, but in my experience, they're decent enough.' She sat with her cup in mid-air, her cigarette glowing in the half-light. 'No,' she continued, pursing her lips. 'It's the Irish you've got to look out for. I don't like to speak ill of my own, but if there's one thing I know, it's that. When an Irishman goes bad, he goes all the way.'

That night, Maureen must have believed all her predictions had come true. My father got to the door and tried the handle. There was a long silence, then he knocked. Not loud, just a knock. If my mother had locked the door on him at home, he would have broken it in without a moment's hesitation. But that was how he worked. It's how so many drinkers work: at some level, a ghost of common sense still operates, and he knew Maureen wouldn't stand for any nonsense. 'Maureen?' He waited. 'It's Tommy,' he said. 'I'm locked out here.'

We'd all been awake, and now we were up, Maureen

downstairs in the hall, my mother, me, Margaret and a Maureen-clone in frozen attitudes all the way up the stairs and on to the landing. Maureen looked at my mother. 'I'm not letting him in,' she said.

My mother shook her head. 'Go back to bed,' she said to me. I didn't want to go, but I didn't want to stay to the end either. Not out there on the stairs. 'Go on,' my mother said. 'It's going to be all right.'

I didn't believe her, but then, as I lingered, Maureen spoke. 'Off to bed, you two,' she said. 'And not a squeak out of you.' She smiled sadly. 'It's all right,' she said. 'Your Dad will be fine.'

That night was the end of our Birmingham adventure. My father tried to hang on, doing what he always did in such situations – acting as if nothing had happened, as if everything was going fine – but with Maureen watching him as closely as my mother had been, he couldn't keep up the pretence. My mother had contacted the council in Cowdenbeath and found out we could have our old prefab back and, soon, we were on the road, traipsing from one bus to another with our boxes and suitcases, stopping off on the way at Blackpool for what was billed as a family holiday. It didn't work out that well, though: after we'd got settled in our digs – a seedy, cramped guest house a few streets from the front – my father disappeared to the pub and we hardly saw him for the next ten days. What I remember best about that holiday is that Emile Ford and the Checkmates were playing in Blackpool while we were there. Somehow, my mother found the money to take me and Margaret to see them. Emile Ford was one of my heroes at the time, an extraordinarily good-looking man from Nassau, whose biggest hit, 'What do you want to make those eyes at me for?' was number one in the Hit Parade for several weeks in 1959.

After the show, we waited around at the stage door till he came out, and I got his autograph on a black-and-white *Postcard from Blackpool* showing the famous tower looming over the sands. Emile Ford told me they had a tower just like it in Paris, then he patted me softly on the shoulder and got into a car. I remembered him for months afterwards and, whenever anyone asked me about our trip to England, I talked about Emile Ford.

That was the year we got television. Till then, we hadn't been able to afford it, and my mother had been against it anyhow, preferring the radio that played all the time in her warm kitchen, making an island refuge of the place while she cooked and boiled laundry on the stove, filling the room with steam and the smell of hot starch. She liked to listen to *Sing Something Simple* on a Sunday night, and there were children's programmes on a Saturday morning, when the same songs were played every week at almost exactly the same times. 'Tubby the Tuba'. 'Thumbelina'. 'Sparky's Magic Piano'. It was more than a preference, this fondness for radio, it was a ritual, a way of connecting back to her mother's house. I remember my grandmother's radio, a large, genial-looking thing that sat high on a dresser in the kitchen-cum-parlour where my grandparents lived at the end of their lives, warmed by the fire, making tea and toast on the range, listening to the wireless. My mother's wireless was tuned to that world, and to the time before she was married. When television arrived, everything changed. She still listened to *Sing Something Simple* in the kitchen, but the main draw was *Sunday Night at the London Palladium* in the living room. On good weeks, my father would give us money to go out to Katie's van and buy ice creams, while Norman Vaughan guided members from the audience through the latest in a line of bizarre games, or Perry Como slumbered through another performance of 'Magic Moments'. My mother resisted for a while; then, all of a sudden and with no warning, she converted with a vengeance. She had imposed all kinds of viewing restrictions on us: one hour of television a night, no frivolous programmes (I remember she approved of *Criss Cross Quiz*, for example, but was against *Crackerjack* pretty much on principle), BBC rather than ITV, unless there was a very good reason to switch over. On weekdays, the television came on at eight o'clock, and went off again at ten, no matter what was on. My father didn't care: all he wanted was the horse racing and the football results on a Saturday. On public holidays, exceptions were made. I remember how strange it felt, the first Christmas we had the box, standing at the foot of our Christmas tree, handing the ornaments and strings of tinsel up to my mother, then turning round and seeing a character in the film that was showing at that moment – June Allyson, say, or Judy Garland – doing exactly the same thing. Outside, it was snowing, and in the film it was snowing too, and because the filmed snow was perfect, bright and clean and perpetual as a mother's love, our snow was also perfect, and our Christmases were white as they had never been before.

It was television that introduced me to Walter Pidgeon. I remember, on Sunday afternoons, or in the four or five snowlit days of the Christmas holidays, how he would step with such ease into the gap my father left and sit there, in my mind's eye, smoking his pipe, reading a leather-bound book, doing something with his hands. He was always a little preoccupied, always thinking about something, as if life itself were a tricky, but rather amusing puzzle. Yet whenever anybody needed him, he was there, all attention, good-humoured but serious, ready to offer action or good counsel. He wasn't perfect: in Fritz Lang's *Man Hunt*, say, he made a terrible mistake, and what hurt most wasn't the pickle he got himself into because of it, but the fact that his original error led to the death of the girl who would do anything for him, played by the delectable Joan Bennett, at the hands of George Sanders' sinister henchmen. That didn't matter, though. Nothing mattered: not the script, not the lighting, not the cinematography. Pidgeon represented something unparaphraseable for me. Later, it might be Montgomery Clift, or Zbigniew Cybulski, or Yves Montand who played out my fantasy of manhood on the screen, but they were troubled older brothers doing things that I might have done, given the opportunity. Walter Pidgeon was the father I couldn't find anywhere closer to home, one of those *real* fathers who can do the impossible.

Most importantly, Walter Pidgeon made decisions and stood by them, no matter what. Maybe this was what made him appear so competent. Whenever I saw a Walter Pidgeon film, I wanted to be a better person in a simple, unexceptional way: more thoughtful, more alert, less self-regarding, humbler, yet more self-assured than before. What I saw was a possibility of goodness, something more than ordinary decency. I clung to this possibility, knowing it for the fantasy it was, but needing something to aspire to. I would be walking through a garden, for example, and I would see a tree that had been so very carefully planted that it moved me. Somebody selected that tree, out of all the possible trees he could have chosen, and I would feel that *this* was a Walter Pidgeon decision, because the tree was exactly right for that spot: elegant, slender, not too dominant, it filled the space in a way that no other tree could have done. This sense of things being done right, this sense of the just act, is something a man should get from his father, just as the impression of gentility mixed with a certain wildness of spirit my mother experienced every time she saw a Franchot Tone movie should have come from her husband. No wonder my father felt lonely after the television arrived. He'd bought it on the cheap, I imagine, in some no-questions-asked deal, just to watch the racing and Scotsport, never realising that he was opening a box of dreams for the whole family, dreams that would forever cloud his house with alien possibilities.

CHAPTER 6

Around about my ninth birthday, my father began to fall apart. Something bad had happened at work, and I think he was finding it harder to get taken on for the better jobs. I didn't know why at the time, but I knew something was wrong, because my parents were arguing more often, not just when my father went on a binge, but even when he was having a sober spell. Much of the problem had to do with money, of course, but it wasn't just about that. There was my father's behaviour at the occasional family gathering, for example, when he would embarrass everyone by drinking too much, then sitting around being maudlin, or making big claims about his past, about how he had almost become a professional foot-baller, or how a woman he'd known in Germany had tried to drown herself when he told her he was leaving for good, to go back to Scotland. Yet what bothered me most, as I remember, was his claim, after a few drinks, that he looked like Robert Mitchum. According to everybody else, he looked nothing like Robert Mitchum, but it wasn't a serious matter. His drinking, his occasional falls, his disappearing act, when he would walk out of a gathering and not be seen again for hours, were what worried my mother's family and our neighbours. The Robert Mitchum delusion was, by comparison, a laughing matter.

'What are you talking about, man,' my Uncle John would say.

'It's true,' my half-drunk father would protest. Nobody knew where the notion came from: perhaps, during some drunken night at the Woodside, one of his cronies had seen the ghost of something pass across his features and pointed out a resemblance that, the very next moment, would seem ill-founded even to that drunken assembly.

'Who telt ye that? A blind man?'

My father would sneak a sly look at my mother, then he would say, 'Well, it was a woman, is the truth of it. With perfectly good eyes and all.'

My uncle would snort derisively. 'What woman was that, then?'

My father would clam up at this point, or he'd revert to his obsession with Norman Wisdom, the slapstick comedian who composed his favourite song, 'Don't Laugh at Me, ('Cause I'm a Fool)'. My father would sing this song at family gatherings, or to passing strangers on his way home from the pub. Norman Wisdom was his hero: as a nine-year-old, Wisdom had been abandoned by his mother; at eleven, he was a runaway, working as a miner, a cabin boy and in various odd jobs, before joining up. In 1946, he entered show business: he was thirty-one, but he quickly became a star as the unfortunate, Chaplinesque Norman Pitkin, a clumsy, sentimental loser in a cockily skewed tweed cap and a crumpled suit and tie that appeared to have a life of its own, especially when a pretty girl was close by. My father loved Wisdom, for reasons I couldn't fathom at the time; looking back, however, it's obvious that Pitkin was some kind of alter ego for him: an abandoned child who seemed unlovable, and had to struggle against the odds, Pitkin would overcome the contempt of the boss, the spite of others, the girl's indifference, and end up winning through by sheer energy and puppyish charm. All the time, he believed in himself, and in the basic goodness of the world around him.

The Pitkin persona was my father's harmless side – a bit of a fool, a bit of a liar – but it embarrassed me, and it embarrassed my mother even more. Still, it was nothing to what was to come, if he had his way: once the women had been packed off home, the men would adjourn to the pub, or to a hotel, and my father would start, picking on strangers, arguing with the barman, making a spectacle of himself. There were ugly moments with other uncles and older cousins who tried to quiet him down and, once, a scary escapade when my Uncle John, who had been led to believe that my father could drive, allowed him to take over the wheel of his new car. They had both been to the pub and, though my uncle was probably under the limit, he let himself be convinced that my father had learned specialist driving skills in the RAF. The truth was, my father couldn't drive at all – as my uncle quickly discovered – but he had seemed confident when he got behind the wheel, confident enough to set off at a lick, racing off down a country road, and not coming to a halt till John grabbed the wheel from his control and forced the car on to the verge. When the story came out, everybody's worst fears about my father were confirmed. The only person who saw the funny side of it all, in retrospect, was Uncle John, a man not easily shaken. He had been in the Black Watch all the way through the war, and he had seen things there that he never talked about, though the presumption was that they were more than a match for a short joyride with my drunken father. The other remarkable thing about John was his seemingly infinite capacity to forgive other men their follies. He

93

was the only member of our extended family who could tolerate my father, in the end. His kindness was hard to spot, behind a gruff, sarcastic exterior, but once you saw through his brilliant disguise, there was no denying it.

When my father came home from one of these adventures that had involved members of her family, my mother would be disgusted with him. Usually she said little, occasionally she would cry. That upset the whole house, but the real upset came when, one night, after we'd been to a wedding, my mother turned round, as we were coming through the door, and said, clearly, so everyone could hear, 'I should have married George Grant.'

My father froze. For a moment, I thought he would hit her. Then he pursed his lips grimly, his worst thoughts confirmed. 'Aye,' he said. 'So you should.'

An explanation of the mysterious George Grant was eventually forthcoming. Or rather, two explanations. My mother's version was as straightforward as possible: before she married my father, she had known – or worked with – a man named George Grant, but they had never been anything more than friends. Not even that, really, just two people who would exchange pleasantries in passing, people both friendly and insignificant enough to one another to be a sight for sore eyes on a hard day. My father, however, told a different story. According to this version, George Grant and my mother had been *cosy*, going out to the pictures from time to time, even planning to get engaged. For a while, it had been a big romance, and the whole family had wanted their Tessie to marry this good, kindly man. Then, along he came and stole her away, displacing George Grant in her affections for ever. Once the cat was out of the bag, my father enjoyed talking about all this, his one victory in life. He knew he was better than his rival, because he had *won* – had he not? – even if my mother claimed, as she had done that night, and as she was to do from time to time in the coming years, that she wished he hadn't. For a while, the house was full of George Grant, a ghostly presence, a bargaining chip, a scapegoat, a joke. Then, one day, it occurred to me that he wasn't as much of a joke as my parents pretended. After all, my mother called my father 'George' (the confirmation name he'd taken when he converted to Catholicism), even though his real name – the name I believed his family had given him – was Thomas. I remember realising this around the time of my own confirmation. I had chosen the name George, pretty much without thinking (no; there was a stupid reason behind it: I had been baptised John Paul, and I added the name George because of the Beatles). Then I saw it. We were both, my father and I, haunted by my mother's first love.

For months afterwards I thought about George Grant. My mother had made light of it all, but she had also been embarrassed, which meant there was something to the story, no matter what she said. Soon, I had convinced myself that she had been in love with George Grant, but some terrible accident of impulse or circumstance had perverted her from her true path, and made her marry my father instead. I spent hours wondering what would have happened if she had married the man she'd really wanted: what I would have been like, had I been their son; whether I would have existed in any identifiable form at all; whether I would have been happier as the different boy I might have been, with somebody else's blood, in somebody else's house, following somebody else's example. For the first time in my life, my mother seemed mysterious to me: a woman with a secret, dignified, even noble, in the sacrifice she had made, and I watched her, furtively, for any sign of regret, or longing. My father, meanwhile, became even more of a shadow on our lives. On the few occasions we saw him during the week, and on the interminable weekends, whether he was in the house, or out somewhere and just about to return at any moment, drunk and vindictive, I could see, all too plainly, that he was an impostor, a phantom, a bulky, uncontainable thing that nobody wanted.

In the daytime, I dreamed of what might have been. It was a makeshift and tender fantasy: my father went away – I was very careful never to let him die, even for a moment, in these daydreams – and he was replaced by George Grant, who regained my mother's affections as easily as a bird returns, at dusk, to a favourite perch. In the evenings, after school, I sometimes sat up late, or lay awake in bed, listening, at the time my father usually got back from Grangemouth, or wherever he was working, and if he was even a minute or two late, I imagined that he wasn't coming back, that he had gone off into the moonlight on some country road between work and home, walking away on some wide road or vanishing down some alley of bricks and nettles, going back to the darkness from which he had come, when he first displaced George Grant in the life my mother should have had. At the time, I knew this was the best thing for everybody, even for him. He would be happier gone, he could even imagine himself missed, a treasured memory, loved more for being absent, but free to live however he chose.

Everything stayed hidden. My father's late-night parties, his occasional drunken rampages around the house, my child's fantasies of death and redemption, my mother's attempts to

96

hold things together, it was all secret – known by anybody who cared to know, but unacknowledged, like a priest's feverish brightness around adolescent boys, or the beatings Mrs Wilson endured on those Saturdays when Dunfermline lost at home. Nobody talked about what was going on, as long as it went on behind closed doors. Then, all of a sudden, late in the summer of my ninth year, everybody was talking at once, and the person they were talking about was our neighbour, the gentle giant, Arthur Fulton.

CHAPTER 7

Nobody thought Arthur was guilty. Someone had made a mistake. People from Blackburn Drive, people in the town generally, would gather in shop doorways and talk quietly about what had or had not happened that day. They all agreed Arthur Fulton wasn't capable of murdering, or attempting to murder, anybody, let alone some slip of a girl just out of her teens, a girl he could have picked up with one hand and crushed the life from the way other men crush beer cans. They said it again and again, in stage whispers, pretending they didn't want the children to hear, relishing the fine physical details: he could have snapped her neck like a twig, he could have squeezed the life out of her in seconds, he could have . . . All the time, they talked about the girl as if she was already dead, as if Arthur – or not Arthur, but whoever had committed this terrible act – had actually succeeded. Some went so far as to suggest that there was something between them, this girl and Arthur, that she wasn't some girl he'd met on the road, but someone he cared about, someone he had *loved*. Otherwise, they reasoned, why would she still be alive? Why would Arthur have left her, unconscious, but still breathing, by the side of the public highway?

Listening in on these conversations, I began to understand. Everybody thought Arthur was guilty; there had been no mistake. He was their gentle giant, but nobody thought he was very smart – and that was his failing. A smarter man would have finished the girl off and thrown her into Loch Fitty, where nobody would find her; maybe he would have burned the body, or fixed the scene to look like a bungled robbery. Now, they were angry with Arthur, not for what he had done, but because he hadn't done it properly. If he really had taken that girl out on to a country road that day to kill her, he should have done what he had set out to do, and left her to rot. Most of all, he shouldn't have allowed himself to be caught because, by making such a mess of it all, he was forcing them to recognise that they had known nothing about him, and nothing about themselves, all along. He was one of their own, and he had betrayed them. It was a quiet, resentful anger they felt, like the anger people felt towards Mary Bell, when she killed those little boys about a year later, the same anger they felt towards Myra Hindley. Arthur had broken the cardinal rule of small-town life: he had failed to be what he seemed. Nobody had believed him dangerous for all those years, because he seemed so slow-witted, too shy and clumsy to be a killer. They thought criminals were clever, or at least cunning, like the bad men they saw at the pictures, smart-talking, ruthless, accomplished creatures with leather gloves and lengths of knotted cord.

Oddly enough, it was my father who made me see all this. He'd always welcomed Arthur into our house at Hogmanay, and on the odd occasion when sociability was unavoidable; now, when everyone else was swearing on a stack of Bibles and mothers' lives that they'd had no idea, he came out on the side of common sense. 'Arthur's big, but he's a baby, really,' he said. 'First sign of trouble, and these big men panic. Remember when they wanted people for the foot-and-mouth? They wouldn't take Arthur – '

My mother was annoyed. She knew my father would have no scruples about repeating such things in public. 'He couldn't have gone anyway,' she said. 'He was driving the long-distance lorries then – '

'That's not the point,' my father said. 'These big, stupid men are like children. You can't really trust them – '

'You sound like you think he *did* do it,' my mother interrupted. 'I don't want to hear talk like that when Mary's around – '

'What if he did?' my father said. 'Do you think they would have arrested him so fast if he was innocent?'

My mother was horrified. 'How can you say that?' she said. 'I thought you liked Arthur – '

'I do,' my father said. 'That's why I'm standing up for him.'

'You've got a funny way of standing up for people – '

'What I'm saying is,' my father went on, with exaggerated patience, 'is that he probably did do it. But he shouldn't get the jail for it.'

'Even if he's guilty?'

'Even if he's guilty. I mean, it was probably an accident. It's not as if he'll be doing anything like that again.'

'And what about that poor girl?' my mother asked. 'What happens to her?'

'I thought you said he couldn't have done it,' my father said. He had adopted that tone of voice he would get, when he had you in a corner. Master of the invalid, but pressing argument.

'I don't,' my mother replied. 'But I still think the girl should get some kind of justice – '

My father laughed bitterly. 'It won't do her any good if Arthur Fulton goes to jail,' he said. 'It's happened. It's over. Time to get on with her life.'

100

My mother considered this for a moment and was about to reply – or so it seemed. Then, just like that, she gave up. Maybe she thought my father was just joking, just trying to get a rise out of her. 'Well,' she said. 'I don't think he did what they said. That would be . . . '

As she searched for the right word, my father smiled grimly. 'These things happen,' he said. 'I don't suppose Arthur planned to do it. If he had, he'd surely have done a better job.' He shook his head sadly; it seemed that what bothered him most about the incident wasn't the possibility that Arthur had tried to kill the girl, but the idea that he'd botched it so badly. 'It was probably just an accident, one way or another.'

My mother didn't answer. There was no point, after all. To her, everything happened, or ought to have happened, for a reason. You made a choice, and if you chose the wrong path, it was a sin and you had to pay the penance – and it struck me, then, how odd it was that these two people should be married to one another. It wasn't just that they were different in temperament, or in what they wanted from life, or in what they believed – it was that they inhabited different worlds. For my mother, life was full of patterns and logic; my father, on the other hand, was haunted by the irrational. Maybe that was what made him so decisive: there was a sense in which no action had any meaningful consequences for him, a sense that there was really no such thing as cause and effect. When he said that Arthur's pathetic attempt to kill the girl was an accident, he was saying something about life itself. What he meant was that it was *all* an accident: the meeting, whatever history Arthur had with the girl, whatever feelings he or she might have had, the mood Arthur was in that afternoon, the fact that he panicked. Everything that happened was an accident. The only power you had was to act decisively when the accident happened and so make your own mark on the proceedings. And the truth was that, in Arthur Fulton's place, my father wouldn't have flunked the job. He would have broken the girl's neck and left her in a ditch somewhere, then he would have gone to the pub and sat all night playing crib with his friends. I think he was disappointed that Arthur Fulton couldn't have acted the same way. The one thing Arthur had done wrong was to get himself caught. Had he been in Arthur's place, my father wouldn't have made the same mistake.

The history we learned in school wasn't true. It was just an exercise in facts, an avoidance of obvious errors, rather than any attempt to get at the truth. It was also an exercise in power. All through school, I wondered why we were supposed to be so interested in people like Robert the Bruce, or Winston Churchill, why no real people appeared in the stories we had to memorise. In the Fultons' house, there was real history. Things had happened there, things I knew about, and things that would always remain a mystery. We heard later that Arthur had known the girl – nobody ever used her name, she was just 'the girl' – for several months. This in itself came as a surprise to most people, but then, the nature of a lorry driver's work meant he could be away from home whenever he needed to be away, so it would have been easy, even for a man like Arthur, to keep the relationship hidden. The girl wasn't young enough to be his daughter, as some had said – I knew that, because I knew Sandra, and she was just a year and half older than me – but she was young and, by all accounts, fairly naive. Some people thought Arthur had been 'taking advantage' of her, but this didn't make much sense if you knew Arthur. Still, rumour was that they had been seeing each other now and again, over those several months, and nobody really knew what had happened during that time, or what Arthur said to the girl about his life at home, or even if he'd said anything. The day he tried to kill her, he'd driven her out to a lay-by somewhere outside town. Nobody knows what happened then – Arthur pleaded guilty when the case came to court – but whatever had been done or said, Arthur must have panicked. At some stage, he had hit the girl and, after that, he was out of control. The fact that he didn't just snap her in two, as our neighbours put it, but scrabbled around looking for ways to kill her, indicated that the crime hadn't been premeditated. It had probably never crossed his mind to kill her. Allegedly, he hit her with his fists, then with something else – the proverbial 'blunt instrument' – but he didn't hit her in the head with it. After that, according to the gossip, he sprayed some kind of chemical in her face, wrapped a length of tow rope around her neck, held something over her mouth, as if to suffocate her – but he saw none of it through. He must have been in two minds all the time and there was some debate as to whether you could call what he did an attempted murder at all. This was a moot point, however, valid only in the people's court outside Brewster's or the Co-op: Arthur entered his guilty plea, the judge sentenced him to ten years, the case was closed. Mary Fulton took Sandra away and the house next door to ours fell silent and empty. I never got to find out what happened after the scarves and belts – or not with Sandra, anyhow.

I vividly remember the day they left. A man I had never seen before drove a light blue Austin Cambridge to the end of our path and parked it right outside number 17, then Mary Fulton carried out several bags, while the mysterious stranger stayed behind the wheel. I happened to be off school with something that day, and I sat at my bedroom window watching it all: I couldn't see Sandra, but Mary Fulton went to and fro, loading bags into the boot of the car, her face set, ugly with grief and shock. I knew people had been talking about her – they always had thought her a cold fish, now they were speculating about why Arthur had done what he did, and what Mary could have done to keep him out of trouble.

'If he'd been happy at home,' Mrs Donaldson said, when we met her and Mrs Banks outside the butcher's, 'maybe none of this would ever have happened.'

'I don't think we can blame her for what her husband did,' Mrs Banks retorted.

My mother didn't say anything, but gave me the quick glance that said I shouldn't be listening to their conversation. I looked away, and kept listening.

'A man needs to be respected in his own house,' Mrs Donaldson said. 'It doesn't matter if he's a bit slow.'

My mother seemed uncomfortable. 'Mary was always good to him, as far as I can tell,' she said.

'Well,' Mrs Donaldson said, 'maybe she wasn't good enough. It's hard work, being happy.'

I look back now, and I wonder if they were as happy as they pretended to be, these good women of Cowdenbeath. I knew my mother was miserable, much of the time. Everything in her life was uncertain; there was always the threat of some terrifying outburst, whenever my father was at home, and when he was out, she never knew when he would get in, or what condition he would be in when he got back. Yet she pretended with the best of them, out on the street, in the queue at the fishmonger's, on the steps of the church. What if they were all pretending? I couldn't imagine marriage was a very satisfying state: like a nautilus shell, it seemed an intricate, unknowable thing; it concealed all manner of secret hurts and slights, every variety of private betrayal and unspoken disappointment. I think I suspected, even then, that nobody should carry all the blame for that state of affairs. I may even have realised that no one can know the inner workings of a marriage: it was a matter of a hundred private moments, all the lies and blows and failures, real or imagined, that went unwitnessed and unrecorded, till the crisis that others see, after years or decades – the breakdown, the affair, the drink problem – appears to come out of nowhere.

I don't know if Mary Fulton ever suspected what Arthur was up to. I'm sure his daughter didn't. For over an hour, I waited at my window, till at last Sandra appeared, pale, but not tearful, clutching a small bag and a raincoat, and got into the car. I wanted to go out and say goodbye, but I knew my mother wouldn't let me, and I knew I wasn't wanted. Mrs Fulton, Sandra, even the stranger in the car, all were ashamed of a crime in which they had played no part and now all they could do was run, and hope to start again. What they left was an empty prefab, a garden that quickly became overgrown, and a dark, motionless place that, for the next few years, was to be my special sanctuary, the house that recurs, even now, in my dreams, a house I would fill with the stories I told myself, and so with the boy I was, whenever I managed to escape from the son I was pretending to be.

I don't think I ever knew real silence before I discovered that house. With the Fultons gone, and nobody wanting to move into a prefab, much less a prefab where the murderer had lived

– of course, Arthur hadn't actually murdered anybody, but there is no such thing as attempted murder in the stories of gossips – I had the place to myself: the garden, the kitchen, the house, the rooms that had been so familiar, with their cheap furniture and damp coats hanging in the kitchen. That was all gone now, of course. The place I inherited was quiet, empty, utterly perfect. It was also, back then, the very edge of my world. The Fultons had lived at the end of our narrow lane, and the privet hedge that bordered their garden, once kept to five or six feet by Mrs Fulton's fervent clipping, soon grew out, a huge shaggy mass of emerald green, darkly jewelled and impenetrable. I had no notion of what might be on the other side of that green wall. It was like the hedge around the palace in the story of Sleeping Beauty; every year it grew thicker and darker, a sanctuary for songbirds and spiders.

When a house falls empty, the angels arrive, coming one by one in the early dark to take up residence, lighting the blackest corners with candles of pollen and wax, blurring the doorways with ice and myrrh, filling the kitchen cupboards with an odd scent, half-incense, half-dust. The first time I broke into the Fultons' house, I was afraid, wondering what I would find, expecting strange figures to flare out of the walls, waiting to be touched by some dank hand as I made my way from the living room to the hall, and into the bedroom, where Sandra and I had played our exquisite games. After that first time, though, I felt at home there, accompanied by Sandra's thin, lithe shadow as I remembered what we had done, what she had said to me, what I had said to her. I had nothing to be afraid of in that house: it was all shadows and cold spots and greenery coming in at the windows. My own house was much more frightening. Better the ghosts of other days than the present misery of the living; better the whisper of the unknown than the angry bawling of the all too familiar. For a while, at least, this empty prefab belonged to me, and to me alone. For a while, at least, I had a place I could think of as home.

CHAPTER 8

In the summer of 1965, my father wanted to be gone again. The Birmingham adventure had ended in humiliation; now he was making more drastic plans, talking about emigrating, bringing home brochures and papers about Canada and Australia. He led us to believe that all he needed to do was fill in some forms, send them off and wait; then, after all the documents had been processed, we would go to Canada, to live in a new house with a shower, a garage and bedrooms for everybody. I could barely contain my excitement. My mother kept warning me not to get my hopes up, that it wasn't so easy to emigrate as all that. You needed a skill, and my father was a labourer on the building.

'But he's a brickie,' I said. 'They *need* brickies.' My father had told us this, when he explained how easy it would be to get paid passage.

'Your father's not a brickie,' my mother said. 'He's a brickie's mate.'

'Well, they must need brickies' mates, if they need brickies.'

My mother snorted. 'They can get brickies' mates anywhere. That's not a skill.' She looked at me sadly. 'That's why you have to stick in at school. People don't want you if you don't have a skill.'

I was confused. They weren't teaching me to lay bricks at

school. I was doing sums and memorising bits of Latin. I was drawing birds and studying the New Testament. I was learning the dates of battles and the capital cities of Africa. Once, the priest had come into Scripture class and asked us a whole lot of questions about Jesus. It was fairly embarrassing, but I was the only one got all the answers right, which prompted him to wonder aloud if I might have a vocation. When she heard this, Anne MacKay, the girl I had tried to kiss in the corridor one lunchtime, gave me a funny look, but I was all puffed up about being the centre of attention, and maybe joining the Church one day. I wondered what religion the Canadians practised. Maybe we could get into Canada on the strength of my impending ordination.

Finally, one Saturday afternoon in 1965, my father came home and announced, with total conviction, that we would be in Canada before the end of the summer. We waited, in a fever of excitement. I was going to play ice hockey and ride a horse. We were going to live in a big house: there was so much space in Canada, and so few people, all the houses were big. We'd have a car. I was more excited than ever, and I was beginning to think my father had vindicated himself, when I noticed that my mother, who had been dead set against the idea from the beginning, didn't look too worried. Slowly it dawned on me. I still had hopes, but as I watched her calmly going about her usual business I realised we weren't going anywhere. My father was lying.

To soften us up for the move, my father booked a holiday in Blackpool. I don't know where the money came from: probably he'd had a little luck on the horses for once, though there were other possibilities. However he paid for it, though, it was a sad holiday. On the first day, I fled from the cramped little room where I was once again condemned to spend a fortnight with my squabbling parents, and sat on the wall outside our guest house, watching the people go by. I was content, idling, not thinking about anything; it was a sunny day, and I was hoping, against hope, that things might go well – like the last time, when I'd seen Emile Ford at the Winter Gardens. Then, out of nowhere, a boy appeared, a small, pale-faced boy with straw-coloured hair, laughing and saying something I couldn't hear. Momentarily, I was looking at him, trying to make out what he was saying – and then I was falling: backwards at first, then turning, twisting, my hands coming up over my face, my head darkening . . .

When I came to, the boy was gone. I was in the basement ground, a fall of around twelve feet on to concrete, and I was hurt. I felt sick and dizzy, cold in my head, tender around the eyes and mouth, but I got on to my hands and knees and started climbing the stairs to the street level. Once out of the basement, I felt the sun on my face, and my head began to clear, but there was nobody there to help me, even though the street had been busy a moment before. Our room was on the second floor of the guest house. Afterwards, I was impressed by the fact that, having crawled up the next flight of stairs to the entranceway, I somehow got the inner door open, and proceeded to crawl up the next two flights, trailing my arm and resting every few steps till I felt strong enough to continue. In all that time, I saw no one – not till I reached the door of our room, where I could hear my parents talking as my mother unpacked. They were arguing about something, still, but it was a casual, passionless argument, something they had gone through a thousand times before, an argument for which they knew the script perfectly. I managed to get to my feet, opened the door with my left hand, and staggered in, collapsing on the nearest bed.

'What is it?' my mother said. 'Did you hurt yourself?'

'I fell off the wall,' I said. I couldn't think clearly enough to explain.

'What wall?' my father wanted to know. Neither of them seemed very concerned.

'The wall outside,' I said.

'Oh.' In retrospect, I see that my father must have thought I meant the low wall to the street, not the wall to the basement. The wall to the street was about two and a half feet high, hardly dangerous. 'Let's see you, then,' he said. I rolled over and sat up, my arm screaming pain. My father studied my face. 'You'll live,' he said.

'My arm hurts,' I said.

He smiled grimly. 'Of course it does,' he said. 'You have to be more careful.'

Everybody, including me, was determined that my fall shouldn't spoil our holiday. For the next fortnight, I sat on the beach in a deckchair, nursing my hurt arm. It was broken, but nobody knew that. I did what I could to conceal the pain. What was needed was an effort of will, nothing more. I remembered the times my father had been hurt at work, how he'd worked on when he'd broken his fingers, or the time when he had to go to hospital, *bleeding like a sheep*, to get stitched up, but had got back to work the same day and finished what he had to do. That was what I wanted to do. When my arm sent urgent, angry messages along the nerve lines to the brain, my brain ignored them, telling the arm to pull itself together, to take it like a man. It wasn't until three weeks later, when the swollen fracture turned black from wrist to elbow, and I was finally packed off to see a doctor, that I understood how bad it was. The doctor, a Polish émigré, took one look at my blackened forearm and jumped from his chair.

'How long has it been like this?' he cried. I thought he was so excitable because he was a foreigner.

'A little while,' I said.

'How long?'

'Since we were in Blackpool,' I answered, shamefaced now, and worried somebody might get into trouble. He stared at me, exasperated. 'About three weeks,' I added softly.

'*Three weeks!*' He was genuinely upset. He probably saw things like this all the time – and I wanted to tell him, then, that it wasn't anybody's fault, that I didn't think my parents were neglectful. It had never once occurred to me that they should have known better than to let me go three weeks, playing football, trying to swim, doing all I could to appear normal, with a broken arm. If I could have explained it, I would have said that it wasn't their fault: they were incompetents, sad, preoccupied, one with his drinking, the other with surviving the fallout from his increasingly erratic behaviour. And at that moment, all of a sudden, I felt superior to them, smarter, more capable. I could have told them this would happen. The arm was broken, anybody could see that. It didn't occur to me that I hadn't seen it myself till the doctor pointed it out. 'This arm is broken. Probably in several places. We have to get you to the hospital right away.' He studied my face for a moment – a placid ten-year-old in bad clothes who had come to see him alone, and was planning to go on to school afterwards – and his face softened. 'Where are your parents?' he asked.

'My dad's at work,' I answered. 'My mum's at home.'

'All right,' he said. 'Stay there. Don't move an inch. We'll sort this out.'

And with that, before I could explain it was all a big mistake, I became one of the neglected, one of the children society has to protect. Looking back, I can imagine the doctor probably didn't even believe my story about falling off a wall, when I got to give it. He probably had his own suspicions about parents who would let their child go three weeks with a black, swollen, obviously broken arm, then send him off to the surgery – if they had even sent him at all – on his own. I didn't know it then, but I had blown our cover as a family. From that point on, nothing we did in Cowdenbeath would be a private matter. It was all subject to scrutiny.

For that fortnight in Blackpool, though, we didn't know any of this. We sat on the beach, we made sandcastles and ate ice creams, Margaret and I went on donkey rides, while my mother watched and my father took photographs. We went to Mass in a strange church and I wandered off and got lost on the way back to the guest house. I liked being lost. It reassured me that it was so easy just to detach myself and slip away. I had fantasies of being found, hours later, by a policeman or a good-hearted stranger who would take me off to some good, clean, friendly place while they tried to find my parents; then, when that plan failed, I would be taken in, shown to my own room, sent to a new school, looked after by kindly women, given new clothes and brand new books, with that straight-from-the-bookshop smell. Every street that led somewhere else, every tree I'd never seen before, every house with strange curtains was a new life, just waiting to be entered. I thought myself stupid when I couldn't work out how to get there.

One afternoon, my father led us to a warehouse far from the seafront, and we walked around looking at the goods on offer – tennis rackets, china, lamps, plastic flowers – searching for bargains. I remember, now, how keenly I felt the sadness to which their poverty condemned them: the sadness of people who had next to nothing and were judged accordingly, the sadness of people who knew that such things mattered. When my father produced a handful of notes, and we picked out what we wanted, I was struck by the sadness of our possessions; or rather, the possessions we aspired to, the trinkets and baubles and cheap ornaments we were buying with this surprise windfall, worthless, ill-made objects, like the junk they gave out at seaside bingo games. At some level, I guessed that having these things – owning *stuff*, dusting it, moving it around, showing it to other people – was an enchantment for my parents. They held these objects as others hold talismans, as protection against death, or at least against invisibility. It made me ashamed. It made me want to run away, to have nothing, to have nowhere to go, like Jesus. That day, I didn't want anything for myself, but I couldn't have begun to explain why, so I accepted a tennis racket and a grey tennis ball, items that had, from the look and smell of them, been in storage for years, waiting for better times. I can't remember what anybody else chose, but I think, for them, it was a good day, right at the end of the holiday, the day everybody would talk about, months later.

I remember that day, too; but what I remember is the cool of the sky that afternoon, when we emerged from the warehouse and walked back to the guest house, clutching our goods, a little sad, a little ashamed. I remember the promenade, the smell of the sea, the smell of Blackpool rock and fish and chips and candyfloss. When the holiday was over, I remember coming home to the same place: the prefabs, school, the cold church, the woods. I remember, on the first day back at school, after the long, empty summer, somebody filled the inkwells with milk during the lunch break, and we had to carry them, brimming and heavy as magnets, to the sink where we did our art work, and carefully pour the pale blue liquor down the drain. I remember the day when a thin, pimply, stone-grey boy called Stanley slipped while he was climbing over the high wall at the back of the school and got his leg caught on one of the old iron spikes. I recall how he hung there, screaming, till a passer-by ran into the playground, climbed the wall, lifted him carefully off and lowered him into the arms of the teachers below. On certain days, I remember it all: the summers, the moorhens' nests, the night-long fasts before Holidays of Obligation, but I also remember being small in the eye of my father's rage and I recall, in cine-matic detail, the first fall that no one was there to break, and then, as if some magical immunity had been broken, the falls that followed: the broken arm, the tipped ladder, the hospital room where I lay sobbing on a gurney for no reason, while the nurse waited for the drugs to wear off. Forty years later, I remember it all, and I dream those same dreams. Night after night I populate the dark.

CHAPTER 9

I could never work out why the Donaldsons lived in the prefabs. Nobody else had a car, but they did. They had a phone too, and a caravan somewhere, and they took holidays in places we'd never heard of. Their son, Daniel, was a strong, unsuspecting, generous-hearted boy with a temper, but he was also the local peacemaker, the one who stopped fights before they went too far, the player-referee in every game from football to rounders, the voice of reason, well served by a workaday imagination and the impenetrable authority of the only child. I suppose, if you had to receive bad news, you would rather Daniel brought it than anybody else – and that is exactly what he did for my mother that winter, just a fortnight after her father finally died of the cancer he'd been fighting for months. She was alone in the house, baking, listening to the wireless in the kitchen, when a shadow appeared at the frosted pane of our back door. I think she would have been happy, that day, even though her father had just passed; she was usually happy when she was allowed to get on with the routine maintenance of our world: the cooking, the cleaning, the baking. Baking was her favourite chore, and she baked a good deal, partly because it was a cheap source of treats and partly, I suppose, because she knew the cakes she made were amazing. Everybody liked them. My cousin Dave, who was notoriously averse to family occasions, would come to our house on any excuse, just to have a slice of my mother's fruit cake and one of those rich, frighteningly delicious confections she called Melting Moments. Like everything else she did, she baked by feel: there was no clock in her kitchen, no egg timer. She knew every cake was different, and she judged how well it was doing by smell.

That day, she was making angel cakes and a Victoria sponge. Nothing got spoiled, because Daniel offered to stay behind after she left and take care of things. He had come to tell her that my father had been hurt in an accident at work: it wasn't anything to worry about, he said, but somebody had telephoned to say they were sending a car to take her to the hospital in Dunfermline. Daniel didn't know how extensive my father's injuries were, but even if he had, he wouldn't have said anything more or less than what he had been told to say: an accident, a fall, nothing to worry about, no hurry, car coming. Nobody would know how bad it was, anyhow, till the ambulance arrived at Emergency, and the doctors examined him: my father had fallen around thirty feet from a scaffold; now, he was unconscious, barely breathing, his lungs weren't working properly, his face was badly battered. I didn't see him for weeks, and even then I didn't recognise him. We found out, later, that his skull had been fractured, all the ribs on one side were broken, one of his lungs was punctured, he had broken teeth, broken bones in his face and hands, his left leg was broken . . . When she came to break us the news, my mother said it was typical of our father, to do nothing by halves. He hadn't broken *every* bone in his body, but he'd broken enough that he could claim he had without fear of contradiction, when it came time to recount the story.

The next two months were slow and subdued. At first, my mother went as often as she could to sit by my father's bed as they waited for him to become fully conscious; later, she took flowers from the garden, papers, books, fruit, gifts from the neighbours. My father was sure they all despised him, but there wasn't one who didn't send a card, or bring round gifts for my mother to take in. Meanwhile, we children waited dutifully for the day when we would be able to go in with her at visiting time, sitting in the waiting room while she took him our drawings and letters: touching, empty letters from children who didn't really know what to say, drawings of trees and flowers, drawings of the prefab with smoke coming out of the chimney and the lilac tree in bloom by the back door.

Finally, we were allowed in. I still recall how damaged he looked, lying in his damp-looking, slightly stale hospital bed, his eyes purple and swollen, his mouth rimmed with dry spittle, his voice a thin croak. This was the biggest shock, for me, that his voice had dwindled so, faded to a shadow of itself – this, and the penitent, humbled air he had about him, the air of one who has been chastened, considerate of others, quiet, thoughtful, plugged in to some undercurrent of fear he'd managed to deny for years, but could no longer evade. He'd almost died, he would say later – and everybody knew he was right. It was a drama, a real event. For once, he didn't need to make anything up: it was all true.

Meanwhile, life at the prefabs was close to idyllic. My mother didn't have any money – even though we'd been told there would be compensation payments, she wasn't holding her breath – but we were strangely happy in our quiet home, all of us working together, doing our best, looking after one another. My father had sent a message that I would have to be the man of the house for a while and look after my mother and Margaret but, at ten, I was smart enough to ignore that particular piece of advice. Best of all were the nights, when we got back from Mrs Banks' house and, having sat long enough with my mother to hear the latest news, we forgot my father altogether and moved on to the ordinary things that were so imperilled when he was there: listening to the radio, reading, playing games, sitting quietly around the fire while my mother knitted a matinée jacket – she was *always* knitting matinée jackets – for some cousin's baby. We were happy then and, though we would never have admitted it to ourselves, none of us really wanted it to end.

NOBODADDY

and we are not afraid as we watch her soul fly on: paired
as the soul always is: with itself:
  with others.

  Two swans . . .

Child. We are done for
in the most remarkable ways.

Brigit Pegeen Kelly

CHAPTER 1

After the accident, my father sat at home taking stock of his life – casual labouring, a wartime prefab that should have been demolished years before, a depressed, chronically anaemic wife, unhappy children – and he decided, once again, that it was time for a change. I'm not sure how aware of his alcohol problem he was by then, but I believe he was at least partly motivated by an impulse familiar to alcohol counsellors, the 'geographical solution', where a drinker leaves behind the bad memories and debts of a place where he has outlived his slender welcome, and moves on to pastures new. I imagine my father understood, at some level, that his wife was sick, and his children confused and fearful, because of his drinking and the uncertainty and occasional violence that went with it. By now, he had forgotten the Birmingham fiasco enough to think he could turn over a new leaf elsewhere; perhaps he thought all we needed was a change of scene to become a family again. Perhaps he thought he'd been changed by his brush with death. Perhaps he even believed that *this* fall would be his last.

All the time he'd been talking openly about Canada, my father had been secretly finding out about Corby, an industrial boom town in the East Midlands. He'd heard that men like him, labourers and the unskilled, could get good jobs at Stewart's and Lloyd's, the huge steelworks that had grown up around the high-grade iron-ore deposits that ringed this little village in Northamptonshire, making work for thousands and creating, first, a huddle of terraced housing that sat, grey and squat, around the blast furnaces and the tube mills, then, later, when the government realised that this kind of sprawl had to be better represented for the electorate, one of the celebrated New Towns. My father, who had always resisted the idea of working indoors, now decided that Corby was for him: a fresh start in a growing industry, far from my mother's family, far from the neighbours who had come to see him as a burden, far from the pity and concern and judgement that he saw around him every day. He'd probably known all along that we weren't going to Canada. Even if Canada had been prepared to have him, my mother would never have moved an ocean away from everything she loved, but Corby was just a coach ride away. The clinching argument would have been that, in those days, anybody who wanted to work in Corby was given ten pounds and a place in a hostel till a house came up. They were building new houses all the time. It would be six weeks, more or less, before a place was available, which gave him plenty of time to work out the lie of the land. He could write home and let her know how things were, and she didn't have to go for good. If she didn't like it, we would go straight back, no questions asked.

The next few weeks were troubled. He did seem different, and we all had hopes that he'd been shocked into a new way of living. I wasn't really convinced, however. I tried, but there was a lingering sense of once bitten twice shy that I couldn't quite escape. Now, when my father talked about Canada, I dreamed dutifully of frozen lakes and shy-eyed deer moving silently through maple woods at dawn; when Australia became the topic of conversation, I conjured up images of Christmas on the beach and tropical greenery at the foot of the garden. But my heart wasn't in it. It just felt cruel, all this dreaming and planning. When we did move – and my mother had agreed, finally, that we *had* to move, if only to get my father off the building sites – I was sure we were going to somewhere as grey and wet as the pit town we were leaving.

Finally, on a damp October day, we all gathered with a few belongings on the southbound platform of Cowdenbeath station, said goodbye to the dying coalfields and set out for Corby. My father had been there for several weeks, getting a job, getting a house sorted out. Now he'd come back to get us, to bring us to our new life – and I hated him for it. He'd gone on letting me dream of Canada till the very last minute, and I knew that I would always long for a homeland that would correspond to the snowy woods and little outlying villages of wooden houses and picket fences of my imagination. I had bought into a wide, still darkness, lit here and there by a farmhouse window, or a late tractor working some huge grain field in Manitoba, dirt roads whitening in the moonlight, overgrown tracks leading to blizzards and nothingness. I had bought into that world, and I knew I would always miss it. Decades later, there are times – travelling home from work on a winter's night, or waiting for a train in a country station – when I realise I am still waiting to complete the journey I began in my ten-year-old mind all those years ago.

To say I was disappointed by Corby is a massive understatement, but that first day's disappointment was nothing compared to the misery that followed. Corby was hideously ugly compared to my dream of a northern wilderness: at that time, all it amounted to was a cluster of cheap housing estates clinging like barnacles to the behemoth of Stewart's and Lloyd's; huddled and polluted, it befouled the Northamptonshire countryside like some medieval plague town wrapped in a grey-gold cloud of smoke and smuts and simmering in the orange glow from the blast furnaces. Meanwhile, things at home went from bad to worse, as this second and final flit south, which was supposed to provide security and economic freedom, proved to be my father's undoing. With more money to spend, his drink problems worsened. Very soon, he lost faith in his old policy of simmering threat, of quiet menace: from now on, he would hit out, secretly, unexpectedly, when my mother's back was turned. I never discovered how often this happened with Margaret – a good deal in her mid-teens, I think – but by the time I was fourteen, I'd come to think of him as just another bully, ready to make me pay for even the smallest mistake: leaving something out that should have been put away, laughing at the wrong moment, staying out too long or coming back too early, there was no logic to any of it. At the same time, he would come home from the pub with his pockets full of change and buy every child playing in the square an ice cream from the van that plied its trade around the Beanfield estate. The local kids would run to him whenever he appeared, his RAF blazer jingling with money, to receive their treat from 'Uncle Tommy'. The only ones he left out were his own children. We didn't run to him, because we knew better. Even in a good mood, he wasn't treating us to ice cream we didn't deserve.

CHAPTER 2

That was the year I began inventing my own companions, building ghosts around the given names and spectral images of my lost kin: my dead sister, my brother Andrew, the abandoned and the imaginary who seemed so much happier, so much truer than the living. It seems a necessary enterprise when I look back at the child I was, a strategy that came from somewhere inside, not thought out on the surface, but rising from the mind's undertow, spontaneous, instinctive. My father was doing me harm, but at some level I could see that he himself was hurt, possibly beyond repair. Every time it seemed that his actions were deliberate, I tried to remind myself that they were not. I am using the language I have now to describe it when I say that he was visiting the sins of a mutant belief system on the only son he had, but I think that, even then, I understood some of what was happening. Meanwhile, my strategy was fairly simple: a simplicity that arose from necessity rather than design. The only thing I could do was resist my father's power with my own will, my own imagination. He was the man of the house, the one in charge; but I had some choice in how things went; I didn't have to *collaborate* with him, or with his sad, angry gods. I had my imagination. He was always saying that to me when I asked him a question he didn't want to address: *What do you think? Use your imagination, for God's sake.* So I did. What I came up with was like a game, but it was more than just play-acting. The game I played, in the language I have now, was *Ghost Brother syndrome.*

The first thing to say about Ghost Brother syndrome is that, to be convincing, it should really be called by another name. Something more exotic, more Central European. *Zastra-Serduk's syndrome. Von Hollstadter's disease.* It was only to be expected that I would suffer from this condition, first as a boy whose father had nothing to teach him, then as an adolescent in the proverbial authority vacuum. With nobody *real* to measure myself against, I had always needed a brother; but for a long time it hadn't occurred to me that it was in my power to invent one. Then, when I was around fourteen, I was travelling home in the late afternoon, on the bus that stopped outside Greenhill Rise shops. It was late autumn; it must have been around Guy Fawkes Day, because I could see the occasional firework, a little too pale against the pearl-coloured sky, and the bus was quiet, almost deserted. I had been at the library, and before that with Norman Edmunds, my music teacher. Earlier that day, Mr Edmunds had been playing me a record of Glenn Gould performing the *Goldberg Variations.*

Norman Edmunds was around seventy years old when he offered to teach me to play the piano. I had wanted to learn for a long time, but my father had forbidden it; he wasn't going to have me practising scales day and night, not when he worked shifts and had to get some sleep. Besides, pianos cost money. It took the intervention of my mother and Father Duane, one of the priests at St Brendan's, to shift him. For some reason, my mother liked the idea; I imagine she thought it would be a useful part of my development. Meanwhile,

Father Duane had taken an inexplicable shine to me. I look back now and realise that he saw a boy at the crossroads: a boy who could either make his family and parish proud, or go to hell with all the stops pulled out. Father Duane was the one who browbeat one of his parishioners into donating a rickety, but more or less viable piano to the cause; he was the one who persuaded Mr Edmunds to give up two or three hours of his time, on a Saturday morning, for almost nothing – and, to his credit, it almost worked. Those music lessons provided me with all the education I ever received. After the lesson proper, Mr Edmunds would talk about music and books; he would play me records from his collection, or give me poems and passages from the classics to read aloud. Or he would talk about his youth, and all the public and private errors he had seen in his lifetime. Mostly, though, we listened to Bach and Schubert, his all-time favourite composers. I hadn't known it till then, of course, but those were the days of the legendary performers: Richter, Curzon, Schwarzkopf, Klemperer. Kathleen Ferrier was ten years dead, but her spirit would never die in Norman Edmunds' stricken heart. And Glenn Gould was alive somewhere, playing the piano or drinking coffee, while I sat listening to him play Bach toccatas.

I didn't know anything personal about Glenn Gould. I didn't know about his eccentricity, or his rejection of the concert hall, or any of the other aspects of his personality that made him a cult figure in the seventies. Besides, for me, personal was exactly what music was not. Unique, individual, idiosyncratic, even, yes; but personal, no. To me, music was no more personal than the soul. I knew Gould was Canadian, as I had almost been. I knew he was best-known for his Bach recordings. I had seen a picture of him on an album sleeve, but he had been muffled up in a winter coat and a flat cap, an enigmatic being who seemed indifferent to the presence of the camera. He was doing a chore: standing outdoors somewhere, pretending to be a famous pianist. Wherever he was, it looked cold.

I liked that photograph, but I wasn't really interested in Glenn Gould, the man. I wasn't even interested in Glenn Gould, musical genius. No: his function in my life was to be the name I gave to the music I had just discovered, the music I imagined as belonging to my missing brother. It was an idea that had been forming for weeks in my mind: now, sitting on the 254 bus, turning the corner at the top of Heathfield Drive, I began inventing the brother I needed from the music I had been listening to all morning. Naturally, this wasn't a conscious decision, and it's almost impossible to describe the process, but at the time, it was remarkably easy to do. The difficult part had been coming to the conclusion that it was even possible but, that afternoon, I started to see things through my imagined brother's eyes.

At the same time, I remembered something that had happened back in the prefabs, a fleeting conversation I'd had with my mother, and didn't even know I remembered. It was when I was six, or maybe just turned seven, and my mother was standing in the kitchen of our prefab, making split-pea soup. It was an ordinary, late-autumn afternoon, the trees around the chicken runs opposite dusted with the lights we cast by being there, in that little condemned house; the windows were slightly fogged, and the room was a little too warm and muggy. I approached my mother the way I always did when I had some burning question I was afraid she might not answer, waiting till she was busy, then sidling in to stand by the cooker, watching her work. It's a pre-emptive defence: ask something casually, when someone is otherwise occupied, and there's at least a chance they won't be annoyed, even if they don't provide the answer you need. A large part of my childhood consisted of asking questions that, as soon as they were asked, proved too embarrassing or trivial to answer. My mother, in particular, seemed to hate answering questions, as if she was afraid she would give something away that might be held against her later.

I have no idea what prompted this particular question – maybe something I had seen in a book, or heard on the radio – but it was one that suddenly needed an answer. No doubt it was suggested, in part, by recent events, when we had all been expecting Andrew, the new brother who had mysteriously failed to materialise, though my mother had gone to the hospital, and we had visited her there, in what we knew was the maternity ward. Considering how little time had passed since that particular stillbirth, my question was horribly insensitive.

'Mum?' I waited patiently till she looked at me. She raised her spoon and smiled vaguely, but she didn't say anything. In her face, I saw age – and I realised, with a shock, that she was as old as the other women who lived out there, on the edge of Cowdenbeath, making ends meet.

'Yes?' She gave the pot another stir, then set down the spoon.

It suddenly came to me that I hadn't planned the question well enough, that what I was about to blurt out had some secret and till now unrecognised capacity to harm us both. Not that this stopped me asking.

'Why don't I have a twin?' I said.

She stood still, staring at me, for a long time. She appeared to be doing some difficult calculation in her head, one with lots of carrying over, or division. Then she shook her head and resumed her stirring. 'What a strange question,' she said.

'Is it?'

'Of course it is,' she said. 'Why do you ask?'

I didn't know what to say, so I didn't say anything. I was thinking of Freddy and Ferdy in the *Rupert* annuals, how they were always together, how they were really just a single character.

'Not everybody has a twin,' my mother said. 'It's not that common.'

'Why?' I persisted. If it could happen at all, I figured, why didn't it happen more often? And why hadn't it happened to me?

'I don't know,' she said. There was upcoming finality in her voice, that I *don't have time for this* tone just edging in.

'Wouldn't they let you have one?' I asked.

'What?' She looked at me again, puzzlement in her eyes.

'At the hospital,' I said. 'Wouldn't they let you have two babies?'

She laughed – I am sure of that. She laughed and her eyes were shining. But she was sad, too, and I knew it was time to stop asking questions. As if to let me know that I should do exactly that, she set to work again, stirring the soup as it thickened so it wouldn't burn at the bottom of the pot. 'We didn't ask for two babies,' she said at last. 'We were happy with just you.'

I remembered, that afternoon on the 254 bus, that I hadn't believed her. At the age of six, I knew several things about babies: I knew that they came from the hospital, where you had to ask for them specially and decide on a name while you waited in the queue for yours to come; I also knew that they sometimes died. I knew that, at least in the case of my sister, Elizabeth, my father was very fond of these dead babies, but found the survivors more of a hindrance than a help. The thing is, my mother knew I didn't believe her and, even then, I guessed the truth. I guessed that she had, in some way, asked and been refused, and this refusal had been because of some failure on her part. Yet I'd had a brother and, even if he wasn't a twin, he was mine. Nobody else had claimed him. Nobody could prove to me that Andrew was dead in the ordinary way, the way my grandmother was dead. How could he have died, if he'd never been alive in the first place? Like my sister, Elizabeth, he had never come home from the hospital; but nobody, not even my father, ever compared me to, or even spoke about, *him*. Nobody wished me dead in his place. Or not aloud. Surely he had been there all along, a ghost companion on the long walk to Mass on a Sunday morning, a fellow swimmer, tracking me stroke for stroke the length of the public baths. It seems impossible that I ever forgot him. My mother and father had done their best to expunge him from their world, but that didn't mean I had to let him go. I had a duty, to Andrew, and to myself, to give him space, to listen for him, to make him welcome. In one form or another, I would keep him by me all my life: my brother, my soul-friend, my other self. He would continue where I left off, and I would live for him, tuned in to the rhythm of an other-world that nobody else could hear, a whole kingdom of ghost brothers, hidden in the dark.

CHAPTER 3

The consensus opinion on my mother was that she was a simple and decent woman. She attended Mass faithfully every Sunday, accompanied by her children, but not by her husband. She was polite, God-fearing, conventional, a woman who kept the best china she had been given as a wedding gift for when the priest came to call. For her, what mattered was family, and she did all she could to conceal my father's excesses from the world. I grew up admiring her from a distance: she was the one who taught me to read and write before I started school, the one who scrimped and saved to buy me 'educational' toys, the one who kept things together when it would have been easier, and more merciful, to let them fall apart. All she wanted was a little common decency in her life. She was one of those people who dream of a bookcase full of leather-bound classics and a vase of freshly cut flowers on the hall table. Of course, there was no hall table, because there was no hall. Obviously, there were no leather-bound classics.

To begin with, there were no books at all. After we moved to Corby, however, there were library books: for me, the voracious and utterly random studies of the child autodidact; for her, Mills & Boon. She never went to the library herself: I think she thought they would want her to demonstrate some kind of eligibility before she could borrow anything. Instead, she got me to borrow books for her on my ticket. This caused some amusement among the library staff, who couldn't quite figure out the boy who turned up every fortnight or so, in his faded blue anorak with the torn pockets, to borrow *The Brothers Karamazov*, a book on chess, and two of the latest hospital romances. I could never remember the titles of the Mills & Boon books, but the lurid cover illustrations stayed in my head and, most of the time, I avoided bringing home stuff she had already read.

Once or twice, on a bus home, I would flick through the books I had chosen for her. To begin with, I couldn't understand why anyone would read books like that. After a while, however, I began to see that the pleasure came not from the stories or the characters so much as from the knowledge that somebody out there knew her daydreams – not just in the broader sense of plot and circumstance, but also in the finer details, in the perfumes and the colours and the late-night conversations. Knew them and, so, knew her finer self: the woman who could have walked on a moonlit beach with some beautiful, difficult man, had things been different; the woman who knew the value of the carefully understated gesture, the tacit agreement, the shared secret. A woman, most of all, who knew the power and beauty of the unspoken. That was what mattered to her, I think: those romances left so much room for the unsayable – and what pleased her most was the idea that somebody out there understood, as she understood, that everything good in life was a secret, a private matter that had to be kept intact in the face of neighbours and Church and common law. It was the only explanation I could work out: she was addicted, not to tacky love stories, but to the unspoken. The unspoken, in which so much trust can be placed, and from which so much comfort can be derived. All the time, I imagine, she was hanging on to an illusion that she saw through, but couldn't bear to discard. For as long as she could, she wanted to ignore the fact that the limits of any marriage are set by the one who has the least to give. So she read Mills & Boon books, because they renewed her belief in love.

The move to England had come as a shock to her, though. She no longer had family and friends around her, and she hated the house on Handcross Court, not just because it repre-sented an exile to which she had never really agreed, but also because it was something my father had chosen, something my father had waited and worked for. There was nothing obvious to find fault with: it had an upstairs; in a manner of speaking, it had three bedrooms. It was an end-of-row house, with a larger garden than most, and it was far enough from the works that we almost never had smuts on the washing. From time to time, the rain ran grey on the window panes, and on summer days, when all the windows were open, we might find dark smears of iron-scented dust on the window sills. But everybody had that – and it wasn't as bad as living in a condemned prefab back in Cowdenbeath, with an aban-doned garden on one side, and dark, dripping woods on the other. Here, there was a square of grass where the children could play, a new swimming pool, beautiful countryside all around and a town that was growing, with plenty of work for all: a chance to do better, a chance to start again. My mother didn't believe it. She knew the extra money would disappear on drink, the days out in the country and the foreign holi-days would never materialise. She'd spent her entire adult life listening to promises.

After a while, though, with the compensation money finally in the bank, she decided to call my father's bluff. She waited until he'd had a few drinks – enough, but not too many – then she raised the subject of our buying a house of our own. With the union money we would have enough to put down a big deposit, and the mortgage wouldn't be much more than the rent we were paying at Handcross Court.

My father listened, nodding all the time she was speaking, then he smiled ruefully. 'I don't know,' he said. 'We can't afford it. It's not just the mortgage, though that's bad enough, it's also the – upkeep – '

'What upkeep?'

'Maintenance. If anything goes wrong, you haven't got the Corporation to just come out and fix it.'

'What could go wrong?'

My father snorted. 'All kinds of things,' he said. 'Anything can go wrong with a house . . . '

I listened for a while as the familiar game played out, then I wandered off. Nothing more was said about houses for a while then, suddenly, like some miracle, we went, as a family, to look at a place my mother had seen in the paper: an old house, with a big, neglected garden, it needed work, as the estate agents said, but it was cheap – cheap enough, my mother thought, that we could *manage*. This was her favourite word, and she used it all the time: *Don't worry, we'll manage*; *I don't know how I'll manage*; *If we put this much down, we can manage the rest*.

My father was less than enthusiastic from the start. Before he had even seen the place, he was finding potential pitfalls, insurmountable problems. He had been paid an undisclosed, but significant, sum in compensation for his battered skull, his punctured lung, his weeks of inactivity, and my mother was trying to figure out how to make some good use of it, before he pissed it all away at the Hazel Tree or the Corby

Candle. With this move to Corby, she was planning a fresh start, the first step into another world – into the new morning of home ownership. It had been unimaginable before, and it was unimaginable still, walking around this empty, slightly shabby house – shabby? what did we care? shabby was genteel compared to our usual habitat: condemned. It had been unimaginable till that moment, but my mother had done her calculations and she carried them in her head all the way round: so much down, so much for decorating, so much in monthly payments, so much for some new used furniture. She had worked it out, and she knew it could be managed. It was inconceivable, in fact, that we would not go ahead: once we had made the down payment, drawn from the compensation money, the remaining payments wouldn't be any more than the rent we were paying the Corporation, and this would be *ours*.

The house was at the end of a residential street, not on an estate, an older, whitewashed house in its own overgrown, but surprisingly substantial, garden ground. It had a proper hallway, with stairs, banisters, rooms off the hall, a coat rack, everything she had ever wanted. It even had French windows at the back, giving out on to a little patio. We walked around the place in awed silence, but I could see in my father's face that he was only going through the motions. I wondered if he could see the hope in my mother's eyes – the hope, the fear, the longing. God, it had *French windows*. Of course it needed work, of course it was shabby – but it was also possible. My mother had worked it out. I could imagine the sacrifices she would have made to live in that house. I could imagine how hard she would have worked. She had been one step up from homeless for so long – a condemned tenement, a prefab – and now, here she stood in a house with French windows and a balustrade. I think she almost believed her troubles would just shrivel up and vanish if she could live in this house. At the same time, I think she knew that she never would.

When my father continued to reject the idea – something wasn't right, it was too risky, there was too much to do – she didn't say anything, not while we children were present. She had tried her best, and she had failed. But at that moment – he had said no in front of us for a reason, to close the conversation – in that awful moment, while we all coped with our dashed hopes, I looked into her face and saw that something had been extinguished. Only this wasn't just some hope – an afternoon's adventure, a mad dream scotched. This was the very light of her, the spark, the soul. Extinguished. It had been there for days, ever since she had first seen the advertisement in the paper and begun to plot, and it had kindled her eyes, till they seemed more alive than I had ever seen – as alive, as full of hope, as they were in her wedding picture. For a while she seemed young again and I remember, still, the gratitude I felt for this sudden apparition, this living woman who was my mother. I loved that light, for her sake – and I came to believe, as she had, in the house we would soon inhabit. It seemed so reasonable. I'd overheard some of the talk and her plan had convinced me. I couldn't believe it when my father refused: it seemed nothing more than spite on his part. That day, the light died, and I didn't see it again. From that moment on, my mother's face was like the broken kaleidoscope I had once tried to fix. The patterns still appeared, but they were muddy, unclear, incomplete-looking. Some time later, I asked her why we hadn't tried for the house.

'Oh, why do you think?' she said.

'I don't know,' I said, but I did.

She sat gazing at me in disbelief. Suddenly, everything had

turned upside down: now I was the one trying to believe the best of things, and she was the cynic. 'Drink, of course,' she said. 'All that money. And we'll not see a penny of it.' It was an unusually bitter moment – the first such I had witnessed. That day, when my father refused even to entertain her dream, something else happened to my mother, beyond her loss of hope.   From now on, she would make far less of an effort to conceal her irritation, even her disgust, with my father. From now on, she was a wife from duty, rather than desire. As a Catholic, and as a mother, she would never have left him, but now, I saw, she thought about it. I would see that look again, in the years to come, and I would see it in her eyes, a few days before she died, when she looked up at me from her dying bed, hazy with morphine, and asked me – at that moment, not her son, but some kind stranger – what it had all been about.

CHAPTER 4

I hated Corby from the first, but it felt disloyal to admit as much. On the outside, I must have seemed detached, or indifferent; inside, I was angry all the time. I was angry with my teachers, angry with the neighbours, angry with the parish priest, angry with the cheap shops on Corporation Street where my mother went shopping, angry with my parents for moving to Corby in the first place. Most of all, I was angry with anybody who showed any interest in me, or in what I was thinking or doing, or in what I might want from life. I didn't want anything from life other than to be left alone. I knew I didn't belong – and that was a problem because, as I soon realised, Corby was far more conformist than Cowdenbeath had been. People had come there from all over, bringing their families from Scotland, or Wales, or Northern Ireland, all desperate to fit in and be accepted. Corby was all about joining in, all about *wanting* to belong, a town of clubs and unions that defined who you were and what you were not: the Catholic Club, the Rangers Club, the Latvian Male Voice Choir, the Silver Band, Steelworkers, Tubeside. I hated that. As far as I was concerned, the group, whatever form it took, was an instrument of tyranny. I wouldn't play for the school football team; I refused to even try cricket; I didn't talk the playground talk about jamrags and cunt-smells and intriguing ways to eat Mars bars.

Meanwhile, my father was changing. He had come to a new place, where he was an unknown quantity, but it hadn't been long before he commanded the same respect – or fear – as he had at home. In fact, he was more frightening now, because he was more unpredictable. His failure to give his wife and children the new life he had convinced himself we wanted had much to do with a new mood of simmering resentment that could spill over at any moment, but something else was going on too, something none of us knew about. Now, when he was in one of his black moods, he hit out at random, without intent, for no reason. His victim might be me, or someone he met on the way out of the pub; it could even be one of his friends. One Saturday afternoon, he came home with his current best friend, a genuinely warm-hearted man called Bill. My mother cooked them both something to eat but suddenly, halfway through the meal, my father announced he was going upstairs to get ready to go out again. He needed a change of shirt, some 'good' trousers. Someone would have to clean his good shoes. Bill remonstrated with him: *There's no hurry, eat your food*, the usual drunkard's banter. I'd seen my father and Bill drunk together – swaying back and forth unsteadily, arms linked, calling each other brothers, that kind of rubbish – but I'd never seen them exchange an angry word. That afternoon, however, Bill misjudged the moment, as he got up from the table and tried to take my father's arm.

For all the misery he caused me, for all the damage he did, I think that was the first time I realised that my father was more than just routinely dangerous, the first time I realised he was capable of doing real and permanent harm. Bill shrugged it off, later, but he never came to our house again – not because he was afraid of my father, but because he was embarrassed for them both.

I had just gone through to the living room, while they sat in what we called the dinette. (The word I most dislike, in the English or any other language, has to be this one: *dinette*. What could be more ugly, more revealing of the way we lived then? *Dinette*. Enough room for a sideboard and a table, and a tacky Highland landscape that my father had brought home from God knows where. The canteen of cutlery that someone had given my parents as a wedding present in the sideboard drawer. Cork place mats. Flock wallpaper, badly hung. Fridge in the corner, because the kitchen was too small to get it in.) Suddenly, I heard my mother cry out. She had been in the kitchen, so nobody else saw what had happened: what we did see was Bill on the floor, and my father stamping on his arm, the expression on his face cold and ugly, as if he knew exactly what he was doing. He was like a man performing a routine action, a man at work, doing something he did every day. I tried to grab him and was thrown back against the wall. My mother was shrieking, trying to push him away from Bill, who had rolled over, his arm turning under him, as he tried to scramble back to his feet. Meanwhile, I got my balance and plucked at my father's sleeve. He turned and grabbed my throat. By that time, Bill was on his feet, my mother had my father by his other arm and, for a moment, we all stood, like a tableau, frozen in the moment, something dimming in my father's face, Bill making soft, conciliatory noises, not words, just sounds, like the reassuring sounds you make to a horse when it gets spooked. My mother was talking too, saying over and over again, 'Come on, George. Come on, George. Come on . . . ' Repetition is key in these situations: repetition; soft, meaningless noises; making space. Nothing more than you would do for a frightened animal. Some of the time, it works.

*

For the first three years of our Corby existence, we made the trip home to Scotland in the summer. We travelled all night on a bus that picked us up at Stamford, stopped a while at Scotch Corner, and terminated in Edinburgh at around six in the morning. Everybody hated these long nocturnal journeys; everybody but me, that is. I loved sitting at the window, staring out at the land as it slipped by: the open fields, the towns, the woods, the rivers, the power stations standing massive and elegant in their own smoke, the sky as it darkened over a meadow, reclaiming the trees and the beasts of the field. Most of all, I loved the towns when the street lamps were lit, orange or white or crimson in the blue gloaming. I would try to catch the moment when they came on, the point where day became night; when I saw a street lamp suddenly brighten into crimson or silver, I would feel blessed.

I didn't like the visits home half as much as the journey there. We would be cramped together, all of us in the one room, my father always wanting to be off to some new pub where nobody knew him, my mother worried about the holiday money, and what he might do with it if she let him out of her sight. We would stop first in Cowdenbeath and traipse around visiting everybody: my cousin Madeleine, my various aunts, our old neighbour, Mrs Black, who loved to talk about her own and other people's various operations. Everybody looked the same as they had when we left, but they were also strangely altered: they seemed far away and muffled now, as if they didn't exist at any other time, and had just come out of storage for the length of our stay, to re-assure us that nothing had changed while we had been gone. Their voices had begun to soften and fold in upon themselves, their houses seemed preserved in water glass, their hallways and front rooms stood at one remove from the world I remem-

144

bered, their wireless sets and china strangely antique, their clothes neat and clean, but somehow wrong, like costumes they were unaccustomed to wearing. Equally unreal was the world my mother described, a world of new possessions and hot water and modern appliances we didn't own. I knew well enough not to say anything, of course, though I would watch her, as we came away, a crumb of salmon on her lip, or a butter-stain on her sleeve, and I would feel sorry for her, not because she lacked the things she had claimed to have, but because she thought they would make a difference.

For a while, I was still doing well at school. My mother could tell her friends and family, when she went home, or when she wrote the little notes she posted back to Scotland with the Christmas cards, that I had got an A in every subject on my report card (not quite true, but nobody cares about Geography or Art). For a while, she could say I was on the athletics team, I played chess, I was in the science club. When it came round to parents' days, I was the one who stepped forward out of the choir and read the poem, or the dramatic monologue that Mr Edmunds had adapted from *Wuthering Heights*. At the open evenings, I was the boy who demonstrated to a succession of bemused, but tolerant visitors the wonders of chromatography. Year after year, I accepted the prize, I ran the relay, I won the chess tournament or recited a soliloquy from *Hamlet* but, even though this was all duly recounted in letters home, nobody that mattered was there to see me. I wasn't surprised: I knew my mother couldn't afford to miss a day's work; I also knew that, had she taken the time off, she would have been afraid that, by being there, she was showing my father up. Meanwhile, because he worked shifts, and given the fact that he and his workmates were forever negotiating swaps, doing doubles, sometimes, to cover for a club social or a night out, my father had more opportunities to see me enact those childish triumphs – and he was the one I wanted there, truth be told. I know it's a cliché, but it's also true that a boy seeks his father's respect, his father's recognition, first. Looking back now, I see that my problem wasn't just that I couldn't win my father's approval but that, even if I had, I wouldn't have wanted it *from him*. I wanted the regard, not of this wounded, inadequate individual, but of the father I had invented from scraps of literature and hearsay. A father who did not exist, any more than my phantom brother existed, but still the only father I had. This was the man I wanted to step down off the stage, or cross the finishing line for – because I *did* win the prizes, I *did* play the leading part in the school play, I *did* make the speech at parents' day, occasionally I *was* the first to cross the finishing line and, all through my school years, he never came.

But then, a father who never shows up is both a curse and a blessing: a curse, because it's a lonely feeling, to win something and have nobody to show it to; a blessing because, after a while, I didn't care to do anything other than for its own sake. Not for the prize, not for the regard, not for the approval, but for the thing itself. That can be a lonely experience, too, but it's a different kind of loneliness, and after a time, it brings its own satisfactions. 'If I do well, I am blessed,' says Marianne Moore, 'whether any bless me or not.' That's a difficult lesson for a thirteen-year-old. Eventually, I stopped doing well in school. It was just as easy to coast through, and there was no satisfaction in what my teachers had to offer. I began reading away from the syllabus; I got thrown out of the maths class; when I did my exams, I chose to answer questions on books or topics we'd not been prepared for. It was a game, now. No more straight As, no more science club. From now on, it was just me, and what I wanted to do. Eventually, all I wanted to do was read Edgar Allan Poe and go out to the woods with the other misfits, to build fires and find things to destroy.

There were four of us, in the beginning. We would hang about in garage blocks and derelict buildings, playing with matches, smoking stolen cigarettes, making bonfires and standing over them while they slowly kindled and quickly burned out, lonely souls, lost in the beguilement of fire. We were always making plans for something bigger, but even then, I knew the others weren't as serious as I was. I had grown up with this *fascination*, in the old, strong sense. I remembered chasing fire engines, back in Cowdenbeath; I remembered the one big fire I had seen when I was about eight, the drama of it, the noise and beauty of the fire, the excitement of watching it burn. It hadn't occurred to me, then, that this was all in my power to create: a wisp of cloth, some stolen lighter fluid, a box of matches was all it took to make my very own art work. Because that was how it felt at the time: a work of art, a piece of theatre. With the others, it was just bonfires, rubbish bins, piles of cardboard and old papers on pieces of waste ground; but when I was alone, I made real fires, fires that destroyed something, fires that made something beautiful happen. I didn't want to hurt anybody. I burned stuff from the construction sites on the edge of town, where it was advancing into the countryside around Great Oakley; I made fires in abandoned garages to see how things burned in an enclosed space, black smoke gathering, then billowing out into the sunlight. When my father brought friends home, I would stick around to hear their stories of the furnaces and the coke ovens and the soaking pit. I thought it would almost be worth working on Steelside, just to see those huge furnaces. Oftentimes, I would cycle up to the other side of town, just to watch the Candle burning.

As things turned out, one of the others – I'll call him Raymond – was on the same path. Like me, he'd grown tired of the little fires we'd been making, and gone out on his own, riding around on his bike, looking for things to burn. Once, he'd found a disused hut next to an old railway line; after he'd set it alight, he'd taken photographs of the blaze with his mother's camera. He showed me the pictures. They weren't expert, but they were very moving.

One day he came round to our house and told me to get my bike, there was something he wanted me to see.

'Where are we going?' I asked, as we cycled out towards Corby old village.

'You'll find out.' He was enjoying this, being mysterious, looking forward to what was about to happen. Raymond was smart, but he didn't like school. The only thing he took seriously was RE. If he'd switched sides, he could have been a big cheese in the Vatican, the time he spent thinking about the minor details of theology and Church law. In the fourth year, we had a new teacher, a pretty, slightly manic young woman who had recently converted. She was trained to teach French and Spanish, but she had made the mistake of volunteering for RE duty, a task normally reserved for hardened nuns. I'm sure she was already in trouble, morally, or psychologically – Pope John XXIII Memorial Comprehensive was probably a real shock to her system – but I can't help thinking, looking back, that Raymond played a part in her eventual breakdown, with his constant, seemingly innocent questions about her new-found faith. I don't think he actually achieved his ambition of making her abandon the Church; it was just that her pride crumbled when she realised that she couldn't answer the theological enquiries of someone she probably saw as an overly curious, but essentially well-meaning fifteen-year-old. Perhaps she even thought she had failed him, that she had failed all of us. I wish, now, that I could go back to her and explain that we'd all been very thoroughly and carefully failed, long before she turned up.

Finally, Raymond and I arrived at our destination: a disused, late-Victorian or early-Edwardian house, set in its own half-acre of summer grass and fruit trees, a place nobody had lived in for years. I'd been there before, of course: everybody called it the Vicarage, and I think it did belong to the Church of England, though it was too far from the old church, I thought, to have been the vicar's house. Not that I cared much about its history. For me, it was a place to go, a curiosity, a house that was locked and boarded up and, for that reason alone, a place to break into. How many of us honed our burglary skills on places like that? If they had been left wide open, with a big welcome sign on the door, nobody would have bothered going in.

Raymond hopped off his bike and looked to see if I was thinking what he was thinking.

'Yeah,' I said. 'So?'

'We can get in round the back,' he said.

'I know that,' I said. 'I've been here before. There's nothing much – '

He took a box of matches from his pocket and shook them next to his ear, grinning madly. 'Let's burn the fucker down,' he said.

I didn't know if he was serious. I *had* been thinking what he was thinking, but now that he said it, I wasn't so sure. It was a house. One day, people could live there again, as they had done once. One day they would scrape the old wallpaper off the walls, repaint the woodwork, wash the windows and polish the floors. Absurdly, I even thought of being that person. I thought of how I could live there, make it into a home, hang pictures on the walls. Invite my mother to tea. Show her my library of leather-bound books: Dickens, Dostoevsky, Tolstoy, Melville, Conrad. 'No, thanks,' I said. I was annoyed that he'd suggested it, not just because it was a house, but because he'd made me see my own limitations. I liked fires, but I didn't want to burn *property*.

'Come on,' he said. 'It'll be fantastic. Can you imagine – '

'No.' I said. The images that had passed through my mind moments before – a fire in the grate, pictures on the walls, a Christmas tree in the corner of the big downstairs room, snow at the windows – made it seem grotesque, as if he was asking me to burn my mother's house. 'It's stupid.'

Raymond gave me a weary look, but he didn't say anything.

'Let's go down to the sludge beds,' I said. I felt like a twelve-year-old.

He shook his head. 'I'm going in,' he said. He propped his bike against a tree and headed round the side of the house, towards the broken window at the back. I waited a moment, then I got on my bike and cycled away. It was summer, late in the afternoon. Soon, it would be evening.

Later, Raymond and I would be expelled within months of one another: for smoking cannabis, for drinking, for not attending Mass – but not for arson. We'd meet on the street now and then, but we didn't talk much, so I didn't get to know what he did with himself after school. I bought some acid from his older brother, Gerry, at Bickershaw in 1972, and I asked about him. Gerry was a tall, thin, long-haired guy with little round NH specs, one of a million bargain-basement John Lennons; the rumour going around about Raymond was that he'd had some kind of religious experience after his expulsion, and was contemplating the priesthood. I didn't believe it, but it didn't sound impossible. When I asked about it, Gerry laughed. He was so stoned, he would probably have laughed if I'd asked him the time, but I immediately knew the rumour was wrong. Raymond wasn't planning to become a priest.

'That's a good one,' Gerry said, shaking his head. 'Got some purple too, if you're interested.' He didn't say anything else. I heard later that Raymond was at art school.

Some time after the vicarage incident, the public library burned down. It was just before Christmas: when I heard the news, I cycled over there in the early morning, a light snow falling, the air blue-grey, nobody else on the streets. In those days, the library was near the woods, just opposite the Corby Bowl, a piece of low-grade quasi-modernism that was a favourite refuge all through my teens, a good place to sit in the warm and study the photographic books after school, when my father was back from day shift. I'd expected some kind of business to be going on: fire investigators, men at work clearing up, making the ruins safe, policemen looking for witnesses. There was nothing. I was free to wander about, picking up charred pages from books I had probably borrowed over the years, my mother's Mills & Boons, the complete works of Dostoevsky in their gold and scarlet dust covers, the atlases and art books and pharmacy texts I'd pored over in the reading room. It was a sad moment, but it was also beautiful. The woods were full of snow, and a wet snow had fallen on the charred beams and broken remains of the building the night before; the remnants of burned books lay scattered over the snow all around, still as monochrome on a day without wind. It was extraordinary: white, touched here and there with black, silent, wonderfully bleak, and as I stood there, I guessed this fire had been no accident. I knew for sure that Raymond hadn't started it, and it had nothing to do with me, but from what I'd learned about fires, I also knew that *this* wasn't a simple act of malice. It was a statement, done for its own sake: a statement, not *of* something specific, but a statement in the way a line of birdsong is a statement. A natural phenomenon, like a storm, or a rose. I stood there a long time, though by the end I wasn't sure if it was regret for the library that detained me, or the beauty of its ruin. Both, I imagine. By that time, a book was the closest thing to holy that I knew, but I couldn't deny the frisson of pleasure I experienced, seeing those ashes – those words, those ideas, the foreign beauty of those texts – melting away in the snow.

CHAPTER 5

There's a series of paintings by George Shaw called *Scenes from the Passion* that make me think of Corby in the seventies. Shaw is a painter, born in the mid-sixties, who chooses – for these works, at least – to work in Humbrol enamel on board, giving the work a strangely flat, yet intense quality, as if something that should have been tiny, like a faraway memory, had gradually expanded, becoming an altarpiece, an obsession, something at once quotidian and sacramental. One painting, *The Middle of the Week*, painted in 2002, shows a row of ruined garages covered in graffiti and littered with the evocative trash you find in such places. Here and there, clumps of dark, virulent weed poke through the concrete; elsewhere, the stone is charred with the remains of bonfires. It reminds me of the garages we smoked in and set fire to when I was growing up, but this isn't nostalgia working here, it isn't even memory: this is the locus of an extreme stillness, a place beyond time or ordinary significance. Nothing can be superimposed on this painting: it's not social commentary, urban realism, autobiographical exploration. It's a fact: a moment, a natural phenomenon.

Another picture in the series comes closer to depicting my father's natural habitat than anything else I can think of. It's a painting called *The New Star*, showing a building that might be anything, but happens to be a pub, and it makes me think of the pub my father settled on when he moved to Corby, the place that was, more than any other, his home. The Hazel Tree was a typical estate pub: anonymous, dull, closed off to the outside world, as much prison block as sanctuary, as much dream as architecture. You could walk past the Hazel Tree every day and see nothing remarkable about it; then, in a certain slant of light, or in the sudden stillness after heavy rain, you might catch a glimpse of something else, some inner truth, something that resembles the *gravitas* of an icon. Shaw's paintings capture this moment perfectly – and I think, by extension, they capture something about the men who frequent such places, about the dreams they conceal and the stunned tenderness they harbour.

My father started taking me to the Hazel Tree when I was fourteen. I'd gone drinking with him before then, but I'd had to sit outside, in the dark, lonely gardens of the Everard Arms, sipping my pint of cider as the traffic slid by on a Saturday evening. My father would come out every now and then with a packet of crisps and another cider, ask if I was all right, then disappear back inside to see his friends. I knew he was just using me as an excuse to get out of the house, but I liked being there, sitting alone with my drink, listening to the men inside talking, people working in the kitchen, the odd bird singing along the fence line. I've enjoyed sitting alone in pub yards ever since, especially in the early evening, or in the morning, before the crowds get in.

At fourteen, though, I was man enough to sit inside with my father and his friends, playing crib or dominoes, man enough to go up to the bar and remember who wanted what in a round of six – beers and shorts – with the tenner my father had just slipped me under the table. This was his idea of an education – and, in a way, it was. I quickly got the hang of crib, and I was a demon at dominoes. We'd play for drinks, and I won more often than I lost.

All this time, my father was getting weaker. I knew this, without being conscious of it. At home, he was becoming more maudlin, more repetitive; all his energy went into keeping up his image at the Hazel Tree. There, he was still the presence he had always been: glowering, dangerous, sarcastic. He was still considered a hard man, and not to be treated lightly. Now and again, though, I saw a softness in him, a hesitation. The accident had taken more of a toll than any of us were admitting. All the clues were there: where he had once been a wanderer, drifting from pub to pub, never hesitating to walk straight into places that other men would think twice about, now he was a regular, always drinking at the Tree, or the Everard, if he had people with him, or at the Silver Band Club, where the other regulars were known to him. Where he had once been so self-possessed, so heavy and still, now he was restless, ready to lash out, brooding and defensive. Where he had been dark and limber and poised, now he was lighter, fatter, looser. One night, a man I didn't know came up to me in the yard outside the Hazel Tree. He was in his mid-twenties, a big man with a wispy moustache and a dark, tight face.

'You're John, right?' he said.

I nodded. In that place, you didn't talk much, especially if you were a hanger-on, as I was. You waited, heard what the other man had to say. Besides, in this situation, I could tell something was coming, and I wanted time to work out how to play it. My father was inside with his usual crew, sitting at their usual table by the high window, throwing banter around and playing dominoes.

155

'I'm Alastair,' the man said. He held out his hand and I shook it. 'Listen, son. I don't want you to take this the wrong way. All right?'

Here it comes, I thought. I shook my head.

'Your dad's a good man,' he continued. 'But he's not the man he used to be. If you get what I'm saying.'

I didn't say anything. There were tiny dark spots on his teeth, like rust marks, that showed when he talked.

'What I mean is, I wouldn't want to see anybody take the piss,' Alastair said. He wasn't bothered by my reluctance to engage in conversation. I knew that he knew that I knew I was just there to listen. Still, the whole thing was going to take all night, if I didn't say something.

'I see what you're saying,' I said. Naturally, I had no idea what his point was.

He nodded. He looked grim now, like he'd just been to the dentist. 'Fine,' he said. 'You keep an eye on him, OK?'

I nodded back. 'I'll do that,' I said. I had no idea what that meant, in real terms, but I knew it was what he needed me to say.

'That's fine,' Alastair said. 'You're a good man. I didn't want to keep you from your dad.'

'No problem,' I said. I looked at his teeth. 'I'm just going to the bar. Can I get you one?'

He almost smiled. I was fifteen years old, and he knew it. I had no idea what I was doing, but I was putting on the most convincing act I could manage, and he knew that too. Trouble was, he was doing the same thing – and, at that moment, I knew that too. It was 99 per cent act, all this hardman stuff. These men couldn't smile, or laugh in a certain way, or talk about certain things. Not in public. It was all about display: the strong silent type; the nutter who was too crazy to mess with; the hard man; the heid case; the ex-army, disciplined, kills-with-his-bare-hands bampot. You had to fit a recognised profile, or you'd better stay away. I was there because my father was who he was. I could talk to these men, I could win their money at dominoes, I could listen to their jokes as long as I behaved like my father's son, and played the game. If I tried to be anybody else, I was yesterday's papers. *Nae use tae naebody.* If my father should fall from grace, then I fell with him. Those were the rules. Nobody told you what they were, but you had to learn them quickly, or you'd find yourself walking home with a bar towel pressed to your face, blood on your shirt, and a voice in your head saying, *What the fuck were you thinking? What the fuck were you thinking?* over and over again.

At home, my father was often ugly and violent; but he could also be the standard maudlin drunk, embarrassing and pathetic in ways that shamed me far more than the nights when he came home and tried to smash up my piano, or sat in his 'big chair' muttering dark stories about George Grant. He would weep and blurt out things that must have mortified him next day, when he was sober. Or he would listen to his music, full volume, always the same three records: the only ones he owned. Two by Mario Lanza, one by Al Jolson. Some songs he would listen to again and again – 'Vesti la giubba' was a particular favourite – and he would try to sing along, weeping all the while, drowsing away and surfacing again to slide the stylus back to the beginning of the track. He would do this when he came home alone, almost too drunk to talk, and I knew he would do it if I was there too, so I usually left him in the Hazel Tree at around ten or so and went off somewhere else. I didn't like the Hazel Tree that much, but I couldn't avoid going. It made life easier if we went through certain motions, played certain games. One game was that we were father and son, going out together, him slipping me money and looking the other way when I smoked cigarettes. My mother liked it that we went out together, oddly enough. She made him promise every time not to get me drunk, but she must have imagined, no matter what, that any time we spent together was a good thing.

It seems sudden, looking back, but this was the time I gave up trying to see his good side, the time when I began to feel contempt for him. This saddens me – because there were moments when somebody else flashed through his act. For example, I can remember now how, when my sister was choking on something she'd swallowed, my father picked her up by her feet and held her upside down, shaking her – gently enough, forcefully enough – to dislodge the object in her throat. I remember the stories he told against himself, stories about his time in the air force, where he made no pretensions to being a hero. In those days, he had been stationed in Germany, and later in Palestine and Egypt. He said he liked the Germans he'd met, and he was clearly disgusted by the post-war prejudice shown towards them; he also liked the 'wogs' who worked around the base in Palestine. He didn't like 'the Jews' (it would be hard to find a British serviceman from that time who did), by which he meant the Zionists who blew up the King David Hotel, the only real enemy he ever had, given that he was too young to see action in the European war. He used to tell a sad, rather ugly story against himself about a night's sentry duty, a 'who goes there' and a donkey. Whether it was true, I have no idea; probably it happened to somebody, somewhere and, liking the tale, my father picked it up and made it his own. His version went like this: he was on watch, still a young man, still not quite sure of himself on this new duty, far from the world he knew. He was in what he thought of as desert, guarding the camp, when he heard a noise, somewhere out in the dark, somewhere in 'the desert'. He called out a warning, but there was no response. He called again, and he realised that something was out there, silent, possibly malicious, something or someone moving towards him out of the dark. He was afraid of 'the Jews' (not the Arabs, of course, for they were allies), and he didn't want to fail in his duty, so he called 'Who goes there?' one more time and, on receiving no reply, fired at the figure he thought he saw moving in the dark.

It was a donkey. 'I never saw an angry German,' my father would say about his service days, 'but I shot a donkey.' He would try to make a joke of it, but I could see, whenever he told this story, that he was haunted by what he had done, disgusted at his own panic, and shaken – at some deeper level – by the miserable fate of this particular casualty of the Palestine operation. At some level, I know, he blamed 'the Jews' for the donkey, just as much as he blamed them for his imagined comrades in the King David – and perhaps because the Zionists were so much at fault, he liked the Arabs, even though he quite freely referred to them as 'wogs'. The only photographs he brought back from his travels in the service were, in fact, a few bazaar scenes, some postcards of Egypt, and three snapshots of Palestinian men he'd known, 'wogs' who had, it seems, performed menial tasks around the place where he was stationed. There's no way of knowing why, but I think he felt genuine affection for those Palestinian men who, in the world to which he belonged, would have been considered nobodies. The word 'wogs' was his one concession to the prejudices of his class and time; secretly, though, he kept those snapshots for forty years, and spoke often of how decent, and how unfairly treated, the Palestinians had been.

I didn't remember this, however. I didn't remember his occasional flashes of extraordinary competence, his presence of mind when presence of mind was needed. All I saw was the side my friends saw – or rather two sides, at odds with one another: the hard man he put on like a suit of armour for the Hazel Tree, and the pathetic, tearful drunk he slipped into at home. Occasionally, he would be stone-cold sober – but that was no improvement. Sober, he would often be angrier than ever, and even more of a bully. One day, my friend Richard was round at our house when my mother and father were trying to paper the dinette. Richard and I were in the living room, going through some photographs he'd developed. They were good pictures, but pretty soon we found ourselves setting the contact sheets aside, to listen in. My father didn't like Richard, for his long hair, mostly, which made Richard all the more determined to like *him*. Eventually, we drifted into the kitchen, so we could sneak furtive glances at the sad little comedy playing out in the dinette. My father was up on the stepladder he'd borrowed from Matt next door, moaning and cursing, haranguing my mother, trying and failing, trying again, failing even more spectacularly. There was ruined wallpaper everywhere. 'God! What do you think you're doing?' he was saying, as my mother tried to rescue yet another Anaglyptic casualty.

My mother was on the verge of tears, as the wallpaper rolled back off the wall and landed in a crumpled, wet heap on the carpet below, my father's smoothing brush clattering to the floor. 'I don't know,' she said, trying to remain calm. 'What do you want me to do?'

'God Almighty! I'd be better off doing it by myself.' He

stepped down off the ladder, crumpled up the fallen sheet of paper and tossed it into the corner. 'You're no help.' He got back up on the ladder and started scraping at the wall.

Richard couldn't believe this. His father was a painter and decorator who would wallpaper entire houses before breakfast. But he was as amused as he was puzzled. 'More paste, less speed,' he muttered.

'What was that?' My father was down off the ladder, clutching the brush he'd just retrieved from the floor.

'I was wondering if you needed a hand,' Richard said, his face the picture of innocence.

My father threw me a significant look, then turned back to Richard. 'No bother,' he said. 'But thanks for the thought.'

Richard nodded, and we went out the back door. He had a ready-rolled joint in his pocket, which he pulled out and lit up as soon as we were away from the house. 'I have to say it,' he said, 'your parents are the craziest people I've ever met. Where did you say your dad worked?'

'By-products,' I answered. 'Safety.'

Richard gave a snort. 'Remind me not to drink the water,' he said, handing me the spliff.

'Not a problem,' I said. 'He's sober now. He's never sober at work.'

'I feel better already.'

'You should,' I said. 'He's only dangerous when he's sober.'

By now, this was almost true. In the mornings, before he went on day shift, my father would half fill a glass with brandy, break an egg into it, add a dash of milk, then gulp it down in one. His version of egg-nog. He said it warmed him up, got him started for the day ahead, but I don't think he could have gone through a day without it. The egg and the milk were just a cover, a way of calling this food, rather than a drink. When I started at the works, in the gap between finishing A levels and college, I remembered this little ritual and tried it myself once, just before I went on night shift. I almost threw up. But then, by that time, I had something better than brandy and eggs to keep me going through the long nights.

I thought I wouldn't hear from Alastair again. I knew he wanted me to pass his 'message' on, but I didn't. To do that would have been an insult to my father, a suggestion that he needed somebody to watch his back. Besides, Alastair hadn't really said anything. I didn't know what he had in mind, or even if he had anything in mind at all. He'd not made any actual threats, or offered any real warning. It didn't take me long to forget him. Or almost. I knew, if I saw him, I would be on guard.

A few weeks after our near-conversation, I was in the Hazel Tree again, with the usual crowd. My father was on good form, but there was an edge to the evening, a certain electricity in the air. It's a cliché, I know, but that *is* how it feels, like electricity, like the charge before a lightning storm. I had no idea what was going on, but I was there, and after a few drinks, I felt included. We were doing the usual stuff, playing dominoes, drinking, talking crap, and I didn't notice anything out of the ordinary, other than that odd charge in the air, until my father got up and headed for the toilets. That was when I saw Alastair. He looked different from the last time I'd seen him, heavier, darker, but I could tell that he'd been watching us, and now he was following my father out into the corridor. I glanced around the table, to see if anybody else had noticed: if they had, nobody was saying anything. Quickly, I got to my feet.

162

'Where are you off to?' somebody said. I think it was Junior, or maybe Mull, my father's best friend among the little group he ran with.

I paused. 'Just to the toilet – '

'Oh, aye?'

I nodded and looked at him. His face was blank, very still, but there was something in his eyes. 'Won't be a minute,' I said.

'Sit down, son,' he said. 'You're no use to him at the moment.'

'What?'

'Your old man can look after himself,' one of the others put in. 'Sit down and get that wee whisky down your neck.'

I sat down. A few minutes later my father came back, looking very calm. When he sat down, Junior looked at him. 'What took you so long?' he asked.

'Needed to wash my hands,' my father replied. 'Couldn't find the soap.'

I looked round. A couple of boys who had been standing at the bar went out quickly and there was a noise in the corridor outside. My father paid no attention, but reached into his pocket and pulled out a banknote. 'Get the boys a drink, son,' he said to me. This time he didn't slip the note under the table, as he usually did. 'A pint and a wee one,' he added, and he smiled dangerously, as if he knew something I didn't know, something secret and, until that moment, beyond confirmation, a little piece of information that had only just come to light, not about the world, but about me.

CHAPTER 6

The dredger is in today. Every winter it comes, its silver and cherry lights too bright for our little harbour, its great scoop churning up the silt and garbage that has settled over the last twelvemonth. My son likes to go down and stand on the waterfront to watch; there is something that satisfies him about the steady work this boat does, in the still part of the year. To be honest, I like it just as much as he does: some nights, I find an excuse to go out, just so I can walk by the harbour and watch the men at work. They seem more real when they are here, wedded to something intimate and physical and, at the same time, perfectly abstract. They seem more true, more defined than they appear in the pubs, absent from themselves, possessed of skills that are written deep in the muscle and the nerves. *Arbeit macht frei*. Why not? On some winter afternoons, after the gloaming sets in, the harbour becomes a theatre of lights and noise, all of it bent to a purpose, to the beautiful, steady work of maintenance, the creation of order.

Elsewhere, that order fails. Up in the town, they're already screaming through the wynds in souped-up cars, wet-pimpled boys racing around the half-lit streets in a fog of carbon and gangsta-rap, their shiny white faces and polecat eyes improbable behind the windscreens, all self-regard and simmering inferiority complex. As the early darkness of winter sets in, they hang around outside the schools they so recently attended, fatherless children waiting for someone to notice them. The pretty girl who was never impressed by their swagger; the teacher who tried for a while to get through, then gave up to concentrate on more hopeful cases; boys in the year they've just left, who still haven't been given their first car; boys like themselves, willing to stop a while and admire the souped-up tin-cans revving and gurgling in the car park opposite the school. I see them all the time, hurtling along the shore road with their stereos blaring, too stupid to know how stupid they look. I feel sorry for them, at one level, but all I can do is all anybody else does: I ignore them. We all ignore them.

When I was a child, people were always asking me what I wanted to be when I grew up. It wasn't just teachers and vaguely familiar uncles at weddings or funerals, everybody wanted to know, from the fishmonger to our neighbour, Mr Black, whose own children were married and gone. Everybody wanted to know; though, of course, they didn't really want to know at all. It was just a thing people say to a boy who is still at school, one of those questions that always begin with *And*.

'And what do you want to be when you grow up?'

I would be waiting for it, ready to feign the awkwardness of a child being taken seriously for a moment by a grown-up stranger, and I would take a moment to think before I answered, as if such a thing was within my power to decide. Most of the time, I said what people expected to hear: engineer, teacher, jet pilot, train driver. Occasionally, because I had mastered the word early, and knew what it meant, I said pharmacist – and, once, when a particularly smug old church lady stopped me and my mother on the steps outside St Bride's after Mass, I gave voice to the one true ambition I nurtured, the one answer, out of all the possible answers I could have come up with, that I really trusted. The uncoguid old lady – I knew my mother didn't like her, though she would never have said as much – posed her question and waited, with a condescending, self-satisfied smile hovering about her lips: 'And what do you want to be, when you're all grown up?'

Without a moment's hesitation, I said 'An Italian.'

I was only half joking. I knew exactly four adult Italians, the father, two uncles and grandfather of a classmate, and they all struck me as the very model of what I wanted manhood to be. Italian men could cook (in this case, they could even make ice cream), they were obvious and natural in their affection for children, they got excited about the things they liked. The fact that they even liked anything in the first place was something of a revelation. Most of the other men I encountered seemed to like nothing at all. Of course, I knew the Italians were not alone: I had met a couple of Poles, a Slav, a Hungarian, even a Frenchman. The Frenchman had shown me how to pick a flower right at the base of the stem, and suck out the nectar inside. I knew he was French because he was wearing a dark blue beret and had that kind of accent. As he stood there, explaining to me that what I was tasting was what bees tasted as they drifted from flower to flower, I kept stealing glances at his beret. When I was older, I decided, I would have one just like it: not quite royal, but not quite navy blue either, it was somewhere in between, subtle, yet bright, like the colours women wore.

That was a time when men of a certain temperament wore

berets. Priests, of course, when they went cycling around their parishes in those flat black berets with little ribbons on them. Young priests in fawn raincoats and charcoal-grey berets, walking around in churchyards, their boots crunching on the frosted gravel. Old priests working in their gardens, too close to God now to hear confession. The beret men weren't just priests, though. They were men from every walk of life: the gentler kind, the intelligent ones, the thoughtful, the artistic, the kind-but-not-soft-hearted. Schoolteachers, janitors, the man who kept the paper shop on Stenhouse Street. It didn't matter what they did. What they had in common was a sure sense of themselves that other men lacked. They were often religious, of course, but in a looser, more everyday way than the devout people I had been instructed to admire. It was as if they had all wanted to be priests, once upon a time, but hadn't passed muster, like my thirty-year-old neighbour who still lived with his mother and went to Mass every day before work. *Many are called, but few are chosen*, Father Connolly would say, and you couldn't help noticing the look on his face, a hurt, slightly awkward look that combined pride and loneliness in equal measure.

I could never work out if that loneliness was a disguise, a way of letting the other men know that having a vocation wasn't all it was cracked up to be, that the big, echoey house by the church and the car were luxuries that he paid for dearly, in the small hours, after Mrs O'Driscoll had washed up and gone back to her own house. Yet it seemed to me that these other men, the beret men, had a vocation of their own. It was informal and unacknowledged, but it was there for anyone to see: the calm, patient, skilful pursuit of ordinary life, a vocation of the commonplace. Those men transformed the most banal event into a ritual by the power of the imagination. Most of all, they were unlike my father in every way, and they weren't ashamed of the fact — and they weren't afraid. They were separate, gentle, self-contained. They looked at my father and saw him for what he was — and I saw it too. They were sorry for him. It wasn't contempt; it was compassion. That look the fortunate reserve for those who have been unlucky, in their lives, in their characters, in their talents. I wanted that look — or, rather, I wanted the calm I saw in their faces, a calm that my father not only did not possess, but would have denied — so I thought then — with his dying breath.

Sometimes, during periods of uneasy truce, I was going to the Hazel Tree with my father; sometimes we did everything we could to avoid one another. Occasionally, violence flared. After the Alastair incident, I was out of favour for reasons I didn't understand, but by now I was moving away, making friends with boys my father didn't like, boys like me. There were complaints from school about truancy, suspected drug use, insolence towards teachers, violations of the uniform code. My father didn't need any of that. It was a distraction; he felt called upon to act in some way; he thought my mother blamed him for how things had gone wrong. One evening, after I'd been sent home for wearing a makeshift safari outfit to school, instead of the Pope's colours, he told me that, if I got into trouble again, he'd get me a full-time job at the works. 'They're looking for new blood in the coke ovens,' he said. 'How do you fancy that?'

'Fine,' I answered.

He gave a contemptuous snort. 'You wouldn't last two days,' he said.

The crisis point came in our kitchen, during a school lunch

168

break. My father had come in and, seeing I was going to be late getting back and was making no effort to hurry, he grabbed me by the throat and pushed me back against the draining board. Without thinking – if I'd thought for a millisecond, I wouldn't have done it – I picked up a long-bladed knife from the sink unit and all of a sudden we were standing face to face: a man and his son, locked in moral stalemate. When I look back, I'm sure he wasn't afraid of that knife; he almost certainly could have taken it from me before I did any serious harm. After all, he was – hadn't Alastair proved it? – one of Corby's undisputed hard men. What he must have seen, however, was the look of pure hatred on my face; a look which, all of a sudden, had finally revealed to us both that, whatever the cost, I would have been quite happy to kill him. Looking back, I think I would. It surprised me, at the time, but it was also something close to a liberation. He must have felt a momentary dismay then, as he became aware of the level to which we had both sunk: after a long minute, he retreated, with a sneer and a glib remark about not picking up a knife unless you meant to use it, and I was gone, out the back door and over the garden wall. I didn't stop running till I reached the woods.

After that, things were quieter between us; but the resentment still simmered. The times when I wanted to do serious damage – the days when I wanted to kill him – began to merge, gradually at first, then with frightening acceleration, into a single, burning need to *do something*. Began to merge, that is, into a plan. I knew I couldn't have stabbed him when we stood face to face, in my mother's kitchen, but that didn't mean I couldn't do something outside, in the cool of the night, stepping out from the shadows, the way men some-times did, with a knife, or a hatchet. Looking back, I'm shocked at how seriously I took this plan, but at the time, it seemed possible. It wasn't such a hard idea to entertain – as long as it was safely tucked away, reserved for some future date.

By the time I was seventeen, I was hanging around with a completely new crowd. After I'd lost my job at the works – one night, I'd dropped acid and gone in on a twelve-hour shift, the next night I'd not gone in at all – I started at Scandura, a factory that made gaskets. To begin with, I was a solitary, working at my jigsaw in the corner of the shop floor, cutting out the small-batch, trickier gaskets that couldn't be made on the presses. I liked that work, it was almost skilled, and I enjoyed working with the jigsaw. There weren't that many small-batch jobs, though, and when I had nothing to do I had to operate one of the presses – a boring task usually reserved for women. I couldn't turn the work out quick enough. I'd get bored, start dreaming and, after a while, I moved to the warehouse, where my physical strength was considered useful.

From that moment on, the people I met after work, the boys I played table football or cards with in the canteen or out on the loading bay, the men I considered my friends, were a bunch of escapees from Glasgow: Tam, Big John, Wee John (who was, of course, bigger than Big John), Mickey. At Scandura, they were the boys who worked in stores, unloading raw materials from the lorries, keeping things in order, walking about in brown warehousemen's coats, limber, slow-moving, placid, and – the merest glance confirmed it – implacable. Nobody got to work in the stores unless Tam and his boys were OK with it, so when I was reassigned there, I was both apprehensive and honoured. It was the beginning of my shift when the floor supervisor, a supercilious ex-RAF type with the cliché handlebar moustaches, came over.

'We need this machine for somebody,' he said. 'We've got a new woman starting. I imagine she'll make better use of it than you do.' He looked me up and down as if faintly amused by something. 'You get yourself over to the warehouse,' he said. 'They need help over there. See Tam when you get there.'

At first, I thought he'd made a mistake. It wouldn't have been the first time. Once, he'd got me to cut out a whole batch of complicated gaskets, using expensive material, only to discover that he'd sent me the wrong blueprint. Naturally, he blamed me. 'Are you sure?' I said, before I could stop myself.

Handlebars bristled. 'You're not here to ask questions,' he said. 'You're here to do what I tell you – '

I smiled. 'I'm here for the pay packet,' I said, 'like everybody else. Whatever else happens is incidental.'

He studied me a moment, then shook his head. 'Fucking students,' he said. 'You won't last a week in stores.'

I'm not ashamed to have fond memories of the Scandura boys. They weren't patronising me when they let me into their circle: they wanted me to see how they lived, but they wanted to be sure I wouldn't get hurt, morally, as much as physically. They weren't like the so-called hard men I'd met before: playground bullies strutting around in Crombies and Doc Martens; skinhead gangs prowling the side streets around the town centre or the Lincoln Estate, waiting to pick off the weak and the stragglers; the Hazel Tree bampots that hung around my father's crowd, waiting to step into their shoes. These boys were warriors. They didn't fight five on to one, the way so many did. They fought real battles, usually against the odds. Their opponents were people they chose to dislike: servicemen; skinheads; anybody who ran in a gang, or conformed to some ugly system they could see at work in the world. When they weren't out on one of their missions, they were funny, like-able, cunning, ironic. They were far from stupid but they knew that, unlike Mr ex-RAF, they weren't going anywhere. When they were out, in their long black coats and baggy, Bay City Rollers-style jeans with a tartan trim, their long hair flowing over their shoulders, Wee John's baby face set, utterly detached, Big John laughing, Tam raising his wild, keening yawp, they were terrifying, like the berserkers of old who 'went without coats of mail, and acted like mad dogs and wolves'. The berserkers belonged to Odin, whose name derives from the old Norse, *odur*, meaning rage or fury; according to the sagas, Odin could assume the form of an animal, or a bird when he chose, and it was said of the berserkers that they, in turn, could assume the forms of wolves or bears. It may sound fanciful, but I came to believe that these boys really were berserkers, mutant sons of Odin, immune to attack from ordi-nary weapons, possessed by a divine *odur*.

Eventually, I started going to the pub with them. Their nick-name for me was Big Yin, which was, of course, ironic. Most nights it was just a drink after work, then I would wander off to the Open Hearth or the Nag's Head, while they continued on to whatever they had planned. I knew this was pretty crazy stuff: some weekends, they would go off to the villages around American Air Force bases and get into fights with 'the Yanks', or they would do battle with skinheads, squaddies, whoever they didn't like. They had no intention of getting me involved in any of that – they were, in fact, quite protective – but one night, outside the shops on Gainsborough Road, I was there

172

when the action came to them. We had been to a couple of pubs, then we'd bought some fish and chips and were standing around, eating, talking. I wasn't usually with them this late, and I can't remember, now, why I wasn't off doing my sensitive-type routine in some dim bedroom somewhere, listening to Tim Hardin or *All Things Must Pass* with some dark-eyed, platonic girl. I imagine they thought it would be a slow night, just another weekday, no big deal; then, from nowhere, a gang of about fifteen or twenty smoothie types appeared, charging into the little square in front of the shops brandishing sticks and chains, knives, hatchets, who knows what. It was too late to do anything but take what was coming: I was sure it was going to be bad and for a moment I felt nothing but icy terror, but then, just as something hit me, I felt a ridiculous surge of righteous anger, a sense of injustice that these creatures, less intelligent than the average mollusc, were about to beat *me* to a *pulp*. I'd been turning round just as I was hit, so whatever it was had struck the side of my head, but it still almost brought me down. It didn't though, not quite, or not right away, and I lunged forward, grabbing my assailant and dragging him to the floor as I lost my balance. I think I wanted to hurt just one person before I got what was coming. I have a physical memory of punching him, battering at his head and face as we went down, but I'm not sure, looking back, if I did any real damage. Then, as I lay flailing about haplessly, something happened and the other boy was gone. I don't know how. One moment, I'd been holding on, the next he'd slipped from my grasp – but it hadn't seemed as if he had broken free so much as someone had dragged him off. Finally, with an effort, I sat up. My glasses had come off and I swatted the ground around me, trying to find them. Then Tam appeared, peering at me with a queer grin on his face.

'You all right, Big Yin?' he asked.

I didn't know. I was aware of having heard noises – people running, somebody shouting, something like a scream – but it was quiet now. I looked away and saw some guy walking across the square, trying to hold his face together with his hands, blood dribbling through his fingers, but in that moment, I didn't connect him with what had just happened. 'Who's that?' I asked Tam.

Tam didn't take his eyes off me. 'There's a wee bit cut on your head there,' he said. 'I'd get that seen to, if I were you.' I raised my hand and found the wet, sticky jag of something in my eyebrow. 'But first, I'd get out of here,' Tam said. 'The polis will be along in a minute. If they can be bothered.'

He straightened up. Somewhere behind him somebody was calling out, shouting the same thing over and over, but it sounded like somebody who wasn't serious, somebody just pretending. I couldn't make out what it was, or where the voice was coming from. The boy with the gash in his face was sitting on the flagstones at the far end of the walk. Tam didn't wait to see what I would do, he just patted me on the shoulder and turned away. I stood up. I felt light-headed, excited, but I didn't really think I was there. All that had happened had happened to somebody else, and I had just come across it by accident, a moment ago. I turned and walked off, suddenly aware of how bright it was under the street lamps. It was half a mile to home along Gainsborough Road. As soon as the thought came to me, I started running, a trickle of blood meandering down my face, my head buzzing. I felt quick and alive; at the same time, I knew I had been granted a unique favour, a singular piece of luck. The police wouldn't see me, nobody would see me, because I was invisible. I had no mass, no volume; I was nothing but movement. If I were to stop running now, I thought, I would disappear altogether. But even while I was running, I was invisible. It made no sense, or it did in a kind of Zeno's Paradox way, but I wasn't thinking about sense, or paradox, or anything else, I was just running. I felt amazing. I felt free; I felt lucky; and I knew I would never, ever go out with the stores boys again.

I went in to work the next day expecting some kind of post-mortem, but the boys just acted as if nothing had happened. Wee John asked me, in front of a group of women in the canteen, how I'd hurt my head – his little joke. Nobody said anything about the night before until later, in the middle of the afternoon, when we were all down in stores. It was a tea break. We'd been talking about nothing much and I was feeling one of the gang, a little pleased with myself, glad to have got away with whatever it was I had got away with. At the back of my mind, I'd had a dim, superstitious fear that they would know how relieved I felt, as I ran home in my cloak of invisibility. The boys seemed more powerful to me than ever, now – and not just physically.

It was Tam who got things started. 'Remind me not to get into anything with this one again,' he said to Wee John, tipping his head towards me.

'Aye,' John said. 'He's scary though, isn't he?'

Tam laughed. 'I've never seen anybody go down that quick,' he said. 'It really was a sight to behold.'

'Maybe he's got vertigo,' Wee John said.

'Maybe so,' Tam agreed. He looked at me and grinned. 'Anyway, he didnae run, I suppose,' he said. 'He stood his ground – '

'Almost,' said Big John.

I'd been offended to begin with, though I didn't know why.

The boys were right. On the night, I'd been a liability. Now, though, I saw the funny side of it. They didn't expect me to be some big hard man. They thought I was smart. They knew they were bampots. I did what I did; they did what they did. Maybe I was their witness – though if I was, I hadn't made a very good one. 'I didn't have time to run,' I said, 'that boy hit me before I even saw him.'

Tam nodded. 'Dinnae worry, Big Yin,' he said. 'Next time, we'll pack you off to the infirmary before the fireworks start.'

CHAPTER 7

In 1971, I dropped my first tab of lysergic acid diethylamide. It would be a gross understatement to say that this was a revelation – and would be a mistake to talk about LSD in the same terms as other drugs. LSD-25 is a sacrament; by which I mean, *something that allows the celebrant to win back some participation in his environment.* All my life, my environment had been controlled by fathers of every persuasion, by corrupt authority, by The System: when I asked for bread from any one of these fathers, he gave me a stone; when I asked for fish, he gave me a serpent. Then, from nowhere, there was this pill, this tiny microdot on a roll of cellophane, and all of a sudden I *was* a participant, the celebrant of one small corner of the world, a corner where the standards are so much higher than they are elsewhere. And I said: *This is it.* I take this little pill and new rules apply. Nothing can touch me. *Too late to stop now. Love Is Gonna Bring Us Back Alive.* Acid was a sacrament and nobody could control it. Nobody could give it to you and nobody could take it away. It was a *sacrament*.

When I was growing up, a promise had been implicit in the communion host, the promise of a sacramental moment which, in turn, promised revelation, a new awareness, grace. I remember the excitement I felt on my first communion day, when I stepped forward, knelt at the altar rail and waited my turn – and I remember the disappointment afterwards, when nothing happened. For me, the host was only a wafer of unleavened bread melting on my tongue, a wafer of bread and another empty ceremony. I didn't need to study theology to know that something was missing from that experience, and I didn't need to know the etymology to know that what I needed from *religion* was exactly what the word promised. That etymology – *religere*, to retie, to reconnect – said explicitly what I had always implicitly known: it said that, when I went to Mass, when I prayed, when I received the host, when I walked through the snow on a Christmas morning to sing carols in a cold church, surrounded by flickering candles, I was supposed to be renewing my place in the world, reconnecting with everything around me, remembering my place in the whole. Only, it wasn't happening.

Acid did what the host failed to do. Acid was the only real sacrament to which I had access. It connected me back to the world, it re-attuned me to the subtler, deeper frequencies of the material. It made me see the possibility of wholeness, of what the alchemists called *pleroma*. Here I was, the boy who had seriously thought about a vocation. Now, though the source wasn't quite what I'd expected, I had one. I knew, of course, that it was a synthetic experience; but I also knew that what was synthetic about it was only the starting point, the first step on a long walk through the chambers of my imagery. One person could drop a tab of sunshine, or black microdot, and go to heaven, another could do the same and go to hell – there were so many variables. Later, when I became interested in meditation, I remember meeting a guy – the husband of a friend – who was so in love with himself meditating, he thought he'd achieved satori after a couple of years of sitting. Thing was, he was trying to talk about it, so I guess it wasn't quite satori, but it was instructive to listen, interesting to hear what he wanted enlightenment to be. I don't want to sound superior – it's not as if I've never been guilty of a little Blue Peter mysticism myself – but at the time I couldn't help thinking that it all sounded like the pretty UFO-type acid trip they show in movies, all lights and bliss and inexplicable warmth. Acid could be like that, too, but it usually wasn't. Usually, it was something you couldn't describe, even if you wanted to. Sure, if you drop a tab or two of pink microdot, or Strawberry Fields, your body will be charged all the time, like the Northern Lights, always moving, always changing. But that's not all. Nowhere near. Problem is, anything you *say* about acid is purely theoretical, just as it is with any sacrament. All I can say is that my experiences with LSD had nothing to do with drugs, and everything to do with the order a child needs, as it grows. It wasn't about having fun, or living some alternative lifestyle, it was about a whole system that didn't work, a system that lacked any real authority.

According to the exemplary story I was told as a child, George Washington, president and father of his nation, 'could not tell a lie'. Yet all the time I was growing up, his successors lied every night of the week on prime-time television, not just on the news but via advertising, infotainment, feature films, game shows, late-night educational programmes. A web of untruths about how we lived and what we consumed and what was considered useful knowledge constituted the very fabric of my world. I would sit in front of the TV, watching some politician or company CEO look straight to camera and tell a barefaced, deliberate untruth, and the thought that almost always struck me was that these men had children of

179

their own, that they were lying to them, as well as to the rest of us. It wasn't just my father who was lying, it was everybody's father. No surprise, then, that my generation's heroes – our ghost brothers – were moral orphans who were determined to invent themselves anew in another world, not by choice but because their fathers had betrayed them. They were the crazies, the yippies, the Weathermen, the people who said 'never trust anybody over thirty'. For me, most of all, they were the eco-lunatics who talked to plants, the crazed boys who swept along the margins of golf courses looking for magic mushrooms, the wild-eyed latter-day berserkers who crushed *Amanita muscaria* for its psychotropic juices, the seekers after truth and alternative scientists who threw away the possibility of acceptance and good careers for a religion that included meaningful sacraments. For them, as for me, fatherhood had been discredited; the Father, as archetype, was a liar. For boys like us, all that remained was our own minds, and what we could do with them.

What I did was to withdraw into the virtual equivalent of solitary confinement. By the time I was sixteen, I was making any excuse to sit out Sunday lunches, wandering off at the last minute, just as my mother was about to call us in – it didn't matter if there was hell to pay afterwards, I just couldn't bring myself to sit down at the same table as my father. This upset my mother: she wanted, more than anything, for us all to keep up an acceptable pretence, to go through the motions. There would even be times when my father would make an effort, bringing home a bottle of Liebfraumilch or Blue Nun from the off-licence and opening it himself while my mother set out her best tumblers. Still nothing could shift me. On the single Christmas Day my father decided to spend at home, I disappeared halfway through the morning, and spent the rest of the day walking along the disused railway line, hiking through cuttings and along embankments in the new snow, alone, happy, growing up. My mother was furious, but my father didn't say anything about it. At the time, I didn't think he cared.

My relations with my mother, by now more détente than lived affection, were breaking down. Not long before that fateful Christmas, she had found a packet of Durex and a copy of *The Communist Manifesto* crammed into the sweet, dusty gap behind the more acceptable books on my shelf. A week or so later, she came downstairs in the small hours when my father was on night shift, and found me in the living room with a girl she didn't know. A Protestant. Not much was going on, but she had stood behind the half-open door, in her nightdress, and said, in a hurt, firm voice, 'I think you'd better get that girl a taxi home. Her parents will be worried.' After she found the subversive book – lent to me by a history teacher at my all-Catholic school, as it happened – and the *prophylactics*, she called the priest in. Had it been Father Duane, he would probably have made her see that things weren't anywhere near as bad as she imagined; instead, the new priest, a peely-wally Englishman with sandy hair and yellowish freckles, came and sat in the front room, ignored the plate of home-baked buns and chocolate digestives my mother had put out, and talked about obedience and chastity, while I sat in my father's 'big seat', next to the dead television set, and stared out of the window at the rain, nodding from time to time, while the town darkened.

It was a stupid idea – perverse, I suppose – but at the time it seemed promising. Proposition: what would it be like to drop half a tab of microdot, then sit down to one of our

Sunday lunches? The whole thing: chicken, mashed potatoes, soggy sprouts, trifle, my father's bad wine. I flirted with the idea for months before I actually got round to doing it, but it was up there on the list of stupid (perverse) things to do. I'd gone to Mass, once, tripping; later, I would take acid on the night shift at the steelworks. I dropped acid in muddy fields, on the bus to Kettering, in the pub, in bed with lovers and strangers, but nothing compared to that Sunday afternoon, when I sat with the entire family, not even trying to hide the fact that I was out of it. The odd thing was, not trying turned out to be the best policy. Things only went wrong when I tried to appear normal; when I was just sitting, eating, letting what little conversation there was drift by, I was entirely functional, a perfect mask for all that was going on at the back of my mind, in the place where stories unfold. At the same time, I was watching, listening, finding tiny details to latch on to that would move me along from one moment to the next, more or less at the same pace as everybody else around the table. That was always the difficult part when you were trying to pretend you weren't tripping: time. It passes at different speeds, tripping and straight; on a trip, it's not so uniform, not so homogenous. You can get caught up in a glint of sunlight on the tine of a fork, or a glance out of the window at the incredible green of the tree by the back wall, and you lose track of what's happening in the clock-governed realm of others. Or you remember a line from a song and you suddenly understand all the things it might have meant. I knew that the way through this ridiculous test I had set myself was to concentrate on the everyday details: to find the magic in them, yes, but also to keep moving, to get to a point where, if it wasn't working any more, there would be a way out. So I listened: to the almost imperceptible creaks and tears in their voices, to the silences, to the sudden, dark, hurt-sounding noise my father made in his nose from time to time, to the sounds people make when they are eating. Normally, at those family lunches, my unattuned ear heard only the crude noise of mastication. Now, it could distinguish even the finest nuances: bright, wet sounds, like a small party of explorers making its way through sodden rainforest; little crunches and snaps in the cheekbones; the several sounds of swallowing, not just one gulp, but a series of operations in the back of the mouth and the throat, delicate, expert, casual. That was how I got through: by listening. Now and then, my mother asked me a question, or tried to start a conversation, but nobody expected much from those Sunday lunches. Getting through was all that mattered, and we were all intent on getting through, one way or another. Then, as I would have done anyhow, I disappeared up to my room to listen to music through my new headphones, quite sure I had pulled off yet another pointless exercise in perversity.

The terrible, yet strangely poignant, tradition of families like ours was that the excesses of Sunday lunch be followed, at around seven in the evening, by a light supper of salmon sandwiches or, when money was short, of a cold, glassy-looking meat paste called potted hough. That day, we were having the best: soft white bread spread thick with butter, and filled with tinned salmon that had been strategically mixed with enough vinegar to remove any fish taste altogether. I wasn't quite straight by the time I was called to this feast, but I went downstairs feeling confident, easy, ready for anything. It didn't take long for me to realise that something was wrong. Margaret looked worried, and my mother was withdrawn and quiet, setting things out on the table, her thin-lipped mouth even tighter and more wounded than usual. Still, nobody said anything. I wondered if maybe my mother and father had had an argument while I'd been upstairs – about me, perhaps – but I didn't think any more about it. I ate my salmon sandwiches, helped clear the table, hung around waiting for the mood to lighten, then lingered a while longer trying to get Margaret on her own, so I could ask her what had happened. She wasn't playing, though, so I went back upstairs. I didn't emerge till the next morning, after my father had gone on day shift. Nobody said anything out of the ordinary. Whatever had happened, it seemed to have been forgotten. I knew it would have had something to do with me, but I wasn't that bothered. Détente – that was as much as I was hoping for. Anything for a quiet life: the basic philosophy of the male. The dark cloud lingered, however. It wasn't there all the time, but it kept coming back, and I knew something would come out, eventually. All I had to do was wait.

Things came to a head in the most unlikely circumstances. After all the risks I had taken and got away with, it was a friend from school – a former friend, really, a boy from whom I had become estranged for no particular reason, other than the usual vagaries of teenage life – who blew my cover. It was about three weeks after the Chicken and Acid Sunday Lunch, on a week night, when my father was at home. My mother had gone to bed early – she often did, climbing the stairs painfully, clutching her Mills & Boon – and my father was watching television. When he had day shift, he often stayed home, stayed sober, got to bed early. It made for a certain tension, but we all had our hiding places for such occasions:

my mother taking her book to bed early, me in my room, smoking, or reading subversive literature, Margaret watching the little television set my father had brought home one day as an early Christmas present. My father was a world leader in early presents; things didn't always fall off the back of a lorry at exactly the moment he needed them.

I dread to think what would have ensued if my father had opened the door when Simon Corston arrived. The one habit of his I most liked was the way he'd stay in his chair when visitors came to the door. If somebody didn't answer right away, he would come to the bottom of the stairs and call out, 'Somebody's at the door. Can you not hear it?' Then, when my mother or I appeared, he would mutter, 'What, are ye deaf or something?' as he shambled back through to the front room and his television programme. That night, it was no different – just good luck that I was emerging from my room when the knock came at the door. I hurried downstairs; my mother had one of her headaches, and I didn't want her disturbed. I imagined it would be a neighbour wanting to borrow something, or looking for a babysitter, or it could have been one of Margaret's friends, but I was pretty sure it wouldn't be for me. My friends knew not to come to my house unannounced. Only by arrangement: that was the deal.

It was Simon. As soon as I saw him, I knew why he was there. He was completely out of his mind. Stoned, was my first thought – and then I saw. 'What the fuck?'

He gave me an important, blissful look. 'Acid,' he said.

'Uh-huh.' I had no idea why he'd chosen to come to my house. I hadn't told him that I was doing acid. I hadn't even seen him in weeks. I could hear my father fussing around next door, then the sound on the television went low. 'All right,' I said. 'Let's get out of here.'

The door to the living room opened. 'What's going on?' my father said. Then he saw Simon. 'Who's that?'

'I'm just going out for a bit,' I said. It was too late to finesse things. I had to get Simon away before he said or did anything stupid. 'Come on.' I virtually pushed him out the front door; then I turned to my father. 'I'll not be long,' I said, grabbing my jacket from the peg in the hall. I hope I didn't sound as lame to him as I did to myself.

'Aye, well, keep it down,' he said. 'Your mother's no well.' Then he disappeared back into the living room, and turned up the volume on the TV.

Every acid head had a duty, in those days, to look after fellow-travellers who might be in need of counsel, companionship, cigarettes or vitamin C. Simon really needed them all, but he was only prepared to admit to wanting the smokes. I took him to my favourite place, an old, twisted oak about a hundred yards from the house, and we climbed up into the branches. I fished some Benson & Hedges, a packet of skins and a pitiful amount of grass out of my jacket. It was all I had. We sat in the tree for a while, talking, looking up at the stars. I can see now that he was a good sort, Simon. I remember, the first time I heard Quicksilver Messenger Service's *Happy Trails* was round at his house. I hadn't seen him for a while, mainly because my other friends – Richard, in particular – didn't trust him. One warm Sunday afternoon during the holidays, when we'd been hanging around the streets, trying to figure out what to do, Simon had come along and hooked up with us – me, Richard, his brother Tom, a guy from the Lincoln Estate whose name I can't remember. Richard didn't like that, the way Simon just insinuated himself. We drifted around some

186

more, then we got tired of drifting. 'Is your dad in?' Richard asked me.

'No,' I said, 'he's on backs.'

'Well, we could go to yours, couldn't we? Your mum will make us some tea. And we can wipe the mud off our boots.'

'Tea,' I said. 'Good idea.' I was trying to ignore his other remark, because Simon knew, *everybody* knew, what he meant – and the truth is, I felt sorry for him. Simon's parents had money, and they didn't think anybody was good enough for their son, but he was a generous guy, quiet, a little shy, fairly smart. I didn't want him getting upset – which, of course, was exactly why I hadn't seen him in so long, why he hadn't turned up or dropped by. It was my pity, not Richard's rudeness, that had driven him away. Now, I was glad to help out. Simon had to be back home soon, and he didn't need his prissy, tight-arsed parents finding out what he'd been up to. Besides, if his parents found out he'd been taking LSD, they would probably blame it on me. They'd always said I was a bad influence. A year before, when I'd been expelled from school, it was Simon I was with on the fateful day, when I was caught drunk and smoking a joint on school premises. I was tossed out right away, Simon was given another chance. If he apologised to the teachers whose classes he'd skipped, he could stay on. His parents had gone down to the school and told the headmaster that their son was easily led, and that it was all my fault. My mother had gone to the school too, but she left it too late. I was expelled, Simon stayed on. In the end, though, we both ended up doing acid.

When I got home, my father was waiting up for me. He was stone-cold sober, very calm, determined to be reasonable. He called me into the living room, and we sat there, the

187

television eerily silent, while he set out his cards. 'I know what's going on,' he said, gazing at me squarely.

'What's that, then?'

'That boy was on something,' he said. 'You could see it in his eyes – '

'He'd just had too much to drink – '

'Don't lie to me, son,' my father broke in. He was staying calm, which impressed me. I'd expected him to explode. 'I'm not buttoned up at the back of the head, you know.'

'All right,' I said. 'So what was he on?' I was wondering how far I could go with this.

'Well, I suppose,' my father said, 'he was on the same thing you were on a couple of Sundays back . . . ' He waited for my to deny it. I didn't. 'Dope,' he added, darkly. I wondered if he'd been reading the literature they handed out at school for parents with children at risk.

'Dope?' I said. 'What do you mean, *dope*?'

He almost lost control, but caught himself in time. 'Cannabis,' he said. 'It's not new, you know. People took drugs in my day – '

I shook my head. 'Well, you're wrong,' I said. 'It wasn't cannabis.'

'What wasn't?'

'What Simon was *on*,' I said. 'Cannabis resin. Grass. Marijuana. Afghan black. Panama red. Reefer.' I paused a moment to suggest that the list could go on indefinitely; that, if pressed, I could give him more names for *Cannabis sativa* than there were saints in heaven. 'That's what you mean, right?'

He set his mouth. He was doing well. 'So what was it, then?' he asked, his voice quiet.

'LSD.' Why not? I thought. I was tired of pretences.

'*L S D* ?' He wasn't just on the point of being angry any more. '*That* boy?' He was close to letting it show that he was afraid. He studied my face. 'Well, I hope *you* don't take that stuff.'

I didn't say anything. I didn't care what he knew, but I wasn't sure that I wanted my mother to find out.

'Well?' He was close to letting his front slide. Afraid, but angry too. Now, there were only three possible answers: *Yes, No,* and *None of your business* – but they would all have meant the same thing to him at that moment. He had already decided, and he was *right* – only he was also *wrong*, because he didn't know anything about it, and anyway, who was he to preach to me about self-control? 'Do you know how dangerous that stuff is?' he said.

I shook my head. 'No,' I said. 'Why don't you tell me?'

That did it. He was angry now. I could see, in fact, that he wanted to hit me. I couldn't understand why he wasn't hitting me already. Somewhere at the back of my mind, I wanted him to be hitting me. 'You think you're so clever,' he said. 'But you're not.' He shook his head, as if he pitied me. 'And you're not going anywhere till you give me a straight answer – '

I stood up. 'What if I do?' I said. 'It's no worse than drink.'

He stayed in his seat. The anger had gone, bled away in a matter of seconds, to be replaced by real, almost tangible fear. He didn't know what to make of this, he didn't know what to say. Acid was beyond his remit. My father dwelt among men he knew, men he could read. Now, all at once, it was dawning on him that the world that I had begun to inhabit – the world where people bought and sold 'drugs' – was a mysterious realm of endlessly shifting and dubious allegiances between wily, doe-eyed hippies who seemed harmless

189

enough until they got you hooked, and innocent, fresh-faced sixth-formers who thought they were signing up for a bit of harmless fun. And he really was afraid. He didn't know what to do with me. He had never known what to do, he knew that, but this was a problem he needed to go away, and he'd worked out for himself that hitting me wasn't the way to achieve that goal. At that moment, I felt a sudden access of power, of freedom, and, at the same time, I was almost over-whelmed by a sensation of helpless pity. I didn't know what to do with him, either. I wanted to tell him that he'd got it all wrong, that I had no intention of becoming one of those scrawny hard-bitten junkies that he saw, or imagined he saw, about the town, zombies and nutters who took to heroin and all those other terrifying drugs he had read about with all the force of the Calvinism in which their souls were steeped. 'It's not what you think,' I said. 'It's not addictive.' I wasn't sure if I sounded smug or naive. A little of both, I suppose.

He stared at me and in his face I read something I couldn't name: disbelief? hopelessness? disgust? a father's ordinary worry? Then he shook his head and stood up. 'I'm not telling your mother about this,' he said. 'Because I know what it would do to her.' He looked crumpled, weak. 'I don't know what more to say to you,' he said. 'I suppose it's up to you now.' He studied my face for a moment, then he turned and went out of the room. I heard him climbing the stairs: a tired man with a five o'clock start the next morning. Now that I am older than he was then, it seems amazing to think that he was just forty-five years old. In retrospect, he seems so worn, so fatigued. At the time, though, what I realised, after he had gone, was that, for the first time in years, we'd had a conversation, an actual *conversation* in the night, when he had been sober. He had been sober, he had tried to get through to me, and I had felt a real, if momentary, desire to explain myself. That last remark, however, said it all: *it's up to you*. It was what he said whenever he gave up and washed his hands of a problem. That night, he was washing his hands of me and, as the door closed behind him, I hated him for it.

CHAPTER 8

Sheffield, the summer of '72. I wake in an unfamiliar church-yard, lying in the corner where the people who tend the graves toss dead flowers and wreaths and, even though it's about six in the morning, it's already warm and muggy. It's surprising, but I don't feel too bad and, if at least I don't recall much about the days that passed between its beginning and its end, I remember where this particular episode started – this 'trip to Lourdes', as my friend Richard used to call my drunken absences – and I know where I am, mostly from the colour of the bus passing on the street, but also because I possess – like a key, or a helpline number scribbled on the back of a beer mat – the half-formed, clouded memory of knocking at a sky-coloured door in the middle of the night, looking for a girl I'd continued to think of as a friend long after she'd decided that, first as a boyfriend, and then as tea-and-sympathy mate-rial, I wasn't worth the trouble. I don't know this yet, but it's four days since I left home, and two since I invited myself to the little terraced house that Marianne – my not-quite girl-friend, not-quite friend – shares with two other women, a nurse and a student, both of them, like Marianne herself, older and wiser than me, able to recognise a lost cause when they see one and moved, as Marianne is, by mere pity when they have allowed me into their kitchen and fed me coffee and digestives, on my two or three previous visits. Not this time, though. Either they had all been out, or they were hiding in their beds, waiting for me to stagger off into the night and away, hopefully for ever.

What happened to the two days since I did stagger away, my footsteps ringing down an empty street, I have no idea. It's not the first or the last segment of my life that I have lost: over the years, I've mislaid whole months, one way or another. Even then, when I was seventeen, this kind of thing happened fairly often and, when it did, it seemed to come out of the blue. One minute I'd be sitting in the bar of the George, the next I'd be picking myself up off cold concrete, or some long-dead sailmaker's grave, my body wreathed in grime and the stale smell of liquor. I would be cold, usually, but more often than not I was clad in a thin vapour of sweat, and I would always be struck by the smell of it, as if I had been translated in the night to another world, where malevolent spirits bathed me in some strange humour, denaturing me, making me alien to myself.

To begin with, this was as far as it went. When I was in my late teens, working in factories over the summer vacation, or on the post at Christmas, a lunchtime drink might end three days later on the strip of waste ground behind a row of shops, or on the floor of some dingy squat, five, or three hundred, miles from where I'd started. Or I would go with somebody to some poky little flat, and it would carry on from there, long and hard into the night, then desperately into the next day, on a train to wherever it came into my head to go, or a bus, or a lift to some mythical party in Northampton, say, or some place out in the country that I'd never even heard of and wasn't quite convinced was real. Once, when I was looking after my parents' house during the holidays, I met a taciturn Glaswegian who said he was on the run from the army, and invited him back to the house. He had money, he'd bought a carry-out and, for a while at least, he must have amused me. The next evening, I got a lift from a guy in a pink and blue van on the Kettering road: I had left the former squaddie unconscious on my parents' leatherette sofa, where he had passed out an hour before. It seems that I didn't stop to worry about what he might do when he woke and found himself alone in a strange house, the back door wide open, his whisky bottle empty. If my mother had known, she would have died. If my father had found out, he would have killed me. Maybe that was why I did it. The only thing I remembered about the soldier was a thick, purplish scar – or rather, not a scar so much as a recently stitched seam that started at his chin and disappeared into the collar of his newly-pressed shirt. Maybe it was the shirt that convinced me he wouldn't do any damage to the house, the fact that it was newly laundered and pressed, the fact that it had short sleeves. I'm not sure why, but I found those short sleeves oddly genteel. Maybe I just wasn't sufficiently self-aware to bother. When these pilgrimages happened, they happened according to their own mysterious logic, a logic I not only didn't understand, but had no part in. Perhaps it was the same logic that suggested, one fine day, that I really could do something about my father. After all, I'd had the knife in my hand, and I'd been ready to use it. All I had to do was see the logic through to its conclusion.

Bert McKain came round every Hogmanay, doing his best to sound like Elvis, though he was only really convincing when he sang the King's worst song, 'Wooden Heart'. Not that this was a problem at our house: my mother loved that song, and my father was reminded of his time in Germany. For once, everybody was happy. The turn of the year was, at times, even pleasurable: formidable lumps of Dundee cake washed down with beer or port and lemon, the whisky waiting in the bottle till the bells rang (ours was one of those houses where the drinking of whisky was *verboten* before midnight, which didn't stop my father sneaking a few rums around ten o'clock). Ten minutes into the new year, we would hear Bert coming along the road, his cheery, confident, not quite regal voice ringing out some old Elvis ballad or movie song. Bert was the only man I ever met who loved Dundee cake, and he didn't mind what he washed it down with. Unlike the other men who roamed the streets on Hogmanay, he drank for as long as he enjoyed it, then he stopped. He knew his limit; he never did anything stupid or embarrassing. The women liked having him around – a steadying influence – and the kids adored him. I liked him too. Whenever I saw him, I caught myself smiling.

Maybe it was Bert who prevented me from killing my father. Maybe it was just plain fear. Men like my father, or the Scandura gang, could do whatever they liked, because they had such a weak sense of the consequences. I wasn't like that. When I came to execute my plan, I was angry, but I wasn't resolute. I'd found out that my father had gone back on his word and told my mother that I was on 'heavy drugs', and I knew he could be heard, late on a Friday night, announcing to all and sundry that he didn't have a son, that he and my mother had found me under a hedge, and had taken me in. Ironic, given what I later discovered about him (though maybe not). None of this was new, of course. My father had been telling me for years that I wasn't his son. Over time, he'd conjured up various explanations for my existence: I was adopted, I was a baby someone had left under a hedge on his road to work, I was the child of a secret lover my mother had known before he married her. He never repeated these stories when my mother was there, or when he was sober, and he rarely said the same thing twice: there would be slight changes, little details he would alter, from forgetfulness, or perhaps just to keep me interested. Once upon a time, I'd believed what he said – and this was why I'd come to the point of making plans, of thinking through the possibility of killing him. It was a cumulative thing, the result of years of hurt. I didn't really have a plan at all, but I had a scheme, and that scheme was in me, part of what I was, a spell written into the fabric of my being.

After the incident with the carving knife, war had been waged on a purely verbal basis, a war of slow attrition, of casual contempt and everyday hatred, a war that I knew would last until I could get away, once and for all. Our arguments were ugly and demeaning; every time I got into one, I felt as much contempt for myself as I did for him, but I couldn't let it go, I had to keep at him, just as he had to keep going at me. We had dropped all pretence of father and son, of drinks and crib games and half-playful disagreement; now, we were bound together only by rage and hatred. Sometimes we skirted around one another, sullen and careful, too tired or disgusted to get into anything. Most of the time, though, the smallest thing would set us off: an ill-chosen word or gesture, something somebody said on television, any of the day's hundred casual misunderstandings. Yet no matter where it all started, those arguments always came down to the same things: drugs versus alcohol, my wasted future, what I was going to do with my life, how I was killing my mother with my selfishness.

It had to end. It surprises me to think it now but, at the time, I would have had no scruple about killing him. To be honest, I have to admit that, in those days, I *felt* that I could have killed anyone. Yet, even though I'd been thinking about it for a while, it seemed an idle notion, a fantasy, something I would never pluck up the courage to do. After all, I'd had a knife to his throat, and I'd let it go, so it was obvious that I didn't have the heart to do it. Then something came into my mind that made me think again. It was a minor thing, an incident that had happened a few months before, but it was also a sign, when I came to think about it.

I had been walking through the town centre on a Saturday afternoon, with my friend Russell, when I spotted my father coming towards us, a faraway look on his face, as if he were dreaming, or not altogether there. It was a look I recognised: most of the time, when he was out of the house, he would take his glasses off and slip them into the inside pocket of his jacket, presumably because they detracted from his supposed resemblance to Robert Mitchum. Without them, he was blind as a bat, though he could see movement, and he had a basic-level sense of what was happening around him that was more to do with instinct than vision. Still, what I knew for sure was that he couldn't make out details. 'Look at the fool,' I said. 'He can't see a thing without his glasses.'

Russell grinned. 'Is that so?' he said; then before I could stop him, he sang out, '*Hiya, Tommy.*'

My father turned to us. What he sensed was a mass, no doubt, that was neither obviously threatening nor particularly interesting. 'All right?' he said, his voice non-committal.

'Aye,' Russell said. 'Yourself?'

'No sae bad,' my father replied, ready to go on. He didn't know who the hell we were.

197

'Haven't seen you for a while,' Russell threw in. 'You keeping all right?'

My father looked puzzled, but remained non-committal. 'Well, ye ken how it is,' he said.

Russell began laughing. 'Don't you know who I am?' he asked.

I'll give it to the old man, he covered up well. 'I ken your face,' he said. He cast around for a name he remembered. 'I'm no sae good with names —'

'Russell.'

'That's right,' he said. 'Russell. The milk boy.'

'But you know this man here,' Russell went on quickly, turning to me. I was already tired of the game.

'Oh, aye.' My father peered at me. 'How's it going, son?' He'd probably got me down as one of Russell's brothers. I didn't say anything.

Russell laughed. 'This is John,' he said. 'Your son.'

My father grimaced. He was only about six feet away from me. 'Aye,' he said. 'So. What are you boys up to?'

I didn't want the game to go on, then. It didn't seem funny any more. But months later, as I sat in one of the disused garages on the Beanfield, soused on cheap wine, this memory was like a gift. A gift; or an omen. A challenge. If I hated my father — and that afternoon, for reasons I can't even remember now, I hated him utterly — I could solve the problem with one decisive action. I couldn't stand face to face with him, when he was sober, able to look into my eyes, able to fend me off. But what about when he was drunk, coming home through the court late at night, no glasses, unaware of who was waiting for him in the dark? If I could pull that off, it would be like any other Saturday night: two strangers meet; one of them walks away. Why not? This wasn't a sober thought

198

– I'd had quite a bit of wine, some speed, other stuff too, I imagine – but that made it all the more compelling. It wouldn't be easy, of course. Even drunk, I knew that. But I knew what to do, and I knew I could get away with it. My father had so many enemies, nobody would think to suspect his own son.

I never really intended to carry it through. I know that, now, and I think I knew it then. What matters, though, is the fact that I worked it all out: the best place to wait for him, as he walked home (a narrow alley at the foot of Handcross Court, just at the point where the footpath forked between the lower side of the square and the upper); the choice and disposal of the weapon (single-blade, nine-inch knife, to be tossed into a pool in the woods afterwards); the cover I would need to provide an alibi, if I was ever suspected (I would be in my room all the time, listening to music: my mother could testify to this, as she'd have brought me a cup of tea before she went to bed, as an excuse to check that I wasn't up to any *mischief*). Convinced I had everything covered, I placed myself where I needed to be, able to see him coming, but out of sight myself, and I waited. I didn't believe it, not for a moment, but there I was standing in the shadows, clutching a knife, on the darkest part of my father's walk home from the pub. It was almost eleven o'clock. He would soon be on his way.

As it happened, he was not alone. Bert McKain was with him. This shouldn't have been that much of a surprise – Bert was an occasional at the Hazel Tree, and his house was just a hundred yards from ours. If anything, I suppose that was a relief. I don't know what I thought I was going to do, if my father had been alone: if I'd been serious, I could have waited for the next chance to ambush him, and I wouldn't have had long to wait. But I wasn't serious. I was acting out a script, a fantasy. The very fact that I could stand there, waiting, in the shadows, was enough for me, really. To know that I wanted to do it, even if I couldn't see it through – that mattered. I knew I hated him, and I knew I was too sensible, or too much of a coward to act. But it still mattered. It was a piece of knowledge that I needed to possess. When I heard Bert McKain's familiar, mock-Elvis voice singing out through the night, I was relieved, sure I was. They were walking straight towards me, Bert talking and joking, my father – who was nowhere near as drunk as I'd expected – walking along quietly beside him. He seemed preoccupied, wrapped up in his own thoughts, though I could see, as they passed through a hoop of street light, that he was smiling. He liked Bert. In an odd, detached way, he liked most of the men he knew. I kept to the shadows and waited till they passed; then I ditched the knife, cut through the court on the lower side – I knew I'd still be home first, that my father would stand blethering with Bert for a while – and climbed through the window of my room, where Country Joe was still singing quietly to the bedside lamp.

The next morning, as soon as I woke, I knew I had to get away. I was certain that my father would see something in my face – or, worse, that my mother would. I was sure you couldn't think about killing a man without it showing. Even if I had never had the nerve to do it, I'd had the thought – and now I had the knowledge. I wasn't a Catholic for nothing. *Thought, word and deed.* There was a truth in the idea that I could understand – and, by mid-morning, my exit strategy was already in motion. I had friends in Kettering; I knew they would offer me refuge, for a while at least, until I could decide what I wanted to do with myself. Not that it mattered what

I did, or didn't do. There was no long-term plan; I just knew it was time to be gone. I'd been running away half-heartedly all my life; now it was time to be gone for good. There would be some explaining to do, especially to my mother, but that could wait for later. For now, all that mattered was to be somewhere else.

DOBERMANN DAYS

C'est l'inconnu qu'on porte en soi, écrire, c'est ça ou rien.

Marguerite Duras

CHAPTER 1

I stayed away for as long as I could. I went to college, for something to do, then I drifted around, stopping in at the house now and then, when I thought the coast was clear. I never stayed long and, much to my mother's disappointment, I was soon off again, wandering from place to place, finding menial jobs, hanging around in pubs with people much like myself, doing odd deals for extra cash. The money never lasted long, but it was put to good use. There were long days in the sun out on Grantchester Meadows, winter afternoons tucked up in bed with a good book and a bottle of rum, trysts in the wee small hours of the morning in Sheffield, or Northampton. I might have gone on like that for much longer, but somebody took the trouble to track me down and let me know that my father had suffered a heart attack. I didn't really want to go home, but I knew my mother would be upset if I stayed away. I'd barely seen my father since I'd hatched the plan to kill him; now, it seemed, he was doing it by himself.

I got back a few days after I heard the news, expecting to find my father at death's door, but it was my mother's appearance that disturbed me most. Of course, once he'd got out of hospital, my father made light of the heart attack. He had been taken to Kettering General, and later discharged with a warning to quit smoking and drinking, something he wasn't about to do. His argument was that his Uncle Willie, who had gone on to the ripe old age of eighty-four, had smoked sixty a day and had practically lived in the pub. The men in his family, he said, had always been strong; there was nothing to worry about: doctors were constantly telling people to stop smoking, but what was the point of living for ever if you couldn't enjoy yourself? 'Anyway,' he said, 'I can get to work. That's the main thing. I've not a missed a day's work through sickness since I was fourteen. I'm not about to start now.' It was the usual stuff, but there was an edge to it this time. He seemed nervous, unsure of himself. My mother saw this too, and I knew, as soon as I walked into the house, that she had been taking every opportunity she could to work on him, wheedling, cajoling, flattering, persuading. So, to begin with, I assumed she looked so tired and dark around the eyes because the worry, and her trying to keep my father in line, had taken its toll. Soon, however, I realised that something else was wrong. She looked slight, a little shaky, her mouth tighter than usual, her face drained. One afternoon, when my father was out at the Hazel Tree – his first time since the heart scare – I sat her down for as much of a heart-to-heart as was possible in that house. It turned out Margaret – who had recently moved to a house in Corby Village and started a family of her own – had done the same thing. Even her workmates had had a go at her. Nobody had got through, and there was no chance of my breaking down her defences. Still, I made her a cup of tea, and launched straight in. 'What's up?' I said. 'You don't look well.'

'I'm all right,' she murmured, wanting not to talk about it, but enjoy her tea, and what she knew was bound to be a fleeting visit from her only son. With my father already back at the pub, she knew I would soon be on my way.

'No you're not,' I insisted. 'Have you been to the doctor?'

'I was worried about your dad,' she said. 'He's worse than he thinks.'

I tried not to show my irritation. 'He'll be fine,' I said.

She shook her head. 'No, he won't,' she said. 'He doesn't look after himself. I know you don't have much patience with your dad, but somebody's got to keep an eye on him – '

'And who's keeping an eye on you?' I interrupted.

She gave me one of her soft, conciliatory smiles. 'All I need is a bit of a holiday,' she said. 'It's just the worry. Now that your father's a bit better, I'll be right in no time.'

I didn't believe it. I don't think she believed it herself. There was something wrong with her, something more than anaemia or fatigue, but I can't imagine she'd guessed it was cancer. She'd had a routine hysterectomy a few years before but, for some reason, the ovaries hadn't been removed. Now, unknown to us all, she was already past help. I remember the doctor saying, some weeks later: *if only she had come in earlier.* It was the first thought I had when I learned the news. It was probably the first thought my father had too: if it hadn't been for him, she might have been saved. I'm sure that idea plagued him, after she died.

Today, looking back, I have difficulty remembering that time. One moment, it's a seamless fabric and I cannot draw a single thread from this cloth without drawing out the texture and flavour and colours of the whole, so even an apparently innocent image of my mother standing on a kitchen chair, reaching for a strand of loose tinsel on the Christmas tree, is loaded with a grief I cannot explain. When I remember her at all, I remember the extraordinarily long ordeal that followed our conversation: I remember her illness, and how long her dying took, and I want to see her as she was before I was born, before she was married: the young woman in the photographs she kept in the Egyptian bag in her wardrobe, a pretty girl, flirting with the camera, dressed in the latest fashions – not a memory at all, for me, but an indelible moment, a millisecond of limitless possibility, sometime in 1947.

She wasn't right in no time, of course. I sensed it that day: there was a darkness about her, an odd, sickly-sweet smell that even she had probably noticed. And at that moment, I resolved to stay home, to make sure she got the care she needed. I'd get a job at one of the factories, and find a way of dealing with my father. If I couldn't stand being in the house with him, I'd find somewhere else to live. I was full of plans, full of good resolutions. First, though, I had to go somewhere. I wouldn't be away long, I told myself, and I'd stay home for as long as I was needed, just as soon I got back. I made her promise to see a doctor, and told her I'd be checking up on her. She smiled, and made the promise. It was the closest we had been for years, conspirators, with our own secret, just like the old days, back on Blackburn Drive, when we sat over *Look and Learn,* or a borrowed novel, learning to read, dreaming of the marvellous future.

Two days later, I was gone. I intended to be away for a week, but I didn't get back till the end of the month. In those days I hitch-hiked everywhere, and my father wouldn't have a telephone anyway, so I couldn't let anybody know I was coming. I just turned up. It was the middle of the afternoon, and my father was alone in the house, doing the dishes, when I got in.

'Hi,' I said. I didn't want to be alone with him; I supposed he felt the same way. 'Where's Mum?'

'She's in the hospital,' he said. He picked up a plate and

began drying it. I should have guessed. Things had to be bad for him to do the dishes.

'Is she all right?'

He looked at me. His face was empty, neutral. '*No,*' he said. 'She's in the hospital.'

'You said. So – what is she in for?'

He turned away, put the plate in a cupboard. I wondered if that was how he always did it, washing one plate or bowl at a time, then drying it and putting it away, and I wanted to tell him to stop, to put the tea towel down and talk to me properly. Instead, I stood and watched as he picked up another plate and placed it in the sink.

'Well?' I said.

He didn't reply right away. He let the plate settle into the sink, then he turned to look at me again. 'You can't go wandering about here, there and everywhere any more,' he said. 'Your mother's got cancer.'

For a moment, I was stunned. In some back alley of my thinking, I had been expecting bad news – maybe I had even been expecting this – but I hadn't prepared myself for it. Least of all, for the way he broke it. A minute in, though, my dismay gave way to anger. He'd done this on purpose; I knew it. He'd rehearsed it in his mind, chosen the words; I knew he had, because they sounded calculated, they sounded unnatural. Not like him. 'Your mother's got cancer.' He would never have said that, in those words, if he hadn't planned to. It was the great taboo, worse than sex even, to say that word. *Cancer.* 'Well,' I said, 'thanks for breaking it to me so gently.'

He didn't say anything.

'Does she know?' I asked.

He shook his head. 'No,' he said. 'And she's not going to know, either.'

209

'What?'

'She can't take it,' he said. 'It would – '

'What?' I waited, but he didn't answer. 'Well? What would it do?'

He turned back to the washing up. 'She's not to be told,' he said, quietly. 'The doctor agrees. She wouldn't be able to take it.' He put another plate on to the draining board, then reached for the tea towel. I watched as he began to dry it.

'You know what?' I said.

He looked at me, curious for a moment. He'd planned this moment, now he wanted to see what I would say, what I would do. 'What?' he said.

'It would be a lot quicker,' I said, 'if you washed all the dishes at once, then dried them afterwards.'

'Is that so?' he said.

'Yes.'

He finished drying the plate, and set the tea towel down. When he spoke, his voice was quiet, bitter, oddly satisfied with itself. 'Do you think I don't know that?' he said.

In the end, she *was* told she was dying – because I told her. I didn't say the word *cancer*, but she had already guessed that. It was a couple of months after my father broke the news – how that slight, anaemic woman hung on for so long is beyond me – and she had wasted to stick-thin and grey, as nature did its work. My father had kept up the pretence religiously, telling her they would go on holiday just as soon as she was better, carrying home piles of brochures from the travel agents so she could look through and pick what she'd like. He'd get whatever money it took, no problem. I was staying in my old room, and it was my job to look after her in the early evenings, picking up her charcoal-brittle frame and carrying her downstairs, where she would receive friends from work, who'd pop round whenever they could with flowers and fruit that she couldn't eat. Before these visits, she would sit up in bed, brush her hair and put on a little make-up, looking at her gaunt, inky face in the dressing-table mirror with a strange, almost curious expression. One day, she turned to me as I came in and smiled sadly. 'I don't think I'll be going on that holiday any time soon,' she said.

I shook my head. 'No,' I said. 'I don't think so.'

By then she was little more than skin and bone and a ribbon of sickly-sweet perfume, and sometimes she was only half there, because of the drugs, but that day she was alert and watchful, as she studied my face. 'Not ever?' she asked, her voice quiet, but steady.

'Not ever.'

She nodded. 'I thought so,' she said. She looked at her face in the mirror. Her lipstick was almost unbearably red on her thin, grey mouth. She turned back to me, and smiled. 'Don't tell your father,' she said.

CHAPTER 2

At the funeral, my father took aside each family member who would listen and explained how my mother had died. It was Margaret and I who had killed her, he said, *killed her with worry*. We'd been taking drugs since we were thirteen. We'd brought all kinds of strange people into the house. My mother had found a stash of dope in my room, hidden among the books I was supposedly studying. I had admitted to him in so many words that I was hooked on LSD. Since I'd been back home, it had become obvious that I had a serious drug problem. Because of all that – all the drugs, and the drinking, of course – I'd been expelled from school and, even though he'd put me through Cambridge, I wasn't doing anything with my life. What was the point of him sending me to college, if I was just going to drift about doing God knows what, drinking and taking drugs? I'm not sure if anybody took anything he said to heart – I think some did – but he was utterly convinced, utterly sincere in what he was saying. He believed that my sister and I had killed our mother because he had to. He needed a scapegoat.

As soon as we got back to the house, after the drinks reception, a pack of cards appeared and, before anybody could protest, his folding card table with the green baize top had been set up in the living room. People were magicking booze from thin air, a half-bottle of rum here, a bottle of whisky there; somebody had gone for a carry-out and come back with twenty-odd cans of beer. It was shaping up to be one of the usual parties, to the disgust of my Aunt Mary and Uncle Dave, who had driven down from Scotland to be there, and were supposedly staying over that night. I could see that this was my father's revenge for all those years of feeling slighted and despised, the brother-in-law that nobody had liked, the faux-convert who'd not even bothered with the duty Mass and confession once a year to put my mother's mind at rest about his immortal soul. Here he was, the master of his own house, with his friends around him, cards on the table, a ring of cigarettes burning in the ashtray, half-consumed glasses of beer and whisky everywhere, the men muttering away to one another, making bets, lighting up, mulling over their hands like the mutant denizens of some shebeen in the boonies.

Uncle Dave had the first go. 'Tommy,' he said, standing over the table, a quiet, considerate man, used to doing things right, 'can I have a wee word?'

My father looked up, just, from his cards. 'Aye? Want to sit in, Dave?'

Dave shook his head. 'Tommy,' he said, doing – being – exactly what my father most resented: patient, adult, responsible, reasonable, 'Mary's a wee bit upset – '

'We're all upset here,' my father put in. 'It's a grievous day – '

'That's right. It's a sad day for everyone. So I think – '

My father laid his cards down and looked him in the face. 'What is it, Dave? What do you want to say?' His voice was dangerous.

My uncle's mouth hardened. He was a reasonable man, but only up to a point. He could see this was useless, but he'd probably known that from the beginning. 'Well,' he said, 'I'd have thought you and your friends would be wanting to show Tess a bit more respect – '

My father stood up. One of the other men took hold of his arm, but Dave stood his ground. My father had always underestimated him, he had always mistaken his kind nature for weakness. They stood toe to toe a minute, silent, my father glowering, Dave deceptively placid. Finally, my father backed down. 'I'm not like you, Dave,' he said. 'I can't be bothered with all this sitting around with the women. A half-pint of mild and a packet of crisps. Not for me.' He looked around the room, at his cluttered, bereft kingdom. 'I don't tell you how to behave in your house,' he said. 'So don't tell me how to behave in mine, all right?'

They stood a moment longer, then Dave nodded. 'It's your house,' he said. 'But I don't suppose Mary will want to stay, under the circumstances.'

'She can do what she wants,' my father said. He sat down and picked up his cards. 'I'm not bothered.' The others around the table, who had been listening to all this with varying degrees of embarrassment, resumed the game. Before he turned and walked out, Dave glanced at me. 'I'm sorry, son,' he said. I nodded, but I didn't say anything. I was still fairly drunk from the afternoon's proceedings and I'd cleared out what was left of my mother's medication the night before. Some of it was in my room and some of it was in my bloodstream.

A few minutes later, my Aunt Mary was standing at the table, glowering at my father. She'd tried for years to get on with him, for her sister's sake; now there was no further need for niceties. 'Tess isn't cold in the ground yet, God bless her,' she said. 'And you've turned her house into a – ' She looked about, lost for words. 'Are you not ashamed of yourself?'

My father didn't even bother to reply. He studied his hand, then lit another cigarette. By now, I'd had enough – I knew my uncle and aunt were about to leave, which meant, sooner or later, it would be just me and him in the house. I wasn't sure I could manage that; besides, I was feeling fairly groggy with the drink and the painkillers. Without waiting for the outcome of the conversation, I took myself upstairs and locked myself in my room. I wasn't alone, though. I had Pink Floyd, a bottle of vodka and the remainder of a dying woman's pain-management regime for company. Better than memory; better than kin.

When I woke, I thought it was the next day. It was light outside, a late morning, summer's light, and, for a moment, I didn't know where I was, or what I was, lying in my narrow bed, heavy as stone, blank inside. I floated like that for several minutes, perhaps longer, then I began to piece together the world as I knew it: my room, the house, a sense of the court beyond, abnormally quiet on the other side of the open window, the sound of a bird singing somewhere, the sense of everything reaching away around me, to the woods, to the exit roads, to the sea. The house was hushed, and still as glass. I could tell nobody was home, and I was glad. If it was late morning, my father would be at the Hazel Tree. He had some holiday due him, so I knew he wasn't at work, but he would have seen no reason to break his normal routine; if anything, it was all he had to keep him going. I wasn't thinking about this, it was simply there, registered: the knowledge, not of the behaviour of a specific man, but of a set of abstract rules, a system.

Eventually, I got out of bed. I was dressed in a T-shirt and jeans, barefoot, not in the least tired or hung-over, but numb at the surface of the skin, numb all over the way a foot or a

215

hand is numb when you wake up and find you've slept in an awkward position. I also felt oddly disjointed, as if one limb weren't quite connected to another, as if I'd been thrown together hastily on an assembly line. I remembered I'd been drinking vodka, and I'd taken some pills, but everything else was fuzzy. I opened my door and looked out. Nobody. I crossed the dark, narrow landing and peered into my father's room. Empty. I was alone.

The back of the house looked out over our neighbours' gardens. From Margaret's old bedroom, I could see a row of narrow plots, some of them neat and tidy, with vegetables planted in well-hoed lines, others – including our own – over-grown, a mix of grass that needed mowing, summer weeds, and the more exotic species, trying to hold their own. What caught my eye, though, was a shrub at the edge of the garden two plots down from ours: a tall, dark, almost blood-red weigela – I thought – perched on a slight elevation by the back fence. It was in full flower, but there was something odd, something almost uncanny about it: it was too large, too vigorous-looking, and it seemed to be flowering, not just profusely, but to excess. I stood for a long time, staring at this red bush, while my body returned, gradually, to its usual state, the numbness bleeding away, the sense of myself as a single, unified entity returning. At the same time, I felt myself detaching, growing apart from everything around me: the house, its history, the objects in this room, my father's eventual return. It had nothing to do with that particular shrub, of course, but those red flowers focused something that had been happening for years, a sense of myself as coming adrift, finally, of a body – not just a mind, not just a life, but a real, living body – beginning anew, whole again, but utterly separate, utterly apart.

*

My father got home at three. He'd been to the pub, but he wasn't drunk. He was in a grey mood, not angry, not spoiling for a fight, but – and I was surprised how obvious it was – a man who couldn't quite keep his fear in check. In his face, there was a darkness I'd never seen before: fear, dread, a cold, inner panic that he could control, but couldn't quite hide. I think he was grateful when he saw I was up and about: it gave him a distraction, a verbal punchbag. 'So you're still with us?' he said.

'What?'

'I thought you were never coming out of that room again,' he said. 'What have you been doing all this time? Sleeping?'

'What of it?'

'You've been asleep?'

'Yes.'

'For two days?'

'What are you talking about?'

'What day is it today? Do you know?' I had to think. Before I could work it out, he was already off again. 'You don't know, do you?' he said. 'You've been *asleep* for two days. More than that.' He sat down in his 'big chair' and gazed at me, like a visitor to a zoo facing a rare, and slightly repellent, exhibit. 'If you *were* asleep, of course,' he added.

'So where have you been?' I asked him.

'None of your business,' he said. He took up his paper.

'Down the Tree, I suppose, telling everybody how bad me and Margaret were to our mother.'

He gave me a sharp look. 'Well, you were. The two of you. You know as well as I do, it was worry that killed your mother, not – '

I waited to see if he'd say the word. *Cancer.* Even now, he couldn't get it out. I laughed softly. 'She never had to worry about you, though, did she?' I said.

217

He ignored that. 'So what are you going to do now?' he said. 'If you're staying here, you'll have to get a job. It's not a free ride, you know. I can't keep you – '

'I'm not staying here,' I said. I was surprised he'd even imagined I would consider it.

'So where are you going? What are you going to do with yourself?' He leaned forward in his armchair. 'Do you even know what a disappointment you were to your mother? She thought you were going to do such great things – '

'Aw, fuck off,' I said, finally rattled. He'd spoiled it all, taken away that sense of quiet, that stillness I'd been granted, looking out of the window at that red bush in the morning sunlight. That August mood.

'It's my house,' he said. 'You fuck off.'

I almost laughed. It was like two boys in the school playground. *Fuck off. You fuck off. No, you fuck off.* 'It's nobody's house,' I said. 'This house is empty.' He stood up. This was it. I had been waiting for this my whole life, and now it was going to happen. We were about equal now: in weight, in strength, in anger, in willingness to do harm. 'You're a bastard,' I said. 'You always have been – '

It wasn't my intention to refer, in any way, to his family history, or lack of it. It didn't matter to me that his parents hadn't been married, that he'd been adopted, or whatever had happened. His illegitimacy made no difference at all to people of my generation. The very idea of legitimacy was quaint, at best. I was just casting around for an insult, a goad, and *bastard* was the best I came up with. What else was there? *Cunt?* It just wasn't a word I used. *Motherfucker?* We still weren't fully Americanised yet. Besides, it was hardly appropriate, given the circumstances. No, *bastard* was the word I needed – and I imagine, at the back of my mind, back where the stories get worked out, the choice was long-pondered and utterly deliberate. It was the goad, the catalyst, the starting gun, and I was ready for the first blow when it came. Except that it didn't come. He was standing eight feet away from me, at the other side of our little living room, and three steps would have brought him to me; instead, he slumped back into his big chair and sat there, his eyes seemingly drawn to some fascinating detail in the carpet that he'd only just noticed. I stepped towards him, then I stopped. He was pale, oddly bluish around the eyes and mouth; he looked as if he was going to faint. Then I saw that he was struggling to catch his breath.

'Tablets,' he said.

'What?'

He slumped back further in his chair, and looked at me. He looked frightened again. 'Get my tablets,' he said. It was ridiculous, like a scene in some bad television drama. Perry Mason confronts murder suspect with what he knows, suspect crumples in a heap, demanding pills. The little green ones in his coat pocket. The pink pills on the dressing table. Big blue and yellow capsules spilling everywhere as Nature exacts her revenge.

I hesitated. Was this a heart attack? His second? Or was it his third? Was it genuine? 'Get them yourself,' I said, finally.

He looked up. He was going to die. One pill from the bottle in the kitchen would save him, but he couldn't get that far by himself. He gave me a look of bitter satisfaction. 'Suit yourself,' he said. His voice was only just audible.

I waited a moment longer, to see what would happen; then, when he didn't move, I walked through to the kitchen and found his tablets. When I got back, he had laid himself back into the chair, breathing, concentrating. I walked over, opened the bottle and handed it to him. Then, just as I was, in my

219

baseball boots, jeans and shirtsleeves, without waiting to see if he was all right, I walked out into the August sunlight and headed for Gainsborough Road, with a promise to myself that I would never darken his door again.

CHAPTER 3

When I think of what Robert Frost said about home – how, when you go there, they have to take you in – the one thing I know for certain is that, for me at least, it's not true. Nobody *has* to take anybody in, it's always a choice, never *only* an obligation. Maybe that's the view of an essentially homeless – or do I mean, unhoused – person, but I knew Tom Morgan didn't have to take me in that day, when I turned up in Cambridge in my shirtsleeves, with nothing but loose change in my pocket. I met him in Belinda's, the day after I left home. I had spent the night in a B&B, and was now spending the last of my money on coffee and cake, waiting for something to happen: to happen, not in the world, but in my own mind, where the plan was laid out, written since the beginning of time – I really thought this – not fate so much as an unread map that was waiting for the circumstances and the moment to come that would allow it to be deciphered. I'd always had that perverse fondness for being lost and, when I was lost, something always happened. It could be an expensive way to make decisions, but I didn't know how else to do it.

I was in this frame of mind, then, when I met Tom. I can't imagine I was making much sense, but he grasped the situation and an hour later I was sitting in his kitchen, listening to Ali Akbar Khan and chomping on muesli. (As far as I knew,

Tom never ate anything else, his life was just tea and muesli and a seemingly endless supply of very good dope.) Nobody, least of all Tom, had to take me in, but for the next few weeks his house was my house. His spare room was empty, so I was welcome to sleep there; he fed me, mostly on muesli, which was no bad thing at the time; he lent me clean clothes; he shared his dope with me; he listened patiently to my ravings. He waited till I got a job – as a kitchen porter at the Arts Theatre – before he let me pay anything towards my keep. There was no debt here. In those days, people like Tom had no time for ideas like debt.

All this time, I felt like someone who had fallen into the world a few days before, some character in a film who turns up, lost, amnesiac, a man without a history who lives entirely in the moment. There was something there, no doubt, at the back of my mind: something I had to remember, but I didn't know what it was, and I wasn't much inclined to push it too hard. I was too busy with my map, too occupied with waiting for the future to consider the past. My mother had just died; I knew that, and it wasn't her death that I was trying to forget – and it wasn't a remedy for my present difficulties that I was seeking from the map in my head. I just needed to stay lost for long enough to know why I had ended up where I was. I had fallen into the world a few days before, and I expected to be treated with suspicion by everyone I met: friends, strangers, acquaintances, workmates. Instead, I wandered about Cambridge like a holy fool, tolerated, sometimes even blessed, by everyone I came across.

My mother had died in August. By September, I had a whole new provisional life in place: a job, digs, a girlfriend called Annie who was funny and easygoing and had no plans for the future – or none, at least, that included me. Life was simple and clear. I was drinking too much, I was also doing drugs every day, but it was mostly dope or bennies, and anyhow, most of the people I knew were doing exactly the same thing. I wasn't unhappy, and I wasn't conscious of any real problems in my life. In the daytime, I would go to work, sit around in the Arts Café, or meet Annie at the YMCA opposite Parker's Piece; at night, I'd sit around in a pub doing crossword puzzles and drinking a fast-acting concoction called snakebite (half-beer, half-cider). Sometimes I would get stoned with Annie and listen to music at her flat. I was going nowhere, which was fine. It wasn't as if I was in mourning, or anything like that. Something had been adjusted in my head: it was as if I had turned the dial on a radio and tuned in to a new station, quickly forgetting everything I had heard before. It was summer, still, summer at night on the river, summer on Grantchester Meadows, summer on Jesus Green and out on Coe Fen. If I wanted to be alone, I could borrow a bike from somebody and ride out into the flat fenland around about and stand under the wide East Anglian sky, or I could go up to Kettle's Yard, next to the church where Wittgenstein is buried, and sit a while, suspended in the light and the quiet. Like Alice, I had fallen out of the world I knew, and now it was summer wherever I turned: the deep green of the trees, the wet shadows of evening, whole days of wandering the meadows, going alone through the drowsing cattle, the bodies of the animals shifting aside, first one, then another; swimming in the long afternoons down by Byron's Pool; nights spent following the cow-paths home in the glimmer of dawn, alone with the mist on the river, eyes on the farther bank. It was an English summer, the idyll I had always imagined. Then, before I knew the summer was over, it was Halloween.

October, that year, was warm, damp, friendly to the ghosts.

Morning and night, I walked back and forth from Tom's house, just off Mill Road, across Parker's Piece, and through town to the Arts; the shadows under the silver limes that lined the Piece were still and cool, but it was like a theatre waiting for the curtain to go up. The shadows, the trees, the wide lawns – it was all as it should be, but it was too still, too heavy, waiting for the day when the dead would return, coming through rain, coming through the wind, seeking out the angles and corners they knew, the faces they could name, the bodies that were flesh of their flesh. I was going about my business in the usual way, but all the time, somewhere at the back of my mind, the irrational questions were forming: would my mother find me here, so far from home? Would George Grant know she was dead, even though he hadn't seen her in twenty-odd years? Was George Grant dead too? Would they walk the earth together, back in Cowdenbeath, or Crosshill, haunting the places they had known before I was even born? What about Elizabeth and Andrew? Were they ghosts, or had they died young and intact enough to enter the next life immediately? Who were they now? Where were they?

At last the fateful day came. Tom had listened to my ramblings about Halloween and had suggested we have a party at his house to mark the occasion. Some friends of his – people I'd met before and liked – were coming over from Paris and two days after All Hallows they were all going off together, to travel in Spain. His friend Olivier was going too, and there would be nobody around afterwards, so I could stay and look after the house, eat Tom's muesli, water the dope plants in the lean-to at the back of the garden. It was a great idea. Everybody brought something special to the big day: good French wine packed into the boot of Olivier's car, eight bottles of Calvados that his friend Leon had smuggled over, some excellent dope, a few hundred bennies, several crates of Italian beer. I had four tabs of blotting paper for my own consumption: I knew none of Tom's set did acid, they were strictly muesli-and-mushrooms types. If I had stopped for a moment to think about what I was doing, I might even have seen that I was preparing for a fall. Somewhere, at the back of my mind, where stories unfold according to their own logic – not common sense, not wisdom, not folly, but story logic, destiny, character, whatever we choose to call it – I think I did see. I just didn't acknowledge the fact. At the front of my mind, as I shopped and planned and waited for the day to come, I was expecting to fly. Maybe that's the secret of this condition, this *addictive personality type*: that desire to combine falling and flying. And wouldn't they seem the same, for moments at a time? I thought of flight as a matter of a day, a night, a few hours, but falling was something else. There are some places you can only get to if you stop thinking about them. For a long time, as you fall, you think of the impact, of landing, of touching down – and you just keep falling. It takes a long time to fall, and the only way to make it end is to stop thinking about an ending. Or so it seems now. Back then, I was just planning the best party of my life. I had no idea what kind of machinery I was setting in motion.

CHAPTER 4

When I walked out of my father's house, I thought I had written him off for good. I didn't want to have to be in the same room as him again, partly because I had no idea what the outcome might be, but mostly because that detachment, that sense of separation I had experienced standing at the window in my sister's bedroom had been so magical that I was ready to do anything to win it back. I didn't realise, at the time, that our lives – my father's, mine – were running on near-parallel lines: like me, he was detached, going through the motions on the surface, but walking the dim chambers of his own mind in the small hours. Like me, he seemed untouched by grief. Even now, when there was nobody to restrict his movements, he kept going to work, preserving the facsimile that had concealed him all his life, fiercely pretending he was the man he said he was. Every now and then, when I spoke to Margaret on the phone, I would get an update: he was no worse, health-wise; he was thinking about getting a dog; one or other of his friends had died or moved back to Scotland. I didn't care about any of this – or I told myself I didn't – but I listened to what was said, and I responded as if it mattered. I said I thought the dog was probably a good idea; it would give him some companionship, and he could take the mutt out for walks, which would help his heart. He was still drinking, still smoking sixty to eighty a day, though the doctor had told him if he didn't quit he would die. Well, I said, there was nothing anybody could do about that. It was up to him. Nobody could do it for him. I caught myself using exactly that kind of language, the language he would have used. Inside that language, it was easy to see how indifferent he had been. Or how indifferent he had wanted to be. It was all too much for him, all that human concern. All that time, he'd just wanted to be left alone to get on with things. Now, I felt the same way.

Margaret would try to reason with him. If he cut back on the cigarettes, if he drank less, he would feel better, live longer, see his grandchildren grow up.

'What difference does it make?' he would say. 'Who wants to live for ever, if you can't *do* anything? The kids will be better off not having me around. Anyway, I'll soon be seeing your mum.'

So it went on. On days off, he would still get up early, wash and shave, put on a blazer, clean trousers, his black polished shoes. Then he would go through the paper, seeing what he liked in that day's racecard. Not that he put a bet on very often. I suppose he didn't see much point. At around noon, he would go to the Hazel Tree for a few pints, then he would go home and watch television. He still had his 'big seat', where he sat, a foot or two from the screen, with his glasses perched on the end of his nose, the sound turned down as far as it would go without becoming completely inaudible. There was no food in the house, Margaret told me. No food, no washing powder, no toilet cleaner. She would go round twice a week to pick up his laundry and do a spot of cleaning, trying to time it so he would be out, or busy with the racing. Now that he was alone, and sliding down, the only person who could be bothered to help him was this daughter he had treated so badly. All her life, he had attacked her – psychologically, emotionally, physically – systematically chipping away at her self-regard, eroding her confidence, bleeding her of any faith she might have had in herself. When I asked her why she bothered, she gave me the same answer my mother would have done in her place. 'He's still family,' she said. 'You can't just turn your back on family.'

My father had always been a conventional man, in spite of his drinking and unpredictable behaviour. He sought refuge in received truths, ideas that were beyond controversy in the world he inhabited, indisputable facts about human nature, politics, religion, warfare, current affairs, the impenetrable labyrinths of history. At one time, he'd been a reader, and he remembered some of the details, very specific pieces of information that, out of context, could be turned to almost any purpose. He was familiar enough with the Bible to be able to misquote it in support of the most bizarre arguments; he had memorised odd snippets of science fact and fiction that he didn't really understand, but he repeated it all often enough to imagine that he did. His truths, in fact, were as well rehearsed as his lies, and just as unreliable. One of his most prized beliefs – based, not only on the literature, but on personal experience – was that dogs were just as intelligent as people. He would talk about the Alsatians he'd seen in the air force, dogs that could be trained to do anything, even things that it wasn't necessarily in their nature or their best interests to do. He'd had a dog himself in those days, he said, and that animal was the only living creature he could rely upon in any situation.

'I could have trusted that dog with my life,' he would say. 'Which is more than you can say for most people.'

All the men he knew agreed with this sentiment, even if they didn't have dogs themselves. It was part of the canon of beliefs: dogs were smart and loyal; women were moody; children were a burden; management was corrupt; union reps were self-serving; clever people were all very well, but you were better off with a bit of common sense. Nobody was surprised, then, when he finally did get himself a dog, after weeks of talking about it. The only surprise was the breed. Margaret had assumed he would get an Alsatian puppy; she had even hoped he might have enough sense to get a smaller, more manageable beast, maybe one that wouldn't frighten her or her kids when she went round to the house to clean or pick up my father's dirty laundry. The neighbours had hoped for something he could look after: a wee Scottie, Matt from next door had suggested. Alan, his friend from up the road, had even offered him a pup from a litter of nearly-spaniels his bitch had dropped, but my father had, at some point, entertained a vision of himself with a Dobermann, a dog that, in his view, was a fitting companion to a person of his nature, and that was what he got: a *Dobermann.*

'Beautiful dog,' he said, when Margaret remonstrated with him. 'Not afraid of anything.'

'But it's too big,' she'd said. 'It's cruel to keep a dog like that in a little house like this – '

'He'll get plenty of exercise,' my father said. 'I'll take him out every day.'

'A dog like that needs more than a walk round the court,' Margaret said. 'This is a *big dog*. He'll want a five-mile run in the countryside – '

The argument went on for hours, then days, but it was useless. My father had got himself a dog – he called it Prince, naturally – and he wasn't going to give it back. He'd paid good money for it, and he was going to train it, RAF style. 'You don't need to be scared of him,' he told Margaret. 'If that's what's bothering you. A dog is only as good or as bad as his master. Once I've got him trained, you'll hardly know he's there. The girls will love him. Your Dobermann is a great family dog. Most people don't realise that. All you have to do is show the animal who's boss.'

He was still drinking as much as he ever had, but his habits had changed. He had refined his use of alcohol, distilling it to a fine art, finding a near-perfect balance between amnesia and ascesis. It surprises me, still, that people think of drinking as a form of self-indulgence, that they can call it a pleasure, or a vice, when it is so obvious that, for men like my father – for men like me – it is an instrument of self-abnegation. The real drinker doesn't do it for the high, just as the real gambler doesn't do it for the money: drinking, gambling, drugs, these are spiritual exercises, a perverse, home-made *via negativa* that the disciple travels without hope or desire, towards a limbo of his own making. On this road, in this condition, the mind occupies itself with all manner of strange and secret pursuits, whole categories of knowledge and skill become a sanctuary from the quotidian world that, if he is not careful, might at any moment tempt him out into the open. Some days, the drinker's entire life flashes before him in an instant, the way it is supposed to do when a man drowns, but that instant includes itself, and everything is repeated, again and again, for hours. Some days, he falls asleep and dreams he is in a cinema in the middle of the day – a matinée, probably not many people in the auditorium, though, of course, it's too dark to see – and he is watching his life play out on the screen, all the blacked-out times late at night, all the conversations and pranks and petty mortifications that he has forgotten, played out, in an excruciating public spectacle, but quietly, almost unnoticed, on a wet Thursday afternoon, among strangers.

Yet it isn't that painful, not always. Sometimes he wakes in the middle of the evening, too late to go out, and he feels that something has touched him, leaving a faint stain on his fingers and mouth that is only just beginning to fade. All he has to do is stop time and he will find it, he will guess the truth he's been looking for, he will reach the white origin where snow begins, or the far, cobalt origin of birdsong and water which is always somewhere else, not wherever he is, isolated, in the real sense of the word: *isolated*, picked out, defined, illuminated. Everything begins elsewhere, he knows that: dawn, Christmas, love, beauty, terror, the wind, the sky, the horizon, his own soul. It begins far in the woods, or out on some windy field by the sea. He wants to be there, not here; he wants to be where things begin, and he is so close, he is so *near*. Only – for reasons he cannot explain – something stands in his way, something he didn't ask for. Reason, terror, unworthiness, he can't even name it, it takes different guises every time, but it is always there, standing in his way, keeping him from his destiny. I'm sure my father felt these things – but these are my words, and *this* is the real lie about my father. I cannot talk about him without talking about myself, just as I can never look at myself in the mirror without seeing his face. These days, when Halloween comes around, I observe the rites and I think about the chosen dead – my mother, my grandparents, the four or five people I have lost over the years – but none of them ever comes. Nobody comes but him, the one I don't choose and would prefer to forget. He comes to the fire and stands just outside the ring of heat and light, not the bully I knew, not the hawk-eyed predator watching for any sign of weakness, ready to pounce whenever he saw an opening, but that quiet man I never knew, that man he became when he was alone in an empty house. He has nothing to say to me, he brings no mercy, no forgiveness. He hasn't come to deliver a cryptic message or show me what he has found on the other side. All he is here to say is what he has said already: that we are not so very different, he and I; that, no matter how precious I get about it, a lie is a lie is a lie and I am just as much an invention, just as much a pretence, *just as much a lie* as he ever was.

He abused the dog, of course. He didn't mean to, but he did. He began by doing all the right things, but after a while he was feeding it scraps, pushing it out into the garden when it needed exercise, or walking it round the square, letting it get all excited by the fresh air and the thought of distance, then dragging it back to the house and locking it inside while he went off to the pub. Margaret was furious. She didn't much like dogs, and she wouldn't let her girls roll around the floor with Prince, but she thought it was cruel to treat any animal like that, and she worried that some bad would come of it. We'd both been bitten by dogs when we were children – and we hadn't forgotten little Beth Simpson, who had her cheek ripped off by the family dog, a normally good-natured, not very large mongrel called Sam. Margaret had visions of Prince hopping the gate and tearing somebody's toddler apart out in the court, while my father sat indoors watching the horses on television. She saw things turning nasty, when my father forgot – as he sometimes did – to feed his charge, or to take it out for a walk.

How it worked out in the end, though, was quite unexpected. After he'd been out for the night, and ended up calling

her from a phone box somewhere – he wasn't quite sure where
he was, up on the Lincoln Estate, he thought, though all these
estates looked the same – she picked him up at three in the
morning and dropped him at the house. She was always doing
things like that, and I know that he never once thanked her.
One summer, he offered to take her and the kids to Florida,
and they all trotted off to endure a fortnight in some ugly
resort where he spent the entire vacation in the bar, trying to
convince the other customers that he was a former RAF pilot.
That night, he'd been worse than usual, but Margaret put it
down to too much whisky and not enough food. She didn't
hear from him for a couple of days, then he phoned up and
said he was a bit under the weather and needed her to pick
a few things up for him. She told him she'd be round the next
day after work: the usual arrangement. When she got to
Handcross Court, however, she couldn't get him to answer
the door. All she could hear was Prince barking. When she
told me the story later, how my father had collapsed in the
hall, and the dog had been there with him all that time,
without food or water, I thought she was going to say the
Dobermann had eaten a chunk out of his face, then settled
down to work its way down to the heart and the liver. I'd
heard that story somewhere, and it made sense, even if it was
an urban myth. All those tales of loyal dogs staying by their
fallen masters in blizzards, or under grapeshot fire, they were
all about dogs whose owners had loved them and treated them
as well as, if not better than, their own children. But Prince
didn't owe my father anything. I could have seen the logic, if
he'd torn off an ear or a slice of cheek. I would have forgiven
him. The animal was hungry, for God's sake. I was almost
disappointed when Margaret told me the dog had done what
the cliché would have had him do: he stood guard, barking

233

anxiously and persistently, until somebody came to call an ambulance and open a tin of Winalot. That Dobermann saved my father's life. It was a story he treasured all his days, I'm sure, though I never got to hear him tell it. I can imagine the extra value his old self would have woven in: freak storms, snow, rescue teams digging their way through, then drilling into a double-locked door while the dog lay beside him, sharing its failing body heat, in the chill of the small hours. But he never did tell that story, as far as I know, and when he got home from the hospital, Prince was gone, passed on to somebody who could look after him properly, somewhere out in the countryside, where my father would have been lost in a matter of minutes.

CHAPTER 5

(les fleurs du mal: a field guide)

My Halloween party at Tom's went on for several days. When Tom and Olivier departed, I continued the celebrations with other friends, then alone, till what I remember of that time fades out, like the moment in a film when the director draws a discreet veil over the proceedings. The next thing I remember is coming to on the floor of my room. Someone was talking to me, but I couldn't make out who it was. I was there, I was present, but I was also somewhere else, unable to talk, unable to see. I felt like an astronaut suspended in a sea of radio waves. I've heard it said that all the messages we send to cosmonauts and moon-golfers will travel on for ever, barely dimming, as they merge and bleed through all the creaks and whispers of infinity. I felt just as remote from my everyday existence, and just as much a part of the unnameable.

Finally, I surfaced enough to see that my visitor was Valerie, Tom's sister. I didn't really know Valerie – she didn't live in the house, and she only came by occasionally – but I knew about her. She was a nurse, which presumably explained the fact that, over the next week or so, she stuck around, travelling back and forth to work when she was on shift, but helping me put body and soul back together the rest of the time. I wondered, then, why she did this, as I was to wonder, later, why others like her – passing strangers, part-time saints, surrogate brothers and sisters – would catch me, part-way through my fall, and try to haul me back to solid ground. Sometimes, they fell a little of the way with me, and only just managed to save themselves. Sometimes they were falling too, only at a different velocity, or in a different space. Valerie wasn't one of those people, though: like Tom, she was solid, dependable, rocklike. Maybe this was why those people did what they did: they knew how lucky they were; they wanted to reach out to others less fortunate than themselves. And maybe there was an element of curiosity in that reaching out; they wanted to see it close up, to get a taste, to know what it was like. Maybe they envied it, just a little. It's hard, keeping things together all the time, being more or less acceptable, more or less normal. It's much easier, falling.

> *il faut être voyant, se faire voyant . . . par un long, immense et raisonné dérèglement de tous les sens. Toutes les formes d'amour, de souffrance, de folie; il cherche lui-même, il epuise en lui tous les poisons, pour n'en garder que les quintessences. Il est chargé de l'humanite, des animaux même; il devra faire sentir, palper, écouter ses inventions . . .*

Arthur Rimbaud

There was a time when everything surprised me. My mother would read me something from the newspaper, or one of the teachers at school would casually give out some item of information, and I would be stunned by the sheer beauty, or horror, or unexpectedness of the world. It might be cold and overcast for days, but I would still be taken aback, as I trudged the half-mile from my front door to the white steps of St Bride's, when the snow came thick and fast, blanking out the woods and the wide, straw-covered pens of Kirk's chicken farm. In summer, it would feel odd, waking up to sunshine on the walls and the birds calling to one another as they settled in our hedge, or darted through our garden, casting swift, furtive shadows on the rosewater-thin curtains my mother had put up while Margaret and I were at school.

Then, when I was falling, nothing surprised me. When I hitch-hiked back to Scotland one summer, and found that the Water Houses had been cleared to make way for a light industrial estate, I thought such things were only to be expected. It was only to be expected that the trees I had climbed as a child would be grubbed out and paved over, or that the places where I had grown up – the prefab, Mary Fulton's overgrown garden – would have disappeared. Later still, it was no surprise when the little garden supplies store where I'd worked during summer vacations was refitted as a hair salon, the florist next door quietly replaced by a tinny little shop selling electronic goods. Even when it was cheap, or ugly, or just plain sad, change was what you expected. The only thing that seemed odd was when things stayed the same: a building at the far end of a street, or a public park suspended in time, picked out, still, in a light from twenty years ago, the same details, the same unremarkable colours transformed by an unnatural stillness. It was like seeing a fox or a snow-shoe rabbit in a glass case at the natural history museum: the creatures were never lifelike; no matter how well the taxidermist had done his job, they were devoid of potential, devoid of latent energy – though that only made them more compelling, like emblems, or symbols, standing for the very things they were not.

So it was that, in those months when I was falling, everything that reminded me of lost time was painfully and obviously not the past, but a deliberate and misleading reconstruction of things I couldn't quite remember. As I went on falling, I did all I could to have no past at all. The past was a story, an invention: camomile, eyebright, books on a kitchen window sill bleaching in the sun, their contents – all the recipes and Greek myths and pirate stories – leaching away, till the very house itself was a fabric of words and shadowy woodcuts. The seasons of the year, the feast days, the turning points, the report cards, the photograph albums: all I ever knew of time beyond the clock was melting away in condensation and frost lines, bleeding into the paintwork, coming off in my hands. It was an illusion, a series of hallucinations. I didn't know if it had really happened, or if I had just invented it. Or if it was invented for me. Something to keep me occupied, something for me to consume. As I was falling, I couldn't help thinking that *this* was the problem of my generation: we couldn't separate what was really ours from everything that had been set down in our paths for us to find. Something had to be torn before the real could glimmer through. What was needed was Rimbaud's '*long, immense et raisonné dérèglement de tous les sens*'. As I was falling, I believed this – and I really did think I could accomplish something new. I wanted to make something of myself, as my father would have said. Not that what I was making was what he had in mind. *I* was an experiment.

I wasn't expecting anything. This wasn't a *road of excess leads to the palace of wisdom* trip. For me, excess was a desperate attempt to preserve something inhuman, to hang on to wildness. I knew that being a man had something to do with that wildness: *wildness*, not savagery, but the wildness of birds and animals, the wildness of a hard wind in the grass, the wildness of the sea, the wildness of things that remain untamed. I knew this had nothing to do with drugs, or alcohol; at the same time, however, I felt that this private, wild self was somehow preserved, somehow ringed about by the mystique those things gave off. The further my actions placed me beyond the social niceties, the more I believed that some part of me, some essential element, was able to remain uncontaminated. There are other ways to protect this private wildness, but I didn't know that: all I knew was that, sometimes, when I was 'out of my mind', I connected with something that was missing in my life-with-others. When I was alone, beyond the pale, I would experience an odd surge of tenderness for the world, and I would think that I had known, sometime, somewhere, what it felt like to belong – to the earth, to water, to the wind, to rain. That was the purpose of the experiment: to resume that belonging, by any means possible, and at any cost. It never once occurred to me to think of this exercise as my own modest variation on the eternal and bitter music of paranoia.

The fact that the great days are the ones that almost kill you is really neither here nor there. Falling ill, going crazy – *dying* in some way – these are not concerns, merely events in the greater scheme of *falling*. To me, it would have been much worse – sinful, in fact – to refuse the invitation implicit in every morning of that time, an invitation to be, at one or another end of the spectrum of being, and not merely to exist. Eventually, I came to see that Halloween party at Tom's house as a pleasant *divertissement*, a mere first step on the road; eventually, the parties were going on for a week, or ten days (the best, the most *fatal* of them lasted for fourteen days

239

precisely) and there were no limits, no boundaries. I was still doing kitchen work, mostly. There were various ways to supplement that income, but money wasn't that much of an issue anyhow. It was a democratic era, the era of punk with its inverted meritocracy: the crazier you were, the more hell-bent, the more welcome you would be at almost any gathering. Nobody was more welcome (and more despised) than a man who was obviously falling – and nothing made for better entertainment. What was better than watching a determined fall when the one falling was someone you knew but didn't much care about, a grotesque Icarus tumbling slowly through the air, half-heartedly clutching at the scenery as he goes? People love a falling man, even when they hate him, and nobody loves or hates him more than the safe ones, the boys and girls who, in spite of their desperate veneer, are only playing the game, while they wait to move on to their appointed roles: son and heir, vice-president, Rt. Hon. Gentleman. Ladies in waiting. Boys most likely to. People with people to catch them.

Summer of 1978: in a little room in the quad of a time-honoured English university, a shy, somewhat paranoid student of Spanish and Portuguese – let's call him Dan – discovers an astonishingly simple wheeze involving high-quality cocaine direct from Brazil, the international post and the assumption that books move from one academic institution to another for purely intellectual reasons. Dan's girlfriend, a well-heeled graduate student in Rio, is so besotted with him, and with the idea of being an international cocaine smuggler, that she spends her entire life cutting wedge-shaped holes in the pages of textbooks, packing them with *blanca* and sending little packages off to her beloved (c/o his Alma

240

Mater, naturally). Now and again, she sends him a huge, outsize, brightly coloured Brazilian beach shirt in a box, declaring on the customs form that the contents are to be considered *a gift*. As it happens, I am in the fortunate position of being a friend of Dan's during these days of plenty, an association in which I am not alone. The gifts arrive, unexamined and intact, with astonishing frequency, so much so that Dan has to recruit perfectly new friends to help him enjoy his good fortune. Eventually, he decides, since he cannot pay his everyday bills with cocaine, that he should go into business, selling off the excess of this new-found largesse in a south London hostelry that he had, on occasion, frequented in leaner years.

Les fleurs du mal. They are so many. Coca, meth, *alcools*, Afghan black, magic mushrooms, bennies, dexies, sulphate. Choose your poison; dope right for your type. I loved them all and yet, for me, the really big discovery was barbiturates. I'd combined alcohol and speed, alcohol and grass, even alcohol and acid, but I didn't get into the serious business of mixing large quantities of booze and downers till I met a thin, nervy, rabbit-faced boy called Jed on a three-day binge in Cambridge. I'd got talking to him because someone had said he had a plentiful supply of magic mushrooms, and things had moved on from there. Jed was no choice of companion for the confused soul I was at twenty-two, but I was hardly in a position to know, or decide such things and, besides, there were less reliable friends in the world. Jed's sidekick, Mark, for example. Mark liked hallucinogens, sure enough, but mixing barbs and vodka was his catastrophe of choice. He was as thin as Jed and just as rabbit-faced, but he had taken the nerviness to a new level. He wore gold-rimmed glasses with an orange tint, which made him look like one of those laid-back stoned-out hippie types that Cambridge drew in from the surrounding fenland like a magnet, but his appearance was deceptive. He wasn't laid-back, and he wasn't a hippie, he was just common or garden crazy. Nobody had a vocabulary for it in those days, but his big thing, besides the drugs, was what we now call 'self-harm'. A favourite trick was to stub cigarettes out on the palms of his hands. He thought the palms were better because they were more sensitive. He was always trying to get other people to try it. That, however, was only the acceptable, public side of his hobby: at home, on his lonesome, he majored in cut-throat razors and hunting knives. The last I heard, he was in hospital, though he's probably out now, in the fen some-where, maybe living with some sad-eyed, downtrodden woman, or maybe buried in one of those rustic graves where the unquiet dead lie side by side, like characters from a Fairport Convention song.

Jed and Mark came along at a magical moment in my life. I'd stopped doing acid, after a 'psychotic' episode when I'd met my doppelgänger under a street lamp. (Abuse the sacrament, pay the price. I'm not sure I was as disturbed by the bad trip itself as by the sheer banality of its imagery: pure Hammer Horror B-movie shiverfest stuff, on routine *Oliver Reed is the Wolf Man* lines.) Now I'd decided to continue the experiment with beer, mushrooms and the odd medicinal dose of meth. The first time I mixed barbs and wine, I just drifted off to sleep, after a dreamy half-hour or so, and woke up hours later with a crick in my neck. No big deal. No good reason, either, for doing it again, but I did, and it carried on from there, life folding into a haze, the occasional periods of lucidity needed to get through a day's work punctuated by long, slow reveries in grimy bedsits with people I didn't know and wouldn't have liked if I had. I did it, of course, for the dreams, and for that feeling of remoteness so perfectly described by the expression 'spaced out'. Imagined space, real stars. It was an idyll, the true *dérèglement*. It didn't matter where I was, I could leave my body and go wandering wherever chance took me, a blissful child of the random. It's not exaggerating to say that some people disappeared out there.

All things must pass. I'm not sure when that particular idyll started to sour, but I do recall the summer night when I found myself in the summer house of a big house in Newnham, hallucinating wildly on deadly nightshade, which I had consumed a few hours before with Jed and Mark. We knew nightshade contained both fatal and psychotropic active ingredients, but we'd worked out that if we took just so much, and no more, we would be fine. I had discovered the deadly nightshade plant – a tall, dark, dangerous-looking bush of it – on a strip of wasteland by one of the gardens where I did jobbing work, and I'd harvested the purple berries a few days before, carrying them home in a jar like some kid coming in from the fields with a hoard of volunteer raspberries. Earlier that night – the details are hazy, since drink was also involved – I'd taken two or three berries, not enough, I knew, to poison me (I estimated it would take about thirty or so to do that) and waited for the effects to show. I'm not sure how much time passed, but the next thing I knew I was lying on the floor of this rich man's summer house, fully clothed – though the girl beside me (I had no idea how she came to be there) was stark naked. Stark naked and giggling wildly as a torch played across the windows of the hut and a worried but determined voice sang out in the dark.

'I know you're in there. The police are on their way. If you have any sense, you'll get your clothes on and – '

He kept on talking, this rich man with the big house and gardens and, though I guessed from his voice that he hadn't called the police, I was pretty sure he would, if we scared him any more than we already had. Meanwhile, my companion was sitting on the floor, still giggling, trying to get into her jeans. I wanted to say something, to ask her who she was, or how we'd come to be there, or whether she knew where Jed and Mark might be, but I couldn't speak. I stood up. The rich man had backed away across his lawn and was heading for his house – maybe I'd startled him. The girl scampered to her feet and pulled on a blouse. I don't know why, but I was waiting for her. Maybe it was gallantry, maybe it was confusion, but as soon as she stood up I saw that she was completely gone, not just high, but crazy, giggling softly to herself as she did up her buttons, and looking at me with eyes the size of saucers as if I was her oldest friend. Or was it something more? A moment later, she darted out into the garden, still barefoot – and I followed after.

These are the snapshots that do not exist on paper, snap-shots I carry in my mind, all the moments sieved from lost weekends and four-day binges: moments of waking naked in a stranger's bed, alone and wondering who undressed me; moments of waking in bad hotels, bruised, bloodstained, with no clue as to how I got there, or even of what town I am in; moments of waking on the floor of an abandoned warehouse, or some country bus shelter on a windy road running from nowhere to nowhere through acres of rainy wheat fields; moments of waking fully clothed but slightly damp on the floor of a girlfriend's flat, while she sits at the kitchen counter nursing a cup of coffee and a hurt expression, waiting to see if I will get up of my own accord before she goes out into the regular world, not wanting, now, to leave me alone with her space and things, not wanting me around at all any more, and not wanting to have to find the words to tell me so. The night before, she'd said, with a small, hurt flaw in her voice, angry and compassionate and lonely in the small hours, with this wreck of a human crumbling into oblivion as she spoke: *Some day you'll meet someone who's crazier than you. I hope you'll both be happy.*

I'd wanted to tell her that I wasn't crazy: that I never had been, wasn't now and never would be. But I didn't. To begin with, half the attraction had been her notion that I *was* crazy: crazy was what was missing in her life, and she liked the fact that I put a little of it there. What she hadn't liked was my taking it too far. One of the characteristics of crazy, I would have thought, but I didn't want to quibble. Meanwhile, I just kept getting up again and moving on. It was what I did: find something; test it to breaking point; wander for a while, happy, in my perverse way, to be lost; find the next thing; break it. When they warn you about all that bohemian stuff, they always talk about the seductive properties of alcohol, or drugs, or loose morals, but they never say how seductive falling is, what a great pleasure it is to be *lost*. Perhaps they don't know. Perhaps only the lost know. Far from home, far from the known, the imagination starts to play beautiful, terrifying tricks on us. Maybe it *is* the road of excess that leads to the palace of wisdom – which is just another word for a certain kind of crazy. Being lost, being crazy: while I was falling, I knew I was on to something. I knew I wasn't anywhere near *there* yet, but I also knew that I couldn't get there from where I was.

*

The road of excess leads to the palace of wisdom. It's a lie, of course; but then, Blake was always a bit of a fraud: the prophet of free love who remained faithful to his wife, he lived a life that was, by all accounts, remarkably free of the Rimbaldian excesses that the church of latter-day visionaries to which I now belonged had come to believe were *de rigueur*. We were asphalt visionaries, of course: DIY amateurs poring over the sacred texts in the mercuric light of our own befuddled minds; spiritual orphans, lacking any kind of discipline or tradition; but we were visionaries, nevertheless. The road of excess leads to so many places: for Roland, a junkie I'd known back in Corby, it led to death by burning (as his best friend remarked at the funeral, it wasn't necessarily Roland's fault: the bed was probably on fire when he got into it); for Dan, to a side street in south London, where his right arm was very thoroughly broken by a pair of dedicated business people; for Mark, a mistaken attempted suicide diagnosis when one of his arm-slashing experiments got out of hand; for me — well, there were people who said I was mad (psychotic, according to medical records), but I wasn't, not really. When they eventually carted me off, I wanted to point out that I wasn't properly insane: not clinically, not in the full-blown way. Even in madness, I had binges: a few days, a week, of cask-strength lunacy, followed by a period of hyper-lucidity is *not*, by any account, the epic poetry of real madness. I can look back now and, for myself at least, I can lay out the perfectly logical steps that led, a few weeks after my midnight waltz with the naked girl, to my administering to myself a near-lethal dose of *Atropa belladonna*. I really didn't intend to kill myself; I just wanted to conclude the most interesting experiment I'd managed to concoct, on my way to the place I could never quite reach. Dying didn't come into it. Still, after they'd pumped the *belladonna* from my system, they decided I was a suicide risk, and transported me to a haven of new drugs and greenery, a place called Fulbourn where, not on my first visit, but eventually, I embarked upon the long discipline of happiness.

CHAPTER 6

Meanwhile, in his parallel world, my father had been falling at his own velocity. He had withdrawn more than ever, closed in on himself, after a second heart attack. I made no effort to contact him, but Margaret kept me informed of his progress, whether I liked it or not. I also understood enough to guess that his fall, like mine, was not continuous, not uninterrupted. There were mornings, I knew, when he got up and slipped into the routine of a good day without even noticing it. Nothing dramatic, just the quiet of his own house, sunlight on the sudden, unbelievable orange of a bowl of clementines Margaret had brought round, a fond memory coming to him like a surprise gift, the smell of summer when he opened a window and looked out at a lone girl playing hopscotch in the court below. Why not? I don't know what his days were like, but I won't deny him moments of insight, or satisfaction, or even joy, in the years before his death, when he would have known he was going to die, listening to the doctor warning him, again, that he had to stop smoking, had to cut down on the drinking, had to eat properly, listening to Margaret and the odd neighbour telling him the same things, and deciding that he was going to go in his own way, with dignity – which, for him, meant dying alone, in the privacy of his own house. It was the one aim he could still achieve, that solitary, dignified death; nothing else was an issue, not happiness, not pain, not what people thought.

I would like to imagine him happy – or contented, at least. I had never seen him happy, though this, I'm sure, was because he was only *really* happy when he was alone. I think he was content, at times, during those first six weeks in Corby, working at a new job, probably not drinking that much, but enjoying the odd night out, feeling his way, full of good resolutions. He was staying at the Church Army hostel, which must have been difficult, but I think he did things during those weeks that he hadn't done for years. He went swimming. He took walks out to the little Northamptonshire villages around the works, to Weldon and Cottingham and Great Oakley. He read books. I remember how surprised I was, one afternoon, when Richard was round at our house, and they started discussing Hemingway.

It was odd, watching the two of them talk. In certain moods, my father could like anyone, even someone like Richard, with his shoulder-length straight black hair, like one of those rebel chiefs we used to see in old B-movies: Geronimo, Crazy Horse, Sitting Bull. I liked Richard for very specific reasons: he had a generous mind; he was funny, in an offhand way; he liked the same music as me; but there was something else, something that was harder to put my finger on, the sense of someone who lived, when he was alone, in a separate world, a world that was large and subtle and full of echoes, a world where he didn't mind feeling small. My father usually regarded Richard with suspicion – he was an obvious dopehead, for a start – but there were times, like that afternoon, when he made a point of getting on with my friends, the more dubious the better. By that time, it was his way of showing me that he was fine with other people, that not everybody regarded him with contempt. He would never have talked to me about books, but here he was discussing the merits of the early stories with my hippie doper friend. I was surprised, but there was no doubting that he had read all, or most, of Hemingway's stories. It was all aimed at me, I knew: he wanted me to know that there was this other side to him, even if he'd never been able to share it with me. The implication being that it was my fault. I had never respected him, I'd never seen him as he really was.

Now, edging towards sixty, he was falling. He'd been tottering all his life, but he'd never had the good grace to fall, he'd always clung on with all the tenacity and self-deception he could muster. He could drink his wage packet away in a night, he could come home and smash the house up, he could force my mother to push me out of a window into the night for my own safety, but he was proud of the fact that he wasn't falling – that, no matter what, he would never lose a day's work through drink. He'd never been unfaithful to our mother, he'd told us, during his drunken rambles, though he'd had plenty of offers. He could have made a heap of money on the horses if our mother hadn't made him give it up. He could have stayed in the air force, but he'd left for her sake. Because, no matter what any of us might think, he had *loved* her. As soon as he registered that she was gone, he began to fall. To begin with, he believed it wouldn't take long, that it would all be over in a matter of months, a year at most. But this is the biggest surprise, this is the biggest shock to the system, worse than any of the damage we do to ourselves or others, worse than the lost joys of the early days, when the drug of choice was so gracious. This is the worst stage, when the end keeps promising to come, but never arrives, and we go on falling, for years, or decades. And after all that falling – so slow, so casual – when the end finally comes and the fall is over, there's nobody there to appreciate the fact.

I rarely saw him during these years. I met him once at a family wedding, when we exchanged a few civil words, then avoided one another; later, at Margaret's request, I visited him in the hospital when he had a serious heart attack. I could say that I didn't want to know, that I was too busy with myself to be bothered. I could say that I had too many unhappy memories to see him as he was then. But this is all after the fact, all construction. It doesn't explain the fact that, now, in some perverse corner of my heart, I would like to imagine him happy, or that I would gladly have imagined him happy, back then. A few minutes' happiness – a good memory, a bright morning, an old song on the radio during a moment of self-forgetting – would have made so much difference to a life like his. A few hours would be a story in itself, the basis for a whole new construction: gentleness, veneration, history, love. After I landed, in the course of my own fall, in a country of tough love and psychological clichés, I heard the same phrase over and over again: *you can't love others until you learn to love yourself.* I thought that idea was suspect from the start, but I didn't know why. Thinking of my father, though, in his lonely house, where nobody could see him, I can imagine him shedding, ounce by ounce, the armoured self he had been taught to carry, as a man, from the moment he learned to walk. When he was three or four, somebody would have set him on a table and told him to jump off, assuring him that he would be caught, that no harm would befall him. It's an old story: the child jumps, and he falls; then, as he picks himself up, or lies dazed and betrayed on a cold stone floor, somebody leans in and murmurs, with dark satisfaction, 'That'll learn you: *trust nae bastard.*' He did the same trick for me when my mother's back was turned, and he picked away at any and every sign of softness that he saw in my character, just as somebody no doubt picked away at him. To my father, a man was not raised for gentleness, or veneration, or joy. Most of all, he was not raised to love. A man acted, a man used, a man destroyed, a man controlled. Love was a sign of weakness.

Still, it is possible – I think Margaret believed it was more than possible – that my father learned to forget some of this when he was alone in his house, waiting to die. He still went out, he still drank and smoked, he still waited, but it is possible that he loved something, for minutes or hours at a time. He stopped growing vegetables in his little plot of garden, and let the flowers my mother had planted grow a little wild. Once, when I paid him that final visit, towards the very end, he told me he'd let the garden go, to enjoy the wild flowers. When I saw what a wilderness the garden had become, I thought he was being ironic, but it's possible that he meant what he said. I'm told that he was gentler towards the end, less angry, more capable of being quiet in himself. So, as foolish as this seems, I want to venture a hypothesis that, roughly expressed, goes like this: you cannot learn to love yourself until you find something in the world to love; no matter what it is. A dog, a garden, a tree, a flight of birds, a friend. I want to say that the old pop-psych cliché is almost true if you reverse it: you learn to love yourself by loving the world around you. Because what we love in ourselves is ourselves loving. I will never know – it would still have been too much a matter of shame for him to admit it – but I can *imagine* that my father learned to love the world a little before he died, and so, in turn, learned to love himself. I hope so, partly for his sake, and partly for my own – because there are times when I look back and suspect, times when I look back and *know*, that I was as much to blame as he was in our failure to be a father and a son. As a lifetime proposition, happiness is a discipline, no doubt; but for moments at a time, it's a piece of luck. A piece of luck and a clue: a hint, not just of what might be, but of what already exists, in the heart of a man's heart, in the private place where clichés no longer hold, in the smoky, golden, myrrh-scented chambers of his own imagery.

CHAPTER 7

Fulbourn. Any resident of Cambridgeshire knows what that word means, and every other community in the country has its equivalent, some innocent-sounding place name signifying madness, an everyday word for life beyond the pale, a word for pleasant gardens with high fences and rooms filled with medicated phantoms muttering to themselves or to other, even less palpable ghosts in day rooms and isolation wards named for local beauty spots or historic figures. On my first visit, I arrived in the middle of summer and, after a few days, I began to take it all in: the cedar trees in the grounds; the flower borders; the long corridor that led from the day room to the cool night beyond; the piano in the recreation room; the crazed, beautiful girl spinning across the floor of the refectory on the day I emerged from the first wave of medication. I could do this, I knew, because I wasn't mad. I knew it, the doctors knew it, the nurses knew it, the one visitor who drove out from the city with a bag full of fruit and books knew it. I had been mad, but that was over; now, I was just a body that was changing, moment by moment, into something new, something more rational than the logic that had put me in that institution could conceive.

Which meant, of course, that I really *was* mad, or if not mad, then at least disturbed, out of order, a suitable case for treatment. Because everybody – the nurses, the doctors, my visitor, even I – knew that the only way out of Fulbourn was to accept the logic, not of some unexpected, yet wholly necessary transformation, but of the rules that had put me there in the first place. In other words, you got out by appearing normal. How anybody could appear normal when he was taking a healthy dose of chlorpromazine every few hours is a puzzle to me now (though I did fall in love with that particular drug later on). Still, that's another story. This story is a lie about madness: it's bound to be a lie, because nothing I say about that first visit to Fulbourn could be true. A lie, or a story, which amounts to the same thing, if what I say differs in any way from my medical records: records I have seen and marvelled at, for their sheer – *what?* Stupidity?

At the point when they took me to Fulbourn, I was emerging from something I am tempted to call a fit of temporary insanity, emerging and, in an extraordinarily tender and vulnerable state, *becoming* something I couldn't anticipate, something I couldn't have described. It was as if someone had happened along, after the imago of an insect had emerged from its cocoon, wet and new and impossibly fragile, and decided there was something wrong with it, because it wasn't a caterpillar any more. There were other people in that hospital who were undergoing worse treatments than mine – my greatest fear, at Fulbourn, was of the ECT room, into which someone like Cathy, the beautiful, wild dancer from my first day's visions, could vanish one afternoon, only to emerge with all the beauty and wildness stripped away. I knew there was some technical sense in which they couldn't treat me without my consent, but there were ways and means, or there seemed to be, to make me do anything. The proof of that was a moment that came every evening, when I walked to the end of the corridor and smelled the night air seeping through the double doors of the exit. If I was a voluntary patient, all I had to do was push open those doors and walk out. It was all so easy – and that was how I knew it was a trick. I wasn't mad, I could walk out any time; but if I did, it would be taken as another confirmation of my madness, another sign that I still hadn't discovered the secret trick of seeming normal.

Go back, go back. The questions I am raising here are phantoms, just as so many of the people I met in Fulbourn – the doctors; the nurses; the visitors; some, but not all, of the patients – were phantoms. I was not mad; I was not suffering from 'psychosis'. I had spent several days in what was, to outward appearances, a psychotic state – hallucinations, mad ramblings, a misguided attempt, not to fly, but to rise a few inches, no more, from the ground – but I was not mad. Medical records from that time describe me as having a history of 'extreme heavy drug abuse' which had caused 'a psycho-stimulant psychosis of a paranoid nature' – but to me, this language means absolutely nothing. I can read the reports with grim curiosity, but they don't interest me in the least. What does interest me is the interior of that description, the process that was happening behind my eyes and under my skin during the weeks I spent at Fulbourn, and during the months I spent as a shadow after I emerged. No mention is made in the notes of the details of my hallucinations, the tiny elephants and circus acrobats parading across the floor of the hospital ward when I was first admitted, no mention of the Water Girl, a beautiful, sinister woman-child with fingers like hunting knives, who followed me about, changing shape as she went, becoming a nurse, another patient, a passing cleaner, only to emerge as soon as I relaxed my vigilance and advance upon me, fingers slicing the air. No mention of the fact that, at one point, I found myself in a shuttered room with a beautiful gunman, a smiling, gentle creature who held a glittering silver revolver to my forehead and very slowly pulled the trigger. No mention of the fact that this moment, when I was being shot, was one of extraordinary joy.

This all sounds like madness, I don't doubt. And yet – I have to insist on this – I did not lose my marbles, get myself committed, take the meds, talk the talk, then emerge cured, normal, suitably treated and ready to take my place in the world. I will not deny that chlorpromazine eased my pain, and quietened the world down – no, not quietened, but held it at bay, held it at arm's length – long enough for me to do the work that I had to do in that place. Chlorpromazine (trade name Largactil) was a friend to me, then and later, but it wasn't just medication, it was an instrument. No more, no less. The real work happened inside the lit circle of my own mind. I say mind, but I mean *psyche*, in the old sense of the word: *psyche*, spirit, mind, soul. A theatre of possibilities that, most of the time, is out of bounds. Inside that space, there was something that, to others, looked like chaos, but for me it was a maze, a complex pattern of angles and turns and dead ends, but a maze nonetheless, and I knew that, for every dead end, for every skewed turn, a transformation was being offered to me, a chance at an aseity that was as beautiful as it was terrible. There were times when I was desperate to get out of Fulbourn, but there were also times when I felt privileged – and this is what the authorised story never says: that it's *beautiful*, this madness; it's beautiful, this amazement.

Most of the time, though, all I could think was that a mistake had been made. When I came to myself, after what remained of the deadly nightshade experiment had been pumped from my stomach and I'd spent hours in a hospital

257

storeroom, barricaded in, terrified of the Water Girl and her strange company, after the blank days of the first stage of medication, I didn't know why I was there. The experiment had gone awry, I accepted that, but everybody around me had got hold of the wrong story, a story of insanity, psychosis, depression, suicide attempts – who knew what else – and the sheer weight of all those people believing what they believed was too much for me to counter. They didn't know – how could they know, and how could I have told them? – that what had happened to me was the outcome of an experiment in which my life was not that important, or rather, was something I was prepared to risk in the process of effecting an absolutely necessary sea change. I wanted to become something other than I had been, and I didn't care what that transformation cost.

And still, while I was there, I tried to go on with the experiment. As soon as I was stable enough to avoid constant supervision, I would take myself off to the recreation room in the evenings and sit there, alone and silent, for all the world like a living vial of some distilled substance, empty of intent or meaning, reflecting nothing but the moonlight through the long windows and the shadows of the gardens. The recreation room was my sanctuary: a piano, a games table, several shelves of foxed, cloth-bound books, half a dozen jigsaws in boxes with labels on the side to say how many pieces were missing. Nobody bothered me there, and I liked being in the same room as the piano – I had an idea that I could play it, still, but I never tried. The keys looked so perfect, it seemed wrong even to touch them. Most of the time, I was elsewhere, and trying to come back – only I didn't want to come back empty-handed, I didn't want to be 'back to normal'. I was like the monkey in the monkey puzzle story: I had hold of something and I didn't want to let go of it, but I would never escape unless I did. On that occasion, I couldn't figure the puzzle out: I was too weak, I hadn't gone far enough, I thought the reason for my stay was something other than it was. I thought I was tired, or wounded, or unhappy. I was coming off a huge dose of poison, and that explained everything. It didn't though, and I suspected that too. Poison has its own logic, its own purposes, and they vary from one person to the next. In every case, they might be a revelation. I was sorry, when I left, that I hadn't been afforded that revelation. The experiment had failed: I had tried to engineer a meeting with the angel, but there had been no annunciation, just a series of hallucinations and delusional symptoms. Still, I knew I'd be back. There was a sense of unfinished business in the air, as I walked back into Cambridge from my temporary heaven, dazed by the sunlight, numbed by the movement and the noise, and I knew I still had work to do.

CHAPTER 8

It took me a few weeks to get myself sorted out. I had no desire to stay in Cambridge, so I sold, handed on, or discarded the little I owned and walked away. I needed new surroundings, space and time to think, a place to be unseen by others. I could have gone anywhere but, as it happened, I ended up in Woodingdean, just outside Brighton. The room I rented was to the rear of a bungalow, otherwise inhabited by an elderly woman who was often away and didn't seem pushy about rent; I had the use of the kitchen, and my bedroom overlooked a shady secluded garden that, after a time, I took charge of, as payment in kind for monies owed. I wanted to be in a place where I didn't know anybody, and could make a fresh start. If I'm honest, I have to admit that I wanted to hide, to be alone with the theatre of my recovery, assuming the pose of a man who has come close to an experimental death, and might as well behave accordingly.

Which was probably what made me attractive to every crazy and visionary in Brighton. By the following Christmas – a Christmas I'd planned to pass in splendid isolation – I had gathered a circle of friends that I'd never intended to find: madmen, artists, slow suicides, masochists possessed by their own brand of dark, demanding joy. Brighton was just coming to the end of a heyday: an alternative world of gay pubs and arty cafés torn between decline and gentrification, a sad old seaside town of crazed ex-hippies, squaddies on two-day passes, NF skinheads, hopheads, acidheads, cokeheads, breadheads, Supremes impersonators, poets, jazzmen, maniacs, thieves, jokers, fools. At the centre of it all stood the Pavilion, the city's bitter soul passing itself off as a psychedelic birthday cake; but what really mattered was the seafront: the promenades, the pebble beaches, the wreck oozing oil by the old pier, the pier itself, falling apart gracefully under the weight of a thousand starlings and the buffeting of the Channel winds. It was on the front, on the beach or the promenade, where we got high, made love, fought our pointless battles, and lay down in our street clothes when we had nowhere else to go. It was in a house on the front, a tall, narrow mock-Regency building that had been adapted to student accommodation, that my little band of friends came to grief, when the smartest and funniest of us all fell right out of the world when none of us was there to catch him.

Rick was like a brother to me. I never knew what that cliché meant until I encountered him, and realised I had been waiting for him ever since my real brother – my ghost, my Andrew – had died back in the prefabs. He was a thin, nervy man-boy with thick, shiny glasses and horribly pale skin. On our first meeting, it seemed he would never stop talking, but I never got tired of listening; he was always funny, always a little wild. It was like watching Keith Moon play Mercutio from *Romeo and Juliet*: everything he said sounded like some bizarre, speedy variation on the Queen Mab speech, all fanciful nonsense and mania that, of a sudden, could stop us in our tracks and make us wonder if he was serious. I think, at times, he was, but he never let on. I didn't know it then, but all this talk was a smokescreen, not for us, but for himself, a diversion to distract him from the knowledge that he was slowly going crazy with disappointment and outrage at the way people behaved. He loved the world; he was a romantic, even a sentimentalist; and he was doing all he could to hide it from us and from himself. On first acquaintance, it seemed that all he wanted was to go from one party to the next, worming his way into the affections of complete strangers by the sheer bravado of his conversation; but it wasn't all parties and, once I got to know him, I saw that he wasn't really the manic, stand-up cynic he pretended to be. Sometimes, at the end of a night, we would find ourselves alone in the small hours, dawn just beginning at the window like a black-and-white film, and we would be there, with coffee and hash, or the last of the wine, talking about whatever he'd just got into – it didn't matter what: the techniques of sword-swallowing, the philosophy of Nicholas of Cusa, it didn't matter at all, he would just open a subject up in front of me like a backgammon board, and we would be playing, trying out ideas, serious, but not taking ourselves seriously. It was the world that mattered, all that real stuff out there that seemed to mystify and enchant him, and for which he felt a mysterious and genuine grief. Nothing could come up without him thinking of it as a puzzle, he was always bemused, always wondering. Sometimes, he seemed worried, as if he thought everything around him might disappear at any second. It wasn't a side he revealed when he was out and about, but I saw it, and I was forced to admit – silently, in my own mind – that his bewilderment was something I not only shared, but prized.

In spite of this, Rick was the star at the centre of the little group to which I had accidentally come to belong. The inner circle – Carl, me, my *girlfriends* Katie and Lara – moved around him the way planets move around the sun. There were others who came and went – Karen, the beautiful bisexual whose meter we'd raid when there was no money left; Brice, a mad French guitarist who could sound like anybody from Duane Allman to Mark Knopfler, but had no sound of his own; Jackson, a Chinese gambler whose bad luck was legendary in every bar with a slot machine all along the south coast – but we five were always there: the wrecking crew, the ones who would do *anything*. At the time, I was drinking vodka, mostly, though I liked to carry a quarter-bottle of black rum in my jacket for emergencies. My drug of choice was speed, though I rarely turned down a night at Carl's mixing barbiturates and Babycham. Carl was the best Elvis imper-sonator I ever met, partly because he made no real attempt to look like Elvis. He had long, dirty-blond hair that he kept straight by throwing it across an ironing board and pressing it before he went out of an evening; usually he wore blue or black drainpipe jeans and a woman's fake leopard-skin coat that he'd found in a junk shop in Hove and had altered to fit him. He was tall and thin, not bad-looking, with delicate well-made features, but when he danced, you would have sworn Elvis had taken possession of his angular, anorexic's body. He liked to drink well enough but, for him, the real fun came at the end of the evening, when he'd go back to his surprisingly attractive flat with whoever else wanted to tag along, and take night-long trips into oblivion. It was reputed that, at one time, he had earned a good living as a graphic designer, and there were always sketches and doodles scattered about the flat, but nobody knew what he did by the time I met him. Now and again, he would show me a sketch for something he said he'd been commissioned to do, but I never heard of any money coming from that source. Carl didn't like Rick that much, but he couldn't help loving him. In truth, Carl didn't like anybody that much, but he was riven with love for everyone. That's what barbiturates do: they drive the devotee insane with an unspeakable love for everything. For rain, for the pattern in a shell, for a stranger passing on the street. At the end, Carl was insane. He lost everything. The last time I saw him, he was standing on a street corner, singing 'Heartbreak Hotel'. He didn't even sound like Elvis.

Carl was insane, but he drove himself to insanity with barbs. Rick was the real thing, a Parsifal, the holiest of holy fools. Back then, I thought of him as my soul-friend and, for almost a year, he was my inseparable companion, partly because he was the funniest man I had ever met, but mostly because we were falling at *exactly the same speed*. He had that sense of humour that comes of having given up, of seeing everything as an event to witness from the vantage point of profound bewilderment. He wasn't funny ha-ha or even funny peculiar so much as funny absurd: he had a Jesuitical sense of the beauty of argument for its own sake, asking the questions that the rest of us never put into words, examining every detail of every object or event that came within his purview and taking the *reductio ad absurdum* to new and unforeseen heights. He was also, unmistakably, doomed: though not for any reason other than his own will to be so. I think we both knew that all along. What made him different from all, or most, of the others, was that he could have survived, and he didn't lift a finger to save himself. *The sins of the fathers are visited upon the sons.* This was Rick's favourite saying. One night, when we were both completely wasted, we decided that, if the sins of the fathers are visited on the sons then, to escape our fathers we must kill their gods. It was an oddly satisfying moment, as if we really had reached some meaningful conclusion that could have been translated into action – but it didn't last. A moment later, he picked up his beer, snorted into it and muttered, 'If we could only be bothered.'

I met Rick on a Saturday lunchtime in the Shakespeare's Head, on Spring Street. I had just lost another three days of my life. I could remember moments, scraps of conversation, faces floating in a bluish haze, and I had one very vivid recollection of sitting in a bar in hell, some dive I had obviously drifted into late on the first day, when I was too messed up and incoherent to get by elsewhere. By then, though, I was sober: anxious, horribly ashamed, my arms covered with odd scabs and scratches that I couldn't explain, and I was already half hoping that this particular binge would be the last. In the meantime, I had stopped into the Shakespeare's Head to see Katie. I'd stood her up two days before, somewhere near the beginning of this particular fall, and I needed to apologise. Instead, I went on another binge with Rick, who was a student at the art school, and knew where all the best parties were happening that night. From that first day onwards, we were inseparable.

Falling takes so long. There are parts of the process that seem to happen overnight, but it's only later, looking back after years, that you see how slow and convoluted it was. How manifold. How mysterious, how seductive at times, like the seduction of casinos where the promise of the big win is overshadowed only by the beauty of losing, the beauty of having everything stripped away, till nothing remains but the soul, bereft and miraculous. I remember, on the way down, how beguiled I was by the story of the man who turned grey overnight, the story of the man who came home after days spent God knows where, his eyes bright, his body whittled away, the story of the man who had touched bottom and then

265

returned – but that idea to which everybody clings, that notion of touching the bottom and coming up again, is a lie. Yes, you touch bottom, at some point or another, in that long fall, but that doesn't mean you rise, or not necessarily. A man can bounce along for quite a while, lifting and falling, lifting and falling. In the end, the only way he can return to the surface is to stay in the murk, to take it into himself. Maybe he emerges into the light, but it's as well for him to remember the darkness. Maybe, at some decisive point, he aligns himself with the angels, but it behoves him to know where the Devil lives, especially when that perverse imp so often resides in his own heart. Which is to say: in the secrets he keeps, for any number of reasons, from his conscious self.

But this is theory. All of it after the fact. No use to man or dog, as Jackson used to say. I have no idea what he meant by that.

It was still the time of vinyl. The soundtrack of our lives was Neil Young, *Zuma* and *On the Beach* mostly, with some Doors and Bowie thrown in. Days were spent in one or other of the pubs off Western Road, and they always ended back at Rick's place, with 'Revolution Blues', or 'Cortez the Killer', or 'On the Beach' trailing off into the city dawn, while we folded into the blue of our own dreams, drunk, stoned, fluttering down into the beautiful grainy silence of barbiturates, it didn't matter, all that mattered was that we were somewhere else. Mostly, it was just the two of us, though now and then one or other of my girlfriends was there, crashed out on the bed while Rick and I sat up, still smoking or drinking or lifting the stylus back again and again to repeat the tracks we loved and somehow couldn't make out. That music was a mystery to us: it opened up distances in our minds and evoked memories of times we had never known; it made us, for hours at a time, into the people we'd always wanted, and could never hope, to be.

'Cygnet Committee'. 'The Bewlay Brothers'. Half the time I didn't understand the words. Maybe they didn't mean anything, they just created an atmosphere, they reflected something that was in our minds. These were the songs we had listened to and, like 'Little Brown Jug' or 'Maybelline' in other decades, it wasn't the words or even the quality of the music that mattered, it was just that those were our songs. It took me years to realise that I loved Rick. He had a quality about him, a wildness, that couldn't be ignored. Years before, on Blackburn Drive, I had waited for some such creature to come into the Fultons' deserted garden – not just the usual foxes and cats, but something half-animal, half-child, so light-footed it would barely mark the panes of ice on the puddles, but strong enough to tip the bin, to get at the scraps and leftovers. I thought I would cross the lawn some evening and find it there, ripping apart a chicken carcass, or lapping at the crusts of fat on a half-eaten salmon. I didn't invent this creature: there were stories from way back of feral children scouting the borders of graveyards and farms, searching for food and shelter and those were the children I believed in, those were my kin. All my life, I'd been afraid of waking up one day and realising I was safe, at home in the wrong place, marooned. Rick used to say the unknowable had gone out of fashion, but I didn't think so. For a long time after he fell, when I was still mad, I would go out at daybreak and find a trail of pawprints crossing the park, and I would think he'd been there, in some other guise, or I would wake in the dark and imagine I had just heard a cry, savage, insistent, yet at the same time almost human.

*

By the time he fell, Rick had become my ghost brother made flesh. I shared everything with him – money, drink, his room, his music, friends. We were inseparable. When I was with Katie, or Lara, and it was too late to get home, we would sleep in Rick's bed, drunk, stoned, laughing at his stupid jokes, making love while he sat in a chair and listened to music, or opened another bottle of vodka. We invited him in, sometimes, but he wasn't interested. He liked both women, but all he wanted was a brother, and that brother was me – by chance, ill fortune, or default, I couldn't have said. I was the one who stepped in when he got into trouble, which was fairly often. He knew exactly the effect drink would have on him, and he knew what he was doing when he waded into an argument with some NF type or loud-mouthed darts player, he just couldn't stop himself. It was a matter of honour, and no indignity, no mysterious injury, no hideous embarrassment could prevent him doing it. I was bigger than him, colder, more detached; I knew when to offer a cynical apology and when to show ready for a fight. Rick wanted to argue with everybody, but he couldn't have fought his way out of a paper bag, and it showed. Faced with physical aggression, he was, quite simply, bewildered. His logic was always irrefutable, and he couldn't understand why somebody who wasn't as bright as him wanted to win the argument by other means. I was the one who talked him down when he flew too high, I was the one who shadowed him when he went too far into Queen Mab's world. I was his brother and his keeper, his twin, his echo. And I was the one who let him fall.

We had been to three parties in a row, crashing at his room, or sitting around in the bar of the Shakespeare's in between. We were all tired. Carl had disappeared back to his place and was probably floating in the isolation tank of some bizarre mix of sweet wine and downers, Katie had crashed out at hers. People came and went, disappeared, promised to return, didn't return, did, went again, came back with new drugs, new rumours. Something hovered in the air around us, that special tension that comes when the end of something has been reached, but nobody is ready to give up. At some point in the evening, Rick decided he was a cat person, like Simone Simon in the old Jacques Tourneur film. He said people could change into animals by sheer force of will, and he was going to become a cat. It was just the usual nonsense he'd talk, trying to get something started – and at the same time, it wasn't. As Rick waited for feline grace and miraculous eyesight to arrive, I was burdened with real foreboding. I almost knew something was going to happen. I could see in his face that he was serious about this cat thing: even if he never reached that stage where the cat emerged, and the old skin slipped from the bone, I think a point came, some time after I left him, when he believed he'd achieved a new awareness, a near-feral poise that made him invulnerable. I'm sure this was metaphorical, at some level in his consciousness: he was always dreaming about a fall, and he'd tell me those dreams, sometimes, as we sat over a vodka breakfast in his room. But maybe a moment came when it became real-world, when he really thought he could make it work. Maybe that was what happened with the window. I'll never know, because I wasn't there – and even if I had stayed at the party, there's no guarantee that I would have been able to save him.

I wasn't around when he fell because a girl called Jennifer was there when we arrived, and I decided to go home with her. I'd been thinking about Jennifer for quite some time, and this was one night when I wasn't going to pretend otherwise. Maybe I knew trouble was brewing; maybe, for once, I didn't want to be Rick's brother and keeper. I did try, though. Before I left – Jennifer had slipped away already and was waiting in her car – I found him at the drinks table and pinned him down. He looked terrible, all of a sudden. 'You need to sleep,' I said quietly. I was afraid of being too concerned for him. Concern always inspired his contempt.

He looked at me in mock disbelief, then he raised the glass and took a long swig. 'Are you going somewhere?' he asked. He would have seen Jennifer at the party earlier, and he would have noticed us exchanging words.

'I'm going back with Jen,' I said. 'We can drop you off.'

'Nah.' He shook his head and grimaced. 'You go and enjoy yourself. They need me here, on the dance floor.'

I waited. I thought he was going to change his mind. I had such a strong apprehension that something bad was going to happen, that I thought he might feel it too. Then I convinced myself that I'd had that feeling before, on other nights than this, and I let it go. 'You sure?' I asked.

He shook his head. 'The girls are going to catch you out, one of these days,' he said.

I nodded. 'I can't help it,' I said. For a moment, I thought he'd be fine. He would get drunk and doze off in a corner, mumbling to himself. Or he'd go on all night and see me the next day at the pub. He'd walk home and ring his girlfriend in Pittsburgh, or wherever she was, on the payphone outside his room. 'See you tomorrow?'

'Yeah.' He nodded. 'Cheerio.' He grinned maliciously. 'Be careful with that girl,' he said. 'She looks dangerous.'

Later, he must have got his second wind. He knew people at the party, but he was always drawn to people he didn't know, and it was probably somebody he didn't know who pushed him through a third-storey window at three the next

270

morning. Or maybe he just fell. Nobody really knew what had happened, though; partly because nobody wanted to know, but mostly because Rick was on the pavement outside for half an hour before anybody realised.

The damage was extensive. I only saw him once, in intensive care, when he was still unconscious; after that, his parents and girlfriend turned up, and decided that I wasn't to see him again, because it would be too upsetting. I know he regained consciousness, and I know he spoke, but Katie wouldn't tell me what he said, when she came back from her visit to the IC ward. I heard later that he'd suffered brain damage, that the doctors were afraid that he'd end up having the mind of a twelve-year-old. I don't know how they work that kind of thing out (why twelve? why not a bright ten-year-old, or a dim fifteen?) but it didn't matter. I tried a couple of times to get in to see him again, but they wouldn't let me. I asked Katie if he'd asked for me, or if he'd said anything about that night, but she wouldn't answer. Maybe she was wondering why I hadn't been there to stop him falling; maybe she already knew. Either way, it was all over. I never saw her, or Lara, or Jennifer again and, by the time Rick was discharged from hospital into his parents' care, I had left Brighton for good.

CHAPTER 9

Je est un autre. Rimbaud

My father had his third heart attack the following spring. By that time, I was back in Cambridge, working in a college garden, trying to engineer my own disappearance. It took Margaret three days to track me down: eventually, I was called to the phone at the Eagle, where I sometimes dropped in during the early evening to drink beer and do the crossword with a couple of barflies who had been practising for years the transparency that I was only just beginning to master. It was the landlady who took the call, a warm-hearted, sympathetic, discreet woman named Wendy, patron saint of the sad and the lonely, a petite beauty with long honey-coloured hair who sometimes turned up in rival establishments with an Indian python draped around her neck.

'It's serious,' Margaret told me. 'He's asking for you.'

'No, he isn't,' I said.

'I know you don't want to hear this, and I'm sorry to disappoint you,' she said. There was a note of irritation in her voice. 'But he is asking for you. *That's* how serious it is.'

I had read somewhere that the third heart attack was always the last, that nobody ever recovered from it. I imagine

Margaret had read the same article – not true, as my father's case demonstrates – because she managed to talk me into going back, the very next morning, to see the man I'd thought to erase from my life for ever. As soon as I put down the phone, I regretted making that promise, but I knew I couldn't go back on it.

'Everything all right?' Wendy asked, as I thanked her for the use of her private phone.

'Fine,' I said. 'Somebody I know is ill.' I gave her an innocent-seeming smile. 'I've not seen him in years,' I said. 'But we go back a long way.'

'Uh-huh.' She studied my face; and I could see in her eyes that she knew there was something I wasn't telling her. 'I'm sorry to hear that.' She lingered a moment, deliberating, then decided, with the tact of the true professional, not to pursue the matter. I believe she knew what I was doing with myself and, because she had seen it all before, she knew the protocols to observe with a man who was trying to disappear.

A person can disappear in a thousand different ways. For a long time, I'd been toying with the most commonly reported method, where he goes out in his shirtsleeves to buy a loaf of bread, or a pack of cigarillos, and, though his wife waits all afternoon and into the evening for his return, coming to the door from time to time and looking out at the empty street, as the daylight turns to lime green, then to grey, then to the deep, sweet blue of night, nothing is ever heard of him again. For me, this was a necessary myth, in spite of its cruelty. I rewrote it a thousand times, on the walk to work, or on Saturday afternoons when the fair came to town and set up its factory of light and rockabilly on a piece of wasteland sweetened with morning dew, and it was always a necessary myth, even if it seemed a little too easy to act upon, or too selfish to set in motion. For a long time, I had to settle for fiction: building new scenarios over days or weeks and storing them away in my library of mental compilations, like an amateur pornographer thinking up narratives of dominance or submission that he would never dream of enacting. I knew, all along, that this part of my life was a story. Not a fantasy, not that at all, but a story, a fiction, a piece of art. We are, all of us, walking libraries of the unspeakable, whited sepulchres where the real life we imagine is concealed behind talk of the weather, sensible shoes and a received morality that we more or less obey and more or less despise. We are trained to conceal the imagery of our dream lives – yet those images form a world in themselves, they make up an ecology, and it is to this world, this ecology, that I imagine travelling, when I entertain a slow afternoon's dream of leaving, thinking myself out into the distance and away, with a handful of coins in my pocket and a fresh wind troubling the grass.

One day, however, it came to me that, while the heart of this story was true, that it was necessary to disappear, I didn't need to actually go anywhere for the vanishing to happen. The most banal element of the story – and the cruellest – was that gestural element, that walk to the end of the street or the corner shop, that cryptic note on the kitchen table, that abandoned car on a coast road with its scatter of misleading clues. One day it came to me that this disappearing act, this removal from a dishonest and dishonourable existence could happen of itself, at any time. Nothing needed to happen, nothing needed to change. One day, if I did what I needed to do, I could just be gone. A person can disappear in a thousand different ways, but maybe the best method

274

was to stay put and do nothing. After Rick fell, all I wanted was to be a gardener and drift to the end of my life undisturbed. I was all set: a college garden, or some such place, would be my home for as long as I was able to work, and I would have all the time in the world to practise my vanishing act. I would also have space to clean up my act. To simplify, cut back, pare down. By the time the call came through about my father's second-to-last heart attack, I thought I was on my way to what the ancients called *anachoresis*, the calculated withdrawal to a good, or at least neutral, place, in order to remain untouched by the sins of the world. I thought I had it all worked out – and then I met Caroline.

My childish experiments with Sandra Fulton, back in the prefabs, had aroused in me some difficult predilections that I could never quite explain, to myself, or to anybody else. Not sadomasochism, nothing like that, but a game that resembles that cliché in superficial ways, a game that involves hurt, though not, in most cases, harm. Over the years, I'd met others who shared a taste for this game – in some, nothing more than that, in others, a preference – but I'd never encountered anyone for whom the interest was exclusive. Most of the affairs I'd had, love affairs, one-night stands, sexual friendships, had been as normal as such things can be expected to be, and that was never a matter of regret, on my part at least. The impulse to enter into a particular game only applies to some partners, just as there are some people with whom we enjoy having dinner, or going to the cinema.

Still, the choice of co-conspirator is crucial: what matters is to inhabit a space where hurting and harming are distinct events, a space where you cannot do to me what I would not have done to myself. It's simply more of a pleasure when you surprise me. There may be times when one player – one of the co-conspirators – causes the other pain, but that is not the point. There are times when one or the other appears to be 'in charge', but that isn't the point either. What matters is that these two – these *conspirators* – are making a game of the power that exists in every encounter. They acknowledge that power is part of the game they are playing, and instead of turning aside and pretending not to see, they make it into something graceful. At its best, this game is about transformation. At its worst, it becomes a gamble in which the stakes could be life and death. I didn't know that until I fell in love with Caroline. She was the one who fulfilled the promise of my early encounters with Sandra, a promise that had lived with me for decades, just beneath the surface, visible to anyone who could see the signs.

I met Caroline on the District and Circle Line late on a wet Friday evening: I had been to see a film, she was on her way home from a party. As it happened, I'd encountered her once before, in Oxford, but we hadn't talked. On that occasion, she had appeared to be biding her time with the tanned-blond, minor-public-school, wine-by-the-river, hot-air ballooning crowd that drifted from pub to pub making a lot of noise and drawing attention to themselves, but it was clear that she wasn't really with them. There was a distant, sardonic expression in her eyes when one of the blond beasts introduced her, a sense she gave out that she could have been anywhere that day, but she just happened to be there. I remembered how striking she was: around five eight, but taller-seeming; long dark hair bound in a tight plait; her eyes dark; her mouth darker. When we met again she was, if anything, even more striking: darker still, her hair and face damp from the rain, her eyes questioning. The way she looked at me, that night, was a warning: whatever else might happen, I was not to imagine that anything would be ordinary between us. Ordinary did not happen in her world.

Still, to begin with, our brief romance proceeded along fairly predictable lines. If at times a tension was there, a sense of other possibilities that excited and perturbed me, I had to wait a while before the extraordinary began to unfold. Nothing happened quickly, there was all the time in the world; it was only gradually that – with exemplary tact and grace – Caroline introduced brief moments and fleeting passages of tender, and infinitely suggestive, pain. From there we built to something that, in its own way, was a work of art, a shifting and uncertain story that we were telling one another as we went along. The game we were playing was, necessarily, one of tacit understandings and invented rules, a play of unspoken questions and careful interpretations of thought, word and deed. I'm really *not* talking about S&M here, or not the S&M of media caricature, all belts and chains and SS uniforms. This was plain-clothes stuff, the unadorned work of the imagination. There was some blood, there were negligible burns, but mostly the darker moments were played out in the realm of possibility. For a couple of months, we went on, inventing, unravelling, remaking the rules as we went. All we wanted was that *film noir* sense of acting out, in our everyday surroundings, the exquisite pleasure of the moment when the plot is figured out: climbing the stairs, as headlamps sweep through the house, or walking home in the rain after a party, we would stop to notice and admire the final twist, that one sweet betrayal that neither of us expected. This, I imagined, was all either of us wanted – the sweet hurt, the grace note of the unexpected gift – and, for a time,

I thought things would stay as they were, because there was no need to take things any further.

A day or so after I got my sister's call, I made the trip home. My father looked bad, and I guessed he wouldn't last much longer, but he hadn't died and that was the kind of thing that he took pride in. We didn't have much to say to one another. I played one part, he played another, in a scene straight from the basic script unit: working-class son, who has not made good, visits sick father, who tries not to see through working-class son's pretence of being better off than he is. We talked about the man who had died in the bed opposite earlier that day and, when we had nothing more to say to one another, I left, planning, but not promising, to visit the next evening. Afterwards, I took a bus over to Corby, where I went out drinking with some of the old crowd, but my heart wasn't in it and soon I drifted off, wandering around town like a lost tourist, a little dismayed by the knowledge that I had grown up there: that I had got drunk or stoned in *these* garages on lonely sunlit afternoons, that I had sat for hours in *this* tree, or stood for hours at *this* gate with a girl whose face I could still remember, talking about everything and nothing, while the snow fell around us like the snow in an old movie. *The Magnificent Ambersons*, maybe. Everything good that had ever happened had seemed so inasmuch as it resembled a scene in a book or a film. Everything else had been vivid and messy and unacceptable. *No wonder we lie*, I thought, as I wandered around the streets where my father had come closest to being at home. *We want life to be good*.

Then, all at once, I stopped walking and looked at myself in a shop window. I wanted to laugh out loud. What was I playing at? What fresh nonsense was this? I couldn't quite put my finger on it, but I felt like one of those characters you see in old sports movies, wandering about his home town the night after his great defeat, alone, disheartened, on the point of giving up. Finally, he comes to a stop and sees himself reflected in a shop window: a half-visible face, confused, hurt, but not quite defeated. He is lost, for the moment, but he is also curious, and ready – too ready – for the moment when the music starts behind him and he decides to go back, to try again, to fight another day. I didn't really fancy having, or even faking, that moment, but I did have a sense of being lost, of having been weighed down by something for too long. Not by my father, or rather, not by the man I had visited in the heart unit that afternoon. No: it was my own mistake, it was the little father in my own head that I had conspired with since I was old enough to talk, who had kept me bogged down. All my life, I had lived in his world: the things he had won, the things he had lost, the things he had been deprived of long before I even got there. It seemed, suddenly, that I couldn't bear the burden of his grief, or his blame, any longer. The next day, I went by the hospital, saw that he had other visitors, and used that as an excuse to hurry away, back to my vanishing act, and back to Caroline, who was just beginning to turn against me, for reasons that I never did figure out.

Our grand romance went sour very quickly. The first sign that something was wrong came on a wet night, a week or so after I got back from my *nostalgie de la boue* trip. We were walking back to her flat, and I was waiting for her to begin the conversation that she'd obviously been wanting to have all afternoon. I was thinking, from her manner, that she

279

wanted to call things off, because she'd got tired or scared, because she'd met someone else, because I wasn't large, or small, or clever, or dangerous enough for her. Instead, she told me that she was very ill: that nobody knew when, but sooner, rather than later, she was going to die. It had been raining, but now the rain had stopped, and the streets were glistening, wet with rain, the lights from the shops and the church on the corner reflecting on the wet pavements for yards ahead, as if we were walking on some shining, imaginary path. I stopped walking. In the church, a choir was singing, an extraordinary, layered sound that, for me, had to do with the pagan fabric of England, with yew trees and meadows and rain on the near hills, a sound as dark and miraculous as some old wood engraving. It was a perfect moment; it was even, in its way, exemplary – and it seemed strangely appropriate. Too appropriate, as if she had been waiting for the theatre of rain and light and song that it afforded. She said she had a disease that affected the blood and told me what it was called, but I didn't really hear, and I still can't recall what she said. I was stunned; yet she seemed very calm, almost content about it all.

'How long have you known this?' I asked. I felt dizzy, confused, unhappy – not because of what she had told me, but because I was beginning to realise, even then, that she was lying. I don't know how I knew, and I couldn't figure out what game she was playing, but I knew it was a serious, possibly ugly variation on the life we had already imagined for ourselves. At that moment, all I could see was a strange, theatrical shade of yellow in everything around me: the street, the rain, the shop windows, the lights of passing cars. It was recognisable as the yellow that might be found in a child's paintbox, but it was strangely faded, on the other side of colour, like the ghastly, jaundiced yellow that suffuses an animal just before it dies. At the same time, it occurred to me that there was no reason not to believe her. She'd always had that brightness, that other-worldly glamour you find in certain characters in old films, like the soldier who pulls out a snapshot in the trenches and shows it to the hero, saying, 'I never showed you a picture of my girl, did I?', or the woman who is doomed from the moment the boy genius, who is destined for other things, begins to fall for her. It was perfectly possible that, as she was saying at that very instant, she had kept the truth from me, not knowing how to tell it, maybe hoping that we could enjoy what time we had before the illness took her – and yet it wasn't possible at all, and I think it showed in my face, if only for a second, that I was unconvinced. A moment later, the necessary mask had slipped into place but, for that one second or two, she had seen, and I saw that she had seen, that I didn't believe a word of her story.

For a time, we continued as we had been, playing the game that, till then, had seemed so innocent and, at the same time, so graceful. For geographical reasons, we didn't see one another that often, so we should have been able to carry on for longer, before things began to seem stale, the game repetitive, the invention strained. That wasn't how it worked out, however: that deliberate and oddly pointless lie – which had gone nowhere, other than to introduce an air of mistrust into our affair – opened the door to a new sense of desperation, a need to go further, to take things beyond their logical limits. To begin with, what happened could be passed off as accidental; then, one Saturday night, I woke in her bed to find Caroline straddling me, her hands gripping my throat. In the eerie light from the street below, her face looked oddly determined, like the face of a child trying to complete some new task, but she wasn't about to kill me, and I knew, even as I twisted her off and rolled aside, gasping a little, but more or less unharmed, that she'd been trying out an idea, and hadn't really believed in her ability to see things through.

The next attack was far more competent, however. It came a couple of weeks after the half-hearted strangling: it was a Sunday morning and we were in Caroline's kitchen, making breakfast, not talking much, just enjoying the easy, slow feeling of being up and about a little later than the rest of the world, moving quietly around the kitchen, performing ordinary breakfast chores. There was a good bakery we used to visit on Saturdays, to pick up some of the dense, nutty wholemeal bread that was just right for thick wedges of buttered toast and those dark, sticky fruit spreads they used to sell in the grungey, grain and beeswax wholefood co-ops we both liked. Opening the cutlery drawer, Caroline had found the long, glittering blade of her best carving knife and, before she'd really formed a conscious intention, it was in her hand: that marvellous weight and balance, that miraculous gravitas of a good instrument, so lovingly made, so compelling in its logic. If I'd not turned around at the very moment I did, this beautiful knife would have lodged in a kidney, or between my ribs; but I did turn and, not altogether aware of what I was seeing or doing, I did fend her off and a moment that might have been — in her eyes, and possibly in mine — one of perfect, almost choreographed grace, ended up in a desperate grappling match, as we fell sideways against the counter and I wrestled the blade from her grasp. I was stronger, of course, and I had been lucky; and those two facts conspired, a moment later, to arouse in me the temptation — that gravity of the blade, that steely logic — to use the carving knife on her.

My choosing not to do so was both a victory for common sense and a terrible betrayal. I had no idea why Caroline had attacked me, but when she saw me hesitate, with the knife in my hand, a sudden contempt darkened her face. I could not see our little game through to its logical conclusion. I could not do what she might have done to me. I doubt, even now, that she'd wanted to kill me, as such. Killing me wasn't really the point. More likely, she was possessed by a desire for blood, a desire for the way into another, the deep cut, the irreversible pact of a wounding. It was a desire I understood, just as I understood the pact she had imagined between us, a union far more decisive, for her, than marriage could ever have been. Yet, even as I saw what was happening, I was also aware of wanting something else – and what I wanted was a separate, isolated state in which I would be forever intact, untouchable and unharmed, amidst the paraphernalia of my own erasure.

Afterwards, she wrote me a beautiful letter. I read it carefully, held it for a moment, then I took it to work and burned it on the great bonfire behind the garden stores. I wanted to go back – I almost did – but I knew that it was over, and I chose to stay away. Not because Caroline had tried to cut me open with a carving knife, but because she had tried and failed. When I left her flat that Sunday morning, walking out into the sunlight and the noise of London, I felt that I was giving up on something that could never be repeated. I know that sounds odd, but fear and desire so often coexist that they seem almost identical, and I knew I would never be able to play that game again. From that moment on, my sense of such things would be by proxy, the way a cinema audience can appreciate it, without really having to be aware of what they are conspiring with: that sense you get in later

Hitchcock films, say, or something by Nicholas Ray, or Jacques Tourneur, when you know things aren't meant to come out right in the end and, even if they do, you know that safety wasn't what mattered, it was that *frisson*, that sweet-bitter taste of *noir* that you wanted. This has nothing to do with the tragic, or the absurd; this is about desiring what you fear and fearing what you desire. This is about the *perverse*. For years afterwards, I would wake in the small hours and think I could hear someone – a woman, though not necessarily a *particular* woman – moving quietly about the lower rooms: going to the kitchen, finding a knife, then stopping to listen at the foot of the stairs, noticing some tiny shift, some change in the fabric of the house that was, in fact, my waking. She would pause a moment, then, waiting to see what might happen next – tense, lithe, radiant with anticipation, she would be, in these half-dreams, unaccountably beautiful – and for that split second before I was fully awake, I wanted to go down and meet her halfway, just so she could see that I hadn't forgotten her, that I had known, all along, that she was there.

Back in Cambridge, things got out of control again. I was living in a one-room bedsit, with a shared bathroom which I never used; the furniture comprised a bed, a wooden chair and a large, battered-looking wardrobe. After I left Caroline, I was alone and I closed up into that solitude like a spring flower closing against the dark. I called in sick to work, saying I'd be back in a couple of days, then I descended, one more time, into my own slow undercurrents. Technically, I imagine, I was suffering from paranoia: I conceived the notion that I was about to be attacked by some phantom who was roaming the streets of Cambridge searching for me, a phantom who was my not-quite-identical twin, the *je* to my *autre*, my own dark self and not myself at all. To protect myself against this imp, I collected bottles, which I then filled with river water, rain water, urine, milk tainted with drops of blue-black ink. It was a fortnight before they found me, but when they did, it was too late for even the most well-meaning intercession. I have no memory of being taken away, watched by the curious, politely concerned fellow tenant who'd found me, but it seems I'd spent days in my room, wrapped in a sheet, surrounded by several dozen bottles filled with various liquids, and covered in words and numbers that I had drawn on my skin with felt-tip markers. As a final, mysterious touch, someone – presumably myself – had laced green ribbons through my fingers again and again, binding my hands, rendering me powerless, beyond the possibility of touch. It took some time before I could be persuaded to part with these favours – and by the time I did, I was already swimming in the smoky underworld of chlorpromazine.

Something wonderful happened during my second stay at Fulbourn. On my first visit, I had wanted to be gone as quickly as possible: as soon as my body got accustomed to the drugs, I started trying to fake my way back to the farce in which I had been so caught up. Now, however, I was more engaged with what was happening: maybe the meds were stronger, maybe I was just more susceptible. Maybe it was just that there were no distractions this time around: no Cathy, no visitors, no desire for normality, no fear of falling off the edge of the social world. This time, there was a story.

As I remember it now – and my memory is at variance with the medical record, which means it is nothing if not suspect – I responded quickly to medication, but as soon as the drugs stabilised me, something new happened. I was, as I saw it, utterly lucid; but I wasn't back to normal: or rather, I wasn't back to the functional, everyday rationality that I had been trained to think of as lucid. After my first visit, I had left Fulbourn restored to that rudimentary lucidity: able to function, as long as I kept taking the pills; more or less well adjusted, as they say in old films; capable of making my way in the outside world without too much fuss and mess. This time, however, it was different. This time, I was super-lucid. Hyper-lucid. I could see everything. I understood *every-thing*. One morning, when I emerged from what the official record calls the 'psychotic' stage, I realised that I could see with *perfect* clarity; or rather, I was able to give everything I saw its due: the window, the chair, the tree in the grounds, that one cloud in the sky.

The turning point came when I was sitting in the day room one morning. There was a vase of tulips on the table, and I was gazing at them, trying to work out exactly what they were. I knew they were tulips, of course, but I also sensed that they were something else, fields of energy, fields of colour, and I was trying to descry in them that otherness, that perfect, Platonic form they embodied. It was mid-morning, some time after breakfast, and I was alone in the day room – or, rather, I was alone but for these tulips, and the light that, falling through the window behind me, suddenly changed. Not so very much, really, but enough for the colours of the flowers to change: lemon, to butter-coloured, to a sudden translucent gold. It was breathtaking. Things were changing all the time, pulsing, and I could see it, I could feel it, just the way it felt on acid, only steadier, less feverish, better tuned. I knew this was significant, but I couldn't have said why – and then I saw that the world itself was an unbreakable secret, not just because I couldn't have put into words what I was seeing at that moment, but also because, even if I had the words, nobody would understand what it was that I wanted to say. Another person could experience this for himself, but I couldn't have told him about it. It was like acid; or rather, it was like acid *without* acid.

Then, quietly, with no great fanfare, it occurred to me that I'd finally become invisible. I had, in fact, been invisible for some time: not altogether, of course, there was something in the world that people could still see, but what they didn't see was the self I was, the self that *sees*, the self that sees *them*. I was invisible – but I hadn't got that way by being mad, or ill, or whatever the social world wanted to call me. I had become invisible just by being there, isolated in that dark garden. I had achieved the Limbo state merely by being prepared for it: I had entered another space, and it would have been perfectly possible to stay there for ever. Not, perhaps, in that place as such, but the choice was there, nonetheless. I could go back to the outside world, or I could pass years in these bright parentheses, learning the etiquette of invisibility till some new life was awakened in my body, some new energy that might begin at the base of the spine, or behind the eyes, or in the quick of the fingernails, a quick within the quick, a life within the life. I was in Limbo, but I wasn't in some strange, altered state. My Limbo was the long corridor to the front door at evening, the view of the great cedar tree in the grounds, the still of the night when I could get up and wander about, or sit in the day room in the blessed absence of television. It was the anonymity of the walls; the wide space of the refectory; the smell of rain on the windows. On my first visit, I had been painfully aware of the other guests; now, I barely noticed them, and the nurses were the merest phantoms, dressed in civilian clothes and, so, almost indistinguishable from their charges, except when they came, at the appointed hours, to dispense the benedictions of Heminevrin and Largactil. Before, I had been intent on *getting well*; now, I had entered the stillest possible world, a world where everything came into view slowly, perfectly, all the good objects surfacing, as if from a sleep, into the light. On my last visit to Fulbourn I'd been too lost, too desperate to get back to the fray of the outside world to see its possibilities. I'd also been distracted, once I'd emerged from the week-long nightmare of *Atropa belladonna*, by the desire to prove myself sane. Now, I didn't care about that: I was beyond human concerns, out in a world of glass and darkness and rain, the world I had always inhabited in my imagination. In heaven, they might dine on ambrosia, or manna, or some other pure substance; in Limbo, I could switch back and forth between Largactil and acid: perfect stillness alternating with endless vibrancy; *sub specie aeternitatis* with forensic detail; Buddhic detachment with monotheist passion. Fullness, pleroma, satori. Chemically induced, of course, but satori nonetheless.

Looking back, I think I came much closer to making myself at home in that artificial Limbo than I realised, once the story was over. I call it a story because, from here on in, everything is narrative: a delusion, in conventional terms, but for me a story, a series of imagined, vividly real moments. As I walked away from Fulbourn after that second, and final, stay, I remembered a time, long before, of walking in a gas-coloured light at the edge of a wide estuary somewhere, and hearing, out across the water, an enormous commotion of geese, moving towards me. Hearing them first, then seeing them: a thick wave of muscle and plumage; flecked, insistent wings and dark, smooth heads surging onwards, wave after wave, including me somehow in their flight, so I felt they would carry me with them, felt that I could almost have burst with joy at their sheer sense of purpose, surging onward for no reason, other than the thrill of the air and the imperative of their migratory blood. That day, on the road back to the city, I knew I would never allow myself to be taken in again. I had nowhere to go, but I had people who would help me – and I had a plan. I was tired of the life I had been living; I was tired of the drugs and the parties; I was tired of the road of excess; I was tired of living at the edge all the time, trying not to fall away into the dark. Most of all, I was tired of *self*. The doctors hadn't been altogether convinced I was ready to leave, but they had never had any real power over me; I hadn't been committed, and I could go any time I chose. So I chose. They were good enough to send me off with an ample supply of medication, and some kind words along with the inevitable warnings – and I was on my way, armed with a pocketful of normality and a whole set of good intentions. I didn't care where I ended up, and I didn't care what I had to do, but I did have a plan, however tentative. To put that plan into action, I needed somewhere new to hide and, given the situation, there was only one thing to do. It was time to go to Surbiton.

For several weeks, I drifted, ending up in Surrey, where I found a job as a dogsbody in a retirement village near Cranleigh. Not exactly Surbiton, but close enough and, to begin with, this was exactly what I wanted. It was my job to keep the grounds neat, maintain the perimeter fencing, mow the lawns and trim the hedges. I was the one who went out in the cold to dig spent mushroom compost into the shrub beds or spread a mulch of chipped bark on the borders. It was all outdoor work, and it had mostly to do with the gardens. Once a week I had to drive a mini-tractor and trailer around the village, collecting the garbage. This was a dull job and, because it brought me into more regular contact with the appalling Supervisor of Outdoor Maintenance, an ex-services type called Graham, one I would have preferred to do without. The only time it engaged me was on those few occasions when one of the residents had died. Not surprisingly, this happened fairly often, and it was the job of the Supervisor of Indoor Services – a hatchet-faced little woman named Alice – to ensure that the decedent's personal effects were disposed of. Sometimes family would come and retrieve anything of monetary or sentimental value; what was left after they had gone was dumped in the miniature garage or shed that abutted each dwelling, for me to bag up and take away.

I enjoyed this job. It was eerie, and strangely pleasurable, handling the ephemera and junk that had accumulated over a stranger's lifetime. Most of what I took to the dump was fairly predictable stuff: mildewed books, empty journals, half-finished toiletries from decades past, unwanted clothes, boxes of old magazines or knitting patterns, cheap ornaments and souvenirs from holidays in Spain or Holland, objects no longer useful, broken possessions, things too worn or too pathetic to keep – but that was exactly what I enjoyed about the work. There was a history in all this junk, a secret history of moments and afternoons, a history more intimate and more expressive than the enduring narratives of years and decades. The obituaries in local newspapers told what these people had been, but the knick-knacks and empty bottles they left behind in death told what they had wanted to be. One afternoon in the late fifties, Mr Alfred Gilmour, a gaunt, scare-faced old man who lived by himself at the far edge of the village, had gone to see a play – one of many, perhaps, or perhaps for the first and the last time – and he had been so moved, or inspired by what he saw, that he kept the programme, folded neatly into a book on salmon fishing, till the day he died. Perhaps he had gone to the theatre with a special friend, or a lover; perhaps he had gone on his own and fallen in love with the actress. It didn't matter: what mattered, to me, was how a few sheets of paper suggested, in their faded, violet beauty, another version of time than the one history imposed, something forensic, something almost homeopathic.

When I had to clear out a dead resident's garage, I always made sure I had time to do the task well. I picked through the relics of each life carefully, but I never took anything away (I was too superstitious, I think, for that), and I always bagged things up with an undertaker's reverence, not for the person who had passed away, but as a gesture of respect for lost time. Yet as I worked, at the back of my mind, I was thinking of my father. Somewhere in all this junk, I half hoped I would find a clue to the keepsake or talisman he would have held on to for half a century, had he lived as these people had. I'm not sure how much of this I recognise after the fact, but I look back now and think that, at the time, I knew I had lost my father – whatever I thought my father had been – and the only way I could bring him back was by this process of sorting and honouring and bagging up somebody else's junk. If I couldn't have my own father, I could, perhaps, distil from the possessions of these many fathers a kind of essence: an abstraction gradually made flesh, a creature of my own invention. A homunculus I could take away and seal up in my imagination, where nobody else could see him, beyond the terms of ordinary logic, and so beyond any possibility of denial.

There is a hummingbird that lives in the cold deserts of Chile and Peru, a tiny, jewelled bird that, every night, when the temperature plunges to below freezing, settles into some half-sheltered spot, some angle of cactus branch, say, and allows itself to die a little, slowing its metabolism till only the heart and the liver still function. Through the dark hours, it sits, ice-cold, immobile; then, when the sun returns, it comes back to life and begins, once again, to flit from cactus to cactus, sipping the sweet nectar. There are worms that live in glaciers, whole lifetimes and generations unfolding in ice, birds that settle on freezing lakes at nightfall and wait, locked in and vulnerable to predators, till morning comes – and there are men who live as I lived then, locked down for weeks or months at a time, only ever coming up for little sips of air, tiny flickers and glimpses of starlight in the long darkness. It suited me, then; and, in modified form, I can see it becoming necessary again, at certain times in this life, an almost Darwinian adaptation, a calculated strategy for survival. It wasn't Limbo, it wasn't even Surbiton, but it was close. I couldn't think of anywhere better to disappear and forget everything that had mattered to me in the past: friends, lovers, enemies, people who thought they knew me, people who thought I owed them, people I owed, people who owed me, helpers and dealers, buyers and sellers. I had been playing for too long and, in the process, I had forgotten what it was I really loved. I'd been sold a very elaborate lie; what I needed to do was practise my new-found invisibility. Draw water, chop logs. Breathe. Say nothing.

This is where I was when I got the news that my father had died. It was my day off and I'd fallen asleep in the afternoon, only waking as it grew dark, chill and befuddled, with that odd, dislocated sense of being in a strange and mysterious place, even if it was the room I inhabited every day, a place where anything could happen. I'd raised myself from the chair where I'd drifted off over a book, and been drawn to the window by that first impulse of every daytime sleeper: the desire to see that the world is still there, where you left it. What I saw was the street I always saw, the parked cars, the hedges, the one street lamp; but around this pale light, flying in an irregular and utterly unpredictable orbit, a bat was describing wide circles, feeding, no doubt, on the tiny insects that gathered there, drawn to the illusory warmth of the lamp. I don't know, now, why this solitary bat struck me as so poignant; I don't know what notion or possibility it represented, but it did seem important, and I stayed a while, to watch, to wait for whatever it was telling me to *register*. I thought it had something to do with the way I was living, something to do with solitude and nourishment and belonging to a wider world, but the thought escaped me and, at that moment, the telephone rang. I didn't want to answer, and I considered letting it go. It was late, I thought, but there was still time to walk down to the railway cutting and taste the cool night air. I often ignored the phone, and I don't know why I was prompted to pick it up on this particular occasion, but I did and, over the next few minutes, as I watched the bat circle in the yellowish light, I listened, responding where necessary, while Margaret told me that my father had died of a heart attack, his fourth and last, the one he had been expecting for so long. When I put the phone down, the bat was gone too, and I had to smile at the thought that crossed my mind: an absurd notion, but one I entertained for several seconds, not just that night, but during the days and nights that followed, sometimes for minutes at a time, like those foolish anecdotes that surround any death, a story that is pleasant in the telling yet, even as it is recounted, is obviously neither fact nor falsehood, simply an anecdote, a fanciful tale that could just as easily have been left untold.

CHAPTER 10

I wake in the dark. Something has just dropped off the end of the bed and landed softly, its claws – the whisper of claws is unmistakable, even if it is the sound of two feet landing, not four – its hard, bright claws retracted for the moment as it skitters away across the wooden floor; and I'm suddenly alert, picking up the ghost figures of silver light on the wall, the grey-blue shadows in the mirror, the bird shapes that shiver across the ceiling. I'm scanning for movement, or some deliberate stillness, something animal in the room, something animal and, at the same time, human, or human-seeming, a living blackness, an attentive shape that ought not to be there. For a minute or more this is fear in its purest form, not anxiety or concern, not the ordinary care of the daylight hours, but ancient, blood-level, irrational, utterly compelling fear. I wonder, sometimes, if animals ever feel it, when they lie down in a familiar place, safe from the weather, safe from predators. Do animals experience terror? Do they wake in the dark from cruel nightmares, believing they have screamed or called out, then lie still for minutes, amazed at the silence? I think of myself as a person without phobias: spiders, open spaces, snakes, water, bats – I am indifferent, or slightly attracted to them all. I am not afraid of death. I have no particular terror or dread I could talk about in the daytime; yet I have this:

the nightmare, the waking, these blood-begotten spirits.

They are not long, these terrors by night. After a minute or so, I am shaking my head, dismissing the phantom, half remembering a dream to explain it all away – but I'll know, too, that I'm being dishonest with myself, that the apparition comes too often not to have some real existence, here in this room, here in my body and mind, and, deeper and older than I am myself, in my blood and nerves, in memory and fore-boding. It's something imagined and something real: the two are not exclusive. It's my fear, is the easiest way to describe it, but it's my excitement too. It's thrilling; it's alive; it's a form of energy I cannot help but recognise as both alien and mine. I've sometimes pictured this phantom – which is always the same, as true and continuous as I am, ageing with me, learning new tricks, becoming darker and more solid as I become darker and more solid – but I cannot fix it long enough to see it whole. All I am left with is the impression of some lithe thing, some creature more malevolent and, at the same time, more innocent than I had expected, half-human, half-animal, a smile hidden in its face, its whole being shaped and drawn from blackness. I do not know what this phantom wants, or whether it even wants anything at all. I do not know if it means me harm, or is the angel of some annunciation that I cannot quite bring myself to accept. I know nothing about it, other than these fleeting impressions, yet I think – or rather, I have convinced myself – that I remember exactly when it was born. No doubt it existed in some embryonic form before I found it and gave it presence, but it was born, it came into being for me, one wet Saturday morning in Crosshill.

That morning my father said something that stayed with me for years, for no good reason, or none that I could think of.

We were standing in a bus shelter, on one of our visits home: I was eleven, maybe twelve, and wishing I didn't have to go back to Corby; my father was sober, which meant he was in a dark mood, unhappy as he always was in the vicinity of his in-laws, who — as he saw it, and probably in their own hearts — judged him harshly and found him wanting. By then, I was as used to my father's dark and unhappy moods as I was to his drink-fuelled mania, but that day something was different. He was sad, preoccupied, even a little tender, as if he was concerned for me, as if it had suddenly struck him that I was actually there, as alive and as capable of suffering as he was. I don't know what could have prompted that recognition in him, and I don't remember where my mother and Margaret were that day. All I know is that we were alone, and it was raining that slow summer rain I'd known all my life, a warm sooty smoor of it on my face and hair as I ducked into the shelter with this difficult, silent man, so unlike the one I usually knew and feared. It was like being abandoned suddenly to the tender mercies of a complete stranger.

The shelter was one of those old-fashioned concrete-and-metal affairs with a flat tin roof and tiny panes of reinforced glass. I still see them from time to time on run-down estates, or out on remote country roads, standing empty in the sun like derelict cages, the glass clouding with rust, the cold walls plastered with graffiti. I don't recall where we had just been, or where we were going, but I do remember that we'd recently heard of the death of a family friend, not quite a relative, but someone my father must have liked. It was hard to know, then, about liking: men didn't show affection in ways that a child could understand; affection, where it existed, was a matter of hints and allusions, all mysterious glimmer and jokey insult, subtle and fleeting and always at risk from sudden outbursts of random anger. Or so it seemed to me, growing up among these dangerous creatures, navigating my way by guesswork through the world of men whose very presence was both a threat and a wonder. The man who had died, a surly but likeable giant called Wullie McFee, had been one of these beautiful monsters, sharp-tongued and cruelly funny among men, but always ready, when women and children were present, with a half-mocking, half-friendly half-smile that I always found reassuring. He had worked underground at the pits all his life, but I remember him as being retired, sitting in the club with my father and his friends, or walking along the high street in Cowdenbeath, strangely awkward and exposed in the ordinary light of day, among ordinary people and objects, like Gulliver in Lilliput. Not long after we had moved south, Wullie had become ill. We had heard about it, along with all the usual news from home, a Christmas or so back, but there had been no further word, and I suppose my father had assumed that no news was good news. As it turned out, Wullie's illness had been much more serious than he had pretended to his friends, to his children, even to his wife. No doubt he had decided, as men often do when they are sick, that such weakness was not allowed. Maybe he had decided to ignore the thing, hoping it would go away of its own accord. Or maybe he had sat in the surgery, one damp autumn after-noon, nodding softly, his mouth set, listening to the doctor's pronouncements and thinking – as all of us had been taught to think – that this was how the world was, birth and work and death and, in my mother's words, *what's for ye will not go by ye*.

There were precious few secrets in that little coal-mining community. People knew one another's business, a man's fate was written in his face, the old folk looked at a ten-year-old boy and saw his life unfolding like a recipe from some well-kent cookbook: school for a few more years, work at the pit, marriage, children the spit of himself and his wife, old age, death, erasure. The chief pleasure of the place, for men and women alike, was the knowing, the sense of *what can ye expect for folk like us*, the gossip they exchanged in grim, satisfied huddles at the club, or round at the drying green, a long narrative of pretension and comeuppance, of hope, or ambition, or blind desperation and the quiet, inevitable falls that followed. The worst offence, for those people, was the keeping of a secret, yet secrets there were, and one of those secrets, till the darkness in his face gave him away, was Wullie McFee's illness. I barely knew the man, but I remember his eyes, and his queer smile, and I think he enjoyed it, in some secret chamber of his being, that he alone knew what was coming, that he had something to think about, something to hold in his mind, something to study and wonder at and raise to the light, like a fragment of stained glass that nobody else could see. He was probably afraid, too, and he probably worried about those he would leave behind, but I'd like to think that this secret was precious to him: that, in a life which had belonged mostly to others, his death had been his own, for a while at least.

Naturally, people would have guessed towards the end. Still, it had come as a surprise, one Wednesday afternoon in the early summer, when Wullie had died, sitting upstairs on the bus to Dunfermline, his cigarette sliding from his fingers and burning a hole in the seat, his dwindled body sliding sideways and down, while two girls from the Co-op watched, not quite knowing what to do as the bus rolled on, then finally ringing the bell madly, five, ten, who knows how many times, till the bus came to an unscheduled stop. The conductor had come upstairs then, followed by a gaggle of curious passengers, some of them neighbours of Wullie's, none of them complete strangers, and I can imagine, now, that Wullie was still there for a minute or so, or maybe longer, while they discussed what to do. Maybe someone loosened his tie, or rolled up a raincoat to stuff under his head while someone – one of the girls, or a keen boy on his way to football practice – ran to fetch help. It was too late, of course, and most of them probably knew that, but they had to do what people did in such situations, and I can imagine Wullie acknowledging that fact, as he slipped away, with something in his head that he wanted to say, and nobody there that he wanted to say it to, or some detail of this life, some wisp of scent, some trick of the light, glowing like an ember in his fading consciousness.

'If there's one thing I couldn't stand,' my father had said, after he had taken in the news, 'it would be that. Dying on a bus, in public. Dying with strangers gawping at you, down on the floor, with some complete stranger poking at you – '

Twenty years later, on his way to the cigarette machine in the Silver Band Club, he suffered his fourth heart attack and died where he fell, with two of his mates, neither of them anywhere near sober, peering down into his face as it turned grey and – in the words of one of his drinking pals, who told me all about it at the funeral – he went out like a light, the life dimmed, the mouth slackened. I have seen three men die in my life and I am grateful I wasn't there when it was my father's turn. When I'd gone to visit him after his third attack, there had been something about his fear – the fear of dying, of course, but also the fear of dying among strangers, in a hospital ward – that made me feel twelve years old again. That fear in my father's eyes brought back a sudden and quite unexpected grief, a grief I had felt years before, and managed to forget, grief for a lost demigod, grief for the beautiful and inexplicably tragic figure he had sometimes cut in my child's world, sitting at family funerals and weddings with the other men, a dark, bruised presence, shrouded in whisky and smoke. I remembered him, for a moment, as a person of simple pleasures: I recalled his fondness for the newly opened pack of Kensitas, I remembered the glitter on that skin of tobacco scent and foil that he stripped away as he drew out the first smoke, a faint glimmer blowing away in the wind, or sculpted into a child's fleeting trinket, later on, his tar-stained fingers shaping frogs or butterflies from silver foil and a trace of whisky. The cellophane would glimmer in the fire, a ghost of matter, blue along the snaking tear-strip, but the pack itself he cradled to his inner pocket, where it perched, birdlike and still. I remember loving the way he tapped out a cigarette with one brisk movement, then lit it with a match from nowhere, smoke appearing like the dead in those old photographs of spirit mediums, ghosts of woodbine conjured from the air. In the evenings, after he had gone out, my mother sometimes left the doors and windows standing open for an hour or longer, long enough for frost to settle on a candlewick bedspread, or the kitchen table, the cold kiss of it on my spiced fingertips perfect and chill, like the moment in the Annunciation story when Mary lifts her head and the angel is there, his wings flexed, his purpose suddenly revealed. Back then, I think, there were days when I imagined my father was immortal.

Then, suddenly, he was small and afraid, and I felt a twelve-year-old's helplessness as he described how he had wakened in the small hours and watched the man in the opposite bed die, unseen, unnoticed, in a strange place, fading out in his own private world, unaware – at the last – that my father was watching from eight feet away. 'But what if he did know?' my father had said. 'What if he could see me watching him? I'd never even spoken to the boy, and there he was, dying right in front of my eyes.'

'Didn't you call for someone?' I asked him.

My father shook his head. 'He was dying,' he said. 'I could see that. Let the boy go in peace, I say.'

'They might have been able to save him,' I ventured.

My father pursed his lips and looked away. It was late afternoon, an unseasonably cold, wet day. The window was freckled with rain and touched with a sulphury light from the parking bay below. 'For what?' he asked, finally. His voice was quiet, buried deep in his chest, as if it was something he wanted to keep to himself, something he begrudged me. 'Anyway,' he continued, after a moment, 'whatever else happens, don't let me go like that. When my time comes.'

I nodded. Maybe that was when I felt like a twelve-year-old all over again, quietly forced into making a promise I couldn't keep. A promise nobody could keep. As it happened, he ended up dying in a public place, and I know he would have hated it, but there was nothing I could have done to prevent that. All I can think is, at least he was among friends, that, in a place like Corby, it could have been worse. I once saw a man die from blood loss on the steps of a pub. He had been stabbed in the neck as he emerged from the Maple Leaf, about a minute before a friend and I pushed open the door to leave: when we found him, he was on the ground, the blood already pooling around him, black and dark-smelling on the night air, and immediately my friend was clutching at my sleeve, telling me we should go, that we shouldn't get involved. I knew that made sense – our pockets were full of acid and grass – but I lingered a moment, against my will, half drunk, curious, touched. The look in that man's eyes was a combination of panic – he knew he was going, and he knew nobody could help him – and dismay that he could be dying like this, a door swinging open in his face and two men he didn't know stopped in their tracks, looking down, then stepping, not quite over, but by him, and hurrying away. My father was lucky not to die like that: the half-drunk faces peering into his after he hit the floor were at least faces he recognised, and by the time a crowd had gathered – so his mates told me – he was long gone.

This is the problem with death: we always imagine dying alone. We forget that, almost certainly, other things will be going on when we make our exit – that, in all likelihood, death, like everything else, takes place, as Auden says, 'while someone else is eating or opening a window or just walking dully along'. It's a fortunate corpse that flickers out when the world's back is turned and, though animals are supposed to find private corners and crannies to die in, most of us have to be prepared for company at the end – and the company of strangers at that. Perhaps this idea horrified my father because, all his life, he had kept strangers at bay, one way or another, with his 'wee stories', as my mother called them, though she had always known they were outright, and often utterly absurd, lies. I suppose even he knew that death was the one occasion he couldn't lie his way out of.

That morning in Crosshill, then, he was thinking about Wullie McFee, and about himself. Thinking about the ignominy of dying on a bus, with strangers gawping into your face, stealing your last breath and tainting it with grease and smoke and cheap perfume – but for my father, Wullie's death was the sign of some greater insult. By that summer's morning, I think, he was ready to feel Wullie's helplessness so keenly because he was just beginning to see how helpless he had become. He hadn't gone to Corby to start a new life, he had gone because there was nowhere else to go. After his accident, my mother hadn't wanted him to work on the building any more, and I think he too had been frightened, in spite of himself: frightened by the way his face changed while he was lying in the hospital and frightened by the sheer random force of events that could take a man like him, a man who had stood proud and intact in his own skin for forty years, never once doubting that, physically at least, he was invincible, and alter him overnight into the broken, bewildered creature he had been on the ward. Physical integrity was all he had: his mind wasn't his own, his history was mostly fake, but he did have his body – to work, to swim, to fight, to drink, to hoist a child high into the air and see its scared, excited face gazing down at him. Now that body had been called into question and he'd been obliged to begin again, to wipe the slate clean, to test himself in new surroundings, coming in from the open air, where he had always worked, to the closed heat and racket of the steelworks. How galling it must have been, when the new start that had cost him so much made no difference to his family, that nobody wanted the Corporation house on Handcross Court, or the leatherette three-piece suite in the front room, or the television and radiogram he bought with his compensation money. How galling to think that they would rather have stayed at home, in Crosshill or Cowdenbeath, back where they started.

This is hindsight, of course, but I believe he was thinking of all these things, of Wullie's death, of his fragility, of the death that was waiting for him, like an old mate, down at the bookies, or on the next street corner, and I believe he was thinking about – or rather, not thinking, but feeling, enduring in its rawest form – the ordinary and seemingly inevitable failure into which he had fallen when, all of a sudden, standing in that dreary concrete bus shelter, he raised his fist and smashed one of the reinforced window panes, scattering slivers and pearls of glass over the concrete floor while I stood watching, horrified, suddenly afraid. He smashed one, then another, then another, only pausing for a moment to give me a twisted, oddly quizzical look, as if he was just as surprised as I was – surprised, but pleased too, as he continued to work, smashing one pane after another, his knuckles bleeding now and crusted with broken glass. I had been afraid of my father before that day, but it had always been an indoors affair, a hidden, secret, forgettable terror that lasted through one drunken night and melted away the next morning. I had seen blackness in my father's face, but it had been a local event, a mood, a passing phenomenon. But that morning, it was different. For the first time, I realised that he wasn't just afraid of death, in the usual way, he was *terrified*. At times, his terror infused him with rage and panic, and he didn't know what to do with himself. I think there must have been times when he wanted to die, just to be free of that almighty fear. Most of the time, though, his fear sat inside his head, a dark, ugly spirit, watching, waiting. I couldn't help thinking, when Margaret called to tell me that he had died, that it was finally gone now, that he wasn't afraid any more. And I couldn't help thinking that a little piece of tainted, fearful blackness had disappeared from my life.

The time comes when each of us sees a blackness in the world: a black in the green of leaf and river, a black in the light of noon, a blackness in the gaze of an animal encountered some early morning in the summer grass. There is a blackness in everything that is, a darkness that is hard to see, more often than not, a blackness that is not only necessary, but also for the best. *For the best.* It's a phrase my grandfather was fond of using, but he used it, not to mean good, or right, or anything else that had to do with human judgement, but as the token of a way of being, a way of accepting what life did that never crumbled into resignation, a way of knowing the difference between submission and surrender. My grandfather saw the black in things and in himself too, and he stood back from it, stood away, holding it at arm's length, the better to see it. He had also been damaged: like my father, he'd been smashed up in an accident at work – in his case, the collapse of a shaft in the pit – but he'd come through it with more resolve, maybe because his body mattered less to him than his faith. The hurt he had suffered, and the changes he'd been obliged to make as a result, had made him stronger, more compassionate and, at the same time, quieter in himself. At family events, at christenings and weddings and funerals, he might sometimes sit off by himself, a still, unmoving phenomenon, but still the way a pond in the woods is still, a not altogether solid thing that was as much potential as it was presence. I liked to loiter just outside his orbit, waiting to be called in, to be questioned in that soft, coal-dark voice he had, a voice that took itself seriously, but was never solemn or self-conscious. Towards the end, when it was an effort for him to get out of the house at all, he would sit in his chair and watch as the children he had raised, and their children in turn, pursued the life he had more or less relinquished, but when he spoke, his voice was still alive, still vivid, still rich with the black of the earth he had dug and the raw gold of his known history. Not that he ever said anything particularly wise or revealing. He was a man of simple faith, as the priests used to say, a man set in his own beliefs and ways. He had nothing to say, in words; all he possessed, by then, was that dark, live voice, an insinuation in it of knowledge he could never have told, but knew beyond question in his blood and in his bones. Part of that knowledge was light – the light off snow at Christmas, the light of church candles, the pale bronze light of the upper room where he had clumsily tended his wife in her dying – but the rest, I think, was composed of blackness: the blackness in himself, the blackness he had seen in the far reaches of the pits, the blackness of pain and the ordinary fears of the deprived and, beyond all that, the abstract blackness of the world, a blackness he had touched, a blackness he had recognised as kith and kin, a blackness he had held at arm's length long enough to accommodate it. He was just a working man from Crosshill, a man like his neighbours who had brought up a family on next to nothing, a man who had aged quickly and watched his wife die by degrees in their narrow house, but that soft, dark glow in his voice spoke of something else which, though it was far more complicated than what we usually think of when we use the word, had a definite undertone of victory.

My father's blackness was different – and that morning, I saw it for the first time. Where my grandfather had held it out and away, the better to control it, my father took it in, like some brother he would rather have done without, but could not turn from his door. He knew he was afflicted, and had decided to relish the affliction. He made it a piece of himself, a distinguishing feature, but it wasn't his to own and, over the years, it came to possess him. That morning was the first time I recognised it for what it was and, though I couldn't have told what I had seen, I knew. I had seen the blackness in things before, out in the fields, in the eyes of a rat draped in a thorn bush, or the hollowed faces of dead lambs; I had seen it in Mr Kirk's hen house after the fox had got in; I had seen it in ponds dense with frogs' spawn and in the black shadows of ivy and, once, in the black silt of the leech-infested loch where Stewart Banks and I had swum one bright afternoon, I had gazed down through the lit water at a black that had to do with time and erosion and forces that were indifferent to all human concerns. Finally, that morning, as my father stood smashing those panes of glass one after another with his reddening fist, I saw the darkness in him and I realised it was continuous, running from field to field, from hedge to hedge, from street to street and in, through the town, to the closed rooms where we ate and slept. Continuous, in the life of everything, and continuous from blood to blood, from him to me, an inescapable fact of existence. His darkness is also mine, or rather, it belongs to nobody. It takes up residence where it can – perhaps where it will – and from that point on, all we can do is try to manage it.

Nowadays, I will turn sometimes and find that same blackness staring back at me from a night-time window, or a half-lit mirror. There are days when that dark face is something I can think of as a friend – a primal energy that carries me forward when nothing else will – but more often than not I am face to face with a stranger, a companion to something I recognise as myself, sure enough, but one who knows more than I do, thinks less of danger and propriety than I ever have or will, feels a cool and amused contempt for the rules and rituals by which I live, the duties I too readily accept, the compromises I too willingly allow. *We make our meek adjustments* – but there is always a dark buzz in the soul that despises any and all adjustments, a careless, erotic energy that wants to break every rule and simply be. This is the creature that rises from my bed in the night and sits there watching, waiting to be realised. When I wake, it drops to the floor and skitters away, dwindling as it goes, fading away into shadows and murmurs, a creature of the night only because I refuse to allow it a daytime existence, I who am a man, in the ordinary and fearful business of living in the world, and keeping my true self hidden. Part of this daytime enterprise is the tissue of lies by which I construct a visible self. Sometimes the lies are authorised, the textbook lies of citizenship and masculinity and employment we are all obliged to tell. Occasionally, they are the lies that reveal the unofficial version of the self, the truth of being. My father was searching for a lie of that calibre all his life. I think he expected to say something, one fine day, and everything would just slip into place: who he was, where he belonged, what was good about his soul. To my knowledge, it never happened. Or maybe it did, and he never realised. Maybe he told the perfect lie, the one that showed him what he really was, just minutes before he stood up, at the Silver Band Club, and walked off to the cigarette machine, half-cut, a little dizzy, and wholly oblivious to the significance of what he had just revealed to a ragtag gathering of old friends and familiar strangers.

CHAPTER 11

By the time I got to Corby, he was safely stowed away at the funeral home. Margaret met me, and drove me to the house, which was even more bare than I remembered: the tea service that my mother had kept intact for so long had vanished over the years; all her clothes, and most of his, had been given away, or burned; the kitchen was empty, my old room was empty, the piano was long gone, my father's room was reduced to a bed and a wardrobe. I wondered what had happened to the things my mother had treasured: the toiletries and knick-knacks on her dressing table; the ornaments that had lined the mantelpiece; the little chiming clock she had won in some raffle – all the objects she had coveted and calculated for and handled with such care. Had they vanished by the usual mysterious processes of time and tide, or had my father disposed of them deliberately? I had visions of him coming home drunk and smashing the little figurines, cascading crockery on to the kitchen floor, pouring old perfume down the sink in the bathroom. More likely, though, these things had just got broken or lost through carelessness.

Before we left, Margaret handed me a package. 'It's not much,' she said. 'All I could find, really.'

I opened it up. It was my father's wristwatch. I stared at it, not knowing what to say.

'At least it's something to remember him by,' she said.

I smiled. 'Thanks,' I said. I didn't say, though we both knew, that I had no desire to remember him.

'He didn't make a will,' she continued. 'So it'll be a while before the money gets sorted out.'

'There's *money?*'

She laughed. 'Yes,' she said. 'Not much, I suppose. About three thousand.'

'Well, that's a surprise,' I said. 'I'd have thought the Hazel Tree would have had it all by now.' I slipped the watch into my pocket. 'Anyhow, I don't want his money. You did all the work. It should go to you.'

'We'll see,' she said. She patted me on the arm. 'I told you he's to be cremated, didn't I?' She seemed anxious. Maybe she thought there was enough Catholic left in me to be upset by his decision.

'If that's what he wanted,' I said.

'Mum wouldn't have liked it,' she continued.

'No.' Thinking about it now, I didn't like it myself. Not because I was troubled by some vestigial Catholic scruple, but because I saw it for what it was: a final gesture of self-disgust, the last defiant act of a man who wanted to be reduced to nothing, to be erased. Ashes to ashes: I had always despised that saying. Living things are wet, dark, mineral, silty. I would have given my body to the earth, to feed insects and plants, the worms, the grass. Someone else might have seen the fire as cleansing but he saw it, I knew, as a removal. At the same time, it was a parting shot at my mother's faith, and so, by extension, her family. A sad little act of revenge on people who would not be there to see it.

*

311

The funeral was surprisingly well attended. It was also a shambles. As soon as the formalities were done with, my father's cronies took over, and the proceedings moved to the Silver Band Club – to the very place where he had died. This was too much for Margaret, but – for no good reason, or none I can think of – I tagged along with Nat and Mull and the others, a party of dour Scotsmen heading for the bar with a perfect excuse to get totally hammered. Two hours later, one of our number, a spare, pale-lipped individual named Billy, was slumped in a corner seat, while the rest of the gang gabbed at me. They had the air of men on a mission, like crazed evangelists out to bring a stray soul back into the fold – which would have been fine, but the stray they had in their sights was me, and I had no desire to be saved. I'd had less to drink than most of them but I was definitely warmed up, and the more warmed up I got, the more convinced I was that tagging along had been a big mistake. When they talked about the man we had just burned, I had to keep reminding myself that it was my father who was the subject of their conversation; they had accepted his stories as gospel, and now they were reminiscing about events they had never witnessed, remembering the achievements and near misses of a golden youth that none of them had shared. I didn't say anything to put them right, of course – even I wasn't ready for that kind of bloody mindedness at a funeral – but some of the boys picked up an incredulous note in my voice, or a flicker of disdain that passed across my face as they were talking about his early footballing career, and eventually, Mull, his oldest friend, pulled me up on it.

'Are you all right, son?' he said.

'I'm fine.' I looked around; as soon as Mull had spoken, they had all turned to look at me.

'Did ye no ken he played for Raith in the old days?'

I smiled sadly. 'No,' I said. 'I didn't know that.'

'Aye.' Mull studied me sourly. 'Your dad must have showed you the pictures, though, didn't he?'

I shook my head. It was a challenge: I was being called upon to acknowledge something, and I wasn't having it. If there were pictures, I would believe; but I knew there weren't. My father had often talked about starting out on a football career before he'd joined the air force. Sometimes he'd played for Raith Rovers, sometimes for Queen of the South. Sometimes his glory days had been cut short by injury, sometimes by money problems. I knew it was all rubbish. 'I've not seen any pictures,' I said.

Mull smiled back. He slipped his hand inside his black jacket and pulled out a brown envelope. The envelope was old and worn, but the pictures inside – small, black-and-white images like the ones you used to get from a Box Brownie – were remarkably well-preserved. He handed one over.

'There's your Dad,' he said. 'Back when he was still playing.'

I took the photograph and studied it. It showed two men in old-style football strips, on a muddy-looking park that might have been the amenity pitch at a local playground. As far as I could see, either of the men could have been my father. 'What's this?' I asked Mull.

Nat was looking over my shoulder. 'Is that no the auld Raith strip?' he said.

'Could be,' Mull said, his eyes still on me.

'They were no a bad team, back in the auld days,' Nat said. He looked closer. 'Some a thae faces look gey familiar.'

'We all know that boy on the left there,' Mull said.

I looked again. I had never believed the Raith Rovers story, as told by my father, and I didn't believe it now, but I was surprised by how keenly these men wanted it to be true. I nodded. 'Sure enough,' I said. I hoped Mull would be satisfied.

'You know who he looked like?' Nat said suddenly. I couldn't believe it. That old Robert Mitchum thing was still coming up. How had he managed it? These men thought he was a great footballer whose promising career had been ruined when he'd had to go into the RAF to fight Jerry, that he was a mathematical savant, who could do five-figure multiplications in his head, that he'd put me through Cambridge University, where I'd probably scored a double first and been captain of the chess team, and now, in spite of the evidence that was right in front of their eyes, they were still talking about his uncanny resemblance to Robert Mitchum.

I shook my head and glanced at Mull. 'Who?' I asked.

'Your dad!' Nat cried, drawing a little ripple of attention from the others around the bar.

'I know,' I said, keeping my voice low. 'So – who did he look like?'

Nat stared at me in amazement. 'You mean, you never *noticed*?' he said, trying to keep his voice down.

'Noticed what?'

Mull gave me a warning look. I shrugged. Nat looked around in mock appeal. 'The boy's no seen it,' he said. Mull shook his head. I knew he had been there on several occasions when my father did his Norman Wisdom–Robert Mitchum routine. 'Why, your dad was the perfect spit of Robert Mitchum,' Nat said. His triumph was wonderful to see. 'You're no goan to tell me a Cambridge college boy like you doesnae ken who Robert Mitchum is?'

I shook my head a little too soon. 'I'm not a Cambridge college boy,' I said. 'I went to the tech.'

'And whereabouts is that?' Mull enquired, his voice quiet and dangerous.

'In Cambridge,' I said, exasperated. 'But it's not – '

'No,' Mull broke in. 'It's Cambridge. Nobody here's ever been to Cambridge, never mind Cambridge college. So you remember that.' He leaned forward and fixed me with his gaze. I had always admired Mull's power, his sense of what was right. Now that I was on the receiving end of it, I felt uncomfortable. 'Your dad was proud of you, going to Cambridge,' he said. 'Don't forget that.'

'I've been to Cambridge,' a slurred voice piped in, from somewhere to my left.

Everybody at the table turned. It was Billy. Like the dormouse, he'd come up for air long enough to chip in, before sinking back into blissful torpor. Nat smiled ruefully.

'You'll miss him,' Mull continued to me, undistracted.

'We all will,' somebody seconded.

'Aye, but this boy here doesnae know that,' Mull continued, suddenly aggrieved. 'And the sad thing is, you *will* miss him,' he continued, studying me sadly. 'More than you know.'

I nodded. 'You're right, Mull,' I said. 'I'm not arguing with you.'

Mull shook his head. He wouldn't be bought off so easily. 'I mean it,' he said. 'Don't give me some glib answer. You don't even know, after all this time, what that man was about.'

The whole table pondered this silently for a moment.

'He was larger than life, your dad,' Mull said. 'Maybe he made some mistakes, but he lived his life. How many can say that, in this day and age?' He gave me a look that suggested, of the few who could claim to be living life to the full, I was not one. I didn't disagree with him.

It was around then that Billy finally passed out and slid,

315

rather beautifully, to the floor. We all turned to look at him, then Nat stood up. 'Better get this boy home,' he said. 'He never could hold his drink, wee Billy – '

I stood up next to him. 'I'll do that,' I said. 'You stay here and have a drink.'

Nat looked at me. 'Are ye sure?' he asked.

I nodded. 'I have to get on, see Margaret,' I said. 'She'll be wondering where I am.' I turned to Mull. 'If you'll help me get him to a taxi, I'll drop him off, before I go round to hers.'

Mull nodded. He knew I was grasping at an escape route, but he didn't begrudge me that. We were too different, now, to sit all night at the Silver Band Club. 'He bides down by the White Hart,' he said. 'I'll walk out with you and tell the driver.'

So it was that, together, we carried Billy – who was light as a feather – down the stairs and out, into the light of day. I was surprised that it was still so bright. I looked at Mull as we waited for a taxi, and saw how similar we were: same build, same face, same fears. He could have been anybody, standing on the kerb, waiting for a cab to pull up, but he was more like me, and more familiar, than my father had ever been. For me, there was no mystery to him, only his keen sense of injustice and his love for a man who hadn't ever deserved it. He knew why I was leaving, and he didn't want to hold me back, but he had been hoping, that day, to say something that would make me see my father in a better light. Now he was disappointed, knowing he'd missed his chance – though he still kept at me, even as I piled Billy into the cab. 'You keep in touch, son,' he said. 'I'll be here. If you ever want to talk, about your dad, or anything, you just give me a ring.'

'Thanks, Mull,' I said. I wanted to say that I had always liked him. I hoped that he knew that. I didn't agree with him about my father, in spite of the photograph, in spite of the very obvious grief of people like Billy and Nat. It could have been any of them, lying on that floor by the cigarette machine. What they were grieving for wasn't so much the death of their friend as what it represented: the lives they'd wasted or had taken away, the impossibility of declaring their love for one another, the lonely death that was coming to each of them. In the end, I thought – an absurd but, at that moment, satisfying idea – people drink for two reasons: because they want to die, or because they are afraid of dying. Two sides of the same coin, I told myself. It was all about time, all about trying to beat the clock.

Mull smiled and shook his head. 'Aye, you'll miss him right enough,' he said.

I nodded. 'I've missed him all my life,' I said. 'I don't suppose I'll stop now.' I was being fatuous, and I knew it; I was also being cruel to Mull, and I knew that too; but it felt like cruelty was all I had to make him see that what I was saying had its own element of truth.

His face darkened, but he wasn't angry. He was considering my words, giving them far more due than they deserved. But he didn't say anything, not for a moment, not as an answer. 'I'd better let you get wee Billy home,' he said. He held out his hand. 'Take care of yourself.'

I shook his hand. 'You too, Mull,' I said; then I climbed into the cab next to Billy, who had slumped sideways and was lying half across the seat, whining softly in his sleep. Mull told the taxi driver Billy's address and the man nodded. Then he slammed the door shut, and we drove away, leaving him alone on the pavement, a mortal man, standing in the sunlight of an ordinary day, watching us go.

LIES AND DREAMS

Jesus said, 'When you see one who was not born of a woman, prostrate yourself on your faces and worship him. That one is your Father.'

The Gospel of Thomas
(Nag Hammadi, Codex 2, Book 2)

A small fishing town on the east coast of Scotland: 1 November 2002, the day after Halloween, the first day of the pagan year. The night was stormy and this morning the wind is still high. Lines of townsfolk have formed at the breakwater to watch the great waves smash against the wall, coming out from rooms haunted by television and muzak, bringing their children to see, bringing cameras and binoculars, a little awed, and letting it show, in spite of themselves. I am taking my son on our usual walk to the lighthouse at the end of the quay, past the boats moored in the inner harbour, past the stacks of creels and old fish crates on the dock, out to where the crab boats come in, on finer days than this. My son is three years old and *here* is his favourite place. He likes to watch the gulls sail overhead and, in season, he tracks our summer visitors: swallows skimming along the line of the breakwater at low tide, catching the flies that are drawn to the tumbles of weed on the shore; Arctic terns hovering over the shallow water, searching for food in the clear light they follow from pole to pole with the changing seasons. Most of all he likes to see the crabs, to exchange a few words with the 'crab-man' and loiter a while for the five-fathom scent of the creels and the black-and-orange crab-bodies packed into old boxes dripping with hairweed and a greeny deepwater-light. This is what we know

321

as life: seabirds; caught fish; the odd twenty-foot wave flaring against a wall; the dark scent of unknown water; and, though we are embarrassed to say it, what we need to say, what we need to remember above and beyond all our other concerns is that *this* is the real world, our enduring mystery.

There were no ghosts last night. Nobody came to my little fire, other than the living. Later, though, as I sat up, observing my customary vigil, a memory came to me of a man who, for the child I was during his lifetime, might just as well have been a ghost. He was someone I had never come to know, though I lived in his house for so long; when I try to picture what he was like, all I find are gaps in the fabric of my memory, little tears and holes where something should have been, wisps of nothingness glimmering through, insubstantial, not quite convincing. Yet every Halloween, I've had the feeling that there is another, *truer* father that I should be able to recall. Till now, all I've come up with is a memory from a film, a character in a book, a surrogate phantom. This last night, however, I sensed that something else was present, and I knew it was real, however flimsy it seemed.

There are psychologists who believe that we record every word we ever read, every picture we see, every event, however small, every window in every house on every street we ever walk in a lifetime of books and streets and pictures. We record it all and file it away, waiting for it to be recollected: the vast, disordered encyclopedia of one human existence. At some point, when they are most needed, we recover images we never knew we had, and make of them what we can: a story, a lie, a dream, a life. The idea makes sense: it is, in its way, Darwinian. In the memory that comes this Halloween, my father is not the brutal, unhappy drunk I knew best, the man who passed his days in a fog of bewilderment, wondering who was to blame for his inconsequentiality, but someone I must have caught a glimpse of, back in Cowdenbeath, even if I don't remember exactly when it was, or why he was there, standing outside our house one night, alone in the dark, rain dripping from the trees around him. In this memory, he has his back to me, but I sense a stillness, a deep quiet that is not necessarily that of a man at rest, as he stands at the edge of Mr Kirk's woods, lighting a cigarette, nameless and, for a moment, free to be whoever he wishes. There must be some ordinary reason why he is out there in the wet, a few feet from his front door, but that isn't what matters now. What matters is that I can see him again, in his white shirt, and I know he is different from the man I learned to fear, the man I wanted to kill. I know his being there is an unusual event, one I may even have misunderstood – in this memory, I am, perhaps, four or five – but it is important that I remember him exactly like this, because this is the father I could bring myself to forgive. I know that it's just as important to remember the damage he did, and the pointless misery he inflicted on his family; yet, now that *I* am a father, I keep this man in my mind's eye: a man alone, at the edge of the darkness, listening out, forgetting himself and, as far as he knows, *unseen*. Suddenly, after all these years, this is the most permanent possession I have of him. More enduring than the watch he was wearing when he died, which I have now lost. More enduring than photographs and mementoes, more enduring, even, than his absurd stories. I know most of those tales by heart, even though I know they are lies; if I learned anything from my father, it was that parents tell their children stories all the time, even when they are not aware of it. Sometimes a father's tales are the same as those a mother would tell, but there are points on the journey where we have different stories to relate, or different versions of the same story, depending on circumstances. Maybe one of the things a father does, for his sons at least, is to let them see the difference between spirits and ghosts, to reveal for them the fabric of the invisible world. Ghosts can be dismissed, or they can be sent on their way, some Halloween night, with a kind word and a warm fire, but spirits are with us always, and it seems that the stories we tell are the only means we have to decide who or what they are, and how they might be accommodated. In the end, ghosts are powerless, but spirits feed our imaginations, and they are capable of anything. The time will come when my son needs me to tell him stories about fathers and sons – about who he is and where he came from – and I want him to be able to distinguish between our ghosts and our spirits. The memory I have of my father, caught between the night and his little prefab, is a story in itself, or at least, the beginnings of one. It is a father's tale, a myth, and I have to work out how to pass it on, in its best form, to the child with whom I am now walking, on this morning of the saints. I will have to give him something, however flimsy, to imagine himself as a man, with his own history, his own images, his own, very particular, spirits – and if I must start with nothing more than a lonely phantom in a white shirt and flannels, waiting to be realised in the eternal cold of a winter's night, so be it. What I need, as a father, is just one story, to start things off. The last thing I would want to do is make a lie of it.

ACKNOWLEDGEMENTS

'Birdland' written by Patti Smith © 1975 Linda Music Corp. All rights reserved. Used by permission.

Brigit Pegeen Kelly, excerpt from 'Dead Doe' from *Song*. Copyright © 1995 by Brigit Pegeen Kelly. Reprinted with the permission of BOA Editions, Ltd., *www.boaeditions.org*.

The author is grateful for the support of the Arts and Humanities Research Council during the writing of this book.

www.vintage-books.co.uk